Hoshin Kanri for the Lean Enterprise

Hoshin Kanri for the Lean Enterprise

Developing Competitive Capabilities
and Managing Profit

Thomas L. Jackson

New York

Most Productivity Press books are available at quantity discounts when purchased in bulk. For more information, contact our Customer Service Department (888-319-5852). Address all other inquiries to:

Productivity Press
444 Park Avenue South, 7th Floor
New York, NY 10016
United States of America
Telephone 212-686-5900
Fax: 212-686-5411
E-mail: *info@productivitypress.com*
ProductivityPress.com

Library of Congress Cataloging-in-Publication Data

Jackson, Thomas Lindsay, 1949–
    Hoshin kanri for the lean enterprise : developing competitive capabilities and managing profit/Thomas L. Jackson.
        p. cm.
    Includes bibliographical references and index.
    ISBN-13: 978-1-56327-342-1 (alk. paper)
    1. Industrial management. 2. Knowledge management. 3. Organizational learning.
4. Total quality management. I. Title.
HD31.J2329 2006
658.4′012—dc22

                                                                    2006020726

10 09 08 07   5 4 3 2

DEDICATION

In memory of Richard Niedermeier.

CONTENTS

ACKNOWLEDGEMENTS

I thank my teacher, Ryuji Fukuda, for tutoring me in his extraordinary methodology. I thank my friends Jamie Flinchbaugh and Jairo Martins for their helpful comments. I thank my partner, Dave Niemann, for reviewing Chapter 8. I thank my editor, Gary Peurasaari, for helping me to make a better book. I thank both Norman Bodek and Professor Peter Ward for encouraging me to address the relationship between hoshin kanri and Toyota's A3 reports. Finally, I thank my wife Daksha and daughter Aditi, for their patience.

INTRODUCTION

A Resource-Based Approach to Strategy

The laws of international trade and finance and the availability of high-speed communications have flattened our world. Your customers are everywhere, demanding good quality, low prices, and special features tuned to their own cultures and lifestyles. Your competitors are everywhere, too, because they have access to the same low interest rates and the same technology that you do. More and more, you must compete based upon your ability to develop special resources that, ideally, are difficult to replicate. Most of these resources and capabilities are intangible assets that Generally Accepted Accounting Principles (GAAP) don't always permit you to carry on your balance sheet. They include strong brands; patented technology and other intellectual property; powerful business processes; relationships with employees, customers, and suppliers; and the development of human assets.

Two of the most powerful combinations of competitive resources to come along in the last 50 years are the Toyota Production System (also known as lean manufacturing and in broader terms, lean thinking or lean enterprise) and six sigma. Lean enterprise is a philosophy that focuses on using continuous improvement to eliminate non-value-adding activities in a company's own production facilities and, eventually, the facilities of key suppliers. In particular, lean enterprise refines the control of time throughout all business functions by eliminating obstacles to the flow of material and information. The most famous of these obstacles are the "seven deadly wastes" of overproduction, transportation, waiting, inventory, defects, overprocessing, and unnecessary movement. By eliminating these wastes, lean enterprises achieve the same level of output with half the human effort, manufacturing space, investment in tools, engineering hours, and time to develop new products—and with a fraction of the inventory of their mass production competitors.

Six sigma is a powerful set of tools that helps to reduce the rate of defects to no more than 3.4 defects per million chances. The term "sigma" is used in statistics as a measure of variation, and six sigma strategy measures the degree to which any business process deviates from its goal. Six sigma recognizes that the number of product defects and wasted operating costs directly correlates with the level of customer satisfaction. The six sigma statistic measures the capability of the process to perform defect-free work. In many ways it is the repackaging of total quality management (TQM), focusing on the reduction of variability through continuous improvement (DMAIC), concurrent engineering (*design* for six sigma), and the improvement of administrative processes (*transactional* six sigma). (DMAIC is an acronym for five interconnected phases: Define, Measure, Analyze, Improve, and Control for the incremental process improvement using six sigma methodology.)

Forward-thinking companies have *combined* waste elimination strategies (the focus of lean) and variability reduction (the focus of six sigma) to form *lean-six sigma* programs. Toyota arguably combined lean and six sigma in 1963, when it won the Deming Prize for its implementation of TQM. Technically speaking, six sigma has been an integral part of the Toyota Production System and lean since that time. Today, evidence continues to mount in the automotive, aerospace, computer, electronics, and other industries—even in retail merchandising—that business systems based on the combined principles of lean *and* six sigma are unbeatable.

At the heart of lean, six sigma, and lean-six sigma is the same unique business operating system: *hoshin kanri*, the subject of this workbook. In a recent study, Dan Jones (coauthor of *The Machine that Changed the World* (New York, 1990: HarperCollins) and *Lean Thinking* (New York, 1996: Simon and Schuster) and colleagues at Cardiff University's Lean Enterprise Research Centre stated four characteristics of highly successful businesses.[1] These are:

1. Hoshin kanri (also known as policy deployment)
2. Process management (with a focus on process improvement as well as financial results)
3. The use of lean systems and tools (including the general TQM tools of six sigma as well as the manufacturing-focused tools of lean)
4. Supply chain integration (in product development as well as logistics)

Hoshin kanri appears at the top of the list because it is the key to attaining *superior organizational learning*. That is, it transforms any organization that practices it (correctly) into a community of scientists focused on a grand experiment—the systematic improvement of doing what needs to be done to make your customers happy and beat your competitors.

BACKGROUND OF HOSHIN KANRI

Hoshin kanri can be many things to an organization. It can be used as a method of strategic planning and a tool for managing complex projects, a quality operating system geared to ensuring that the organization faithfully translates the voice of the customer into new products, or a business operating system that ensures reliable profit growth. It is also a method for cross-functional management and for integrating the lean supply chain. But, most of all, it is an *organizational learning method and competitive resource development system*.

The Japanese characters for *kanri* mean *management*. You can translate the characters for *hoshin* as *direction* and *shining needle* or, taken together, as *compass*. Usually the characters are translated as *policy*, which is why you will often see hoshin kanri translated as *policy management* or *policy deployment*. For most English speakers the word "policy" immediately evokes the world of bureaucracy, which could never be associated with organizational learning. So in this workbook we'll stick with the original Japanese, hoshin kanri.

Hoshin kanri emerged during the 1950s and 1960s as Japanese companies struggled with structural changes to become competitive in the open, postwar economy. Under the influence of Peter Drucker's teachings on market focus and long-term planning, the Japanese Union of Scientists and Engineers (JUSE) added "Policy and planning" to the Deming Prize Checklist in 1958. After that, all Deming Prize applicants had to address "Policy and planning" as part of their implementations of total quality management. In 1964, Bridgestone Tire coined the term hoshin kanri and in 1965 published its *Hoshin Kanri Manual*, which codified the principles of hoshin, based on an analysis of what Deming Prize winners had been doing. Toyota and Komatsu successfully combined Bridgestone's version of hoshin with their own innovative implementations of cross-functional management and daily control of quality, cost, and delivery (the so-called QCDs). Since that time, hoshin has been a hallmark of lean manufacturing as well as total quality management, including its derivative, six sigma.

---

1. Peter Hines, Dan Jones, et al., *Value Stream Management: Strategy and Excellence in the Supply Chain* (Harlow, England, 2000: Financial Times/Prentice Hall).

HOSHIN KANRI, PROFIT MANAGEMENT, AND MANAGEMENT BY MEANS

Hoshin kanri is also the backbone of Toyota's practice of profit management and the closely related techniques of target and kaizen costing, the real secrets to Toyota's remarkably reliable profit performance.[2] As this workbook demonstrates, hoshin integrates the traditional budgeting process within a framework of a multiyear profit plan. Using an innovative negotiation process known as catchball (the subject of Chapter 5), hoshin involves management teams at every level of the organization in providing high quality financial information about current and future operations *before* the annual budget is finalized. Simultaneously, financial targets are carefully related to specific cost drivers and process improvements that ensure those targets will be met. In a sense, hoshin kanri incorporated "open book" management decades before the phrase was coined in the West to describe the sharing of financial information with front-line employees. The theme of profit management runs through the entire workbook in the form of a value stream profit and loss statement (introduced in Chapter 2) that we will update periodically as we learn more information about the two companies featured in our case study: Cybernautx and its key supplier Nonesuch Casting.

Profit is actually a result of properly managed means. Hoshin might well be called "management by means," because it focuses on the development of competitive capabilities as the means to the end of profit. Indeed, hoshin not only anticipated "open book" management, one of its central features has always been a "balanced scorecard" of process improvement targets specifically designed to achieve related cost and profit targets. Hoshin kanri can be used to manage just about anything that moves. For example, you can use it to:

- Integrate value stream activities within a single plant, office, hospital, etc.
- Integrate a total value stream involving multiple suppliers
- Launch a new product or service
- Manage a brand portfolio or bundle of related products and value streams
- Manage strategic change programs
- Manage the implementation of lean manufacturing or six sigma
- Manage any complex project that involves cross-functional cooperation
- Manage companies in an equity fund portfolio to systematically improve their profitability

As you can see, the benefits of adopting hoshin kanri are many. In particular, this workbook will focus on using hoshin kanri to integrate a *total value stream*, where hoshin kanri and

---

2. For a good explanation of the relationship of target and kaizen costing to profit management, see Robin Cooper and Regine Slagmulder, *Target Costing and Value Engineering* (Portland, OR: Productivity Press, 1997). The role of hoshin in profit management is not sufficiently emphasized, but is clearly alluded to in Yasuhiro Monden's *Toyota Management System: Linking the Seven Key Functional Areas* (Portland, OR: Productivity Press, 1993), pp. 47–50. In their Shingo Prize-winning book, *Profit Beyond Measure: Extraordinary Results through Attention to Work and People* (New York, NY: Free Press, 2000), H. Thomas Johnson and Anders Bröms refer to a process that is either hoshin or certainly based on hoshin, which they call "management by means." The fact is that Toyota manages everything through hoshin kanri, including quality and delivery lead times, as well as cost and profit. Like all total quality management tools, hoshin eliminates variability in the processes to which it is applied, in this case, the process of producing profits for shareholders. Toyota's profitability growth is so steady and boring, that is, without surprises—positive or negative—that Wall Street may actually undervalue the shares of the great company. See Miki Tanikawa, "Toyota / Many unhappy returns: Can this stock price be saved?" *International Herald Tribune*, Saturday, March 6, 2004. A plausible alternative explanation for this undervaluation may be that, with $13.8 billion in cash (on its balance sheet for 2005), Toyota simply doesn't need Wall Street.

"lean accounting" are an integrated process. A total value stream is everything you do—from concept to cash—to get new product ideas, procure capital and raw materials, transform them into products and services, and deliver them to your customers. (We will discuss value streams when we analyze the Cybernautx case study in this workbook.)

There are good reasons for organizing the book around the value stream focus. First, it helps to simplify the presentation of hoshin kanri. Second, value streams reflect the way lean companies like Toyota and six sigma companies like GE and Allied Signal manage their product costs and profits. Third, many readers are already familiar with value stream mapping, the popular method of visualizing the flows of material and information that lead to customer satisfaction. Fourth, integration of the total value stream is the next challenge on the horizon for those companies that are implementing lean manufacturing and six sigma.

Along with integrating a total value stream, using this workbook will show you the mechanics of implementing hoshin kanri, so that, as the need arises, your company can:

- Systematically improve brand equity
- Patent new technologies and copyright new ideas
- Implement lean manufacturing and six sigma
- Integrate suppliers into a lean and six sigma organization

All of these things will help grow the required capabilities to create better products and bring them to market faster—promoting good-paying jobs without, as is often the case in the West, asking for self-defeating trade restrictions so your company can compete in a global economy.

Hoshin Kanri, PDCA, and Organizational Learning

The key to organizational learning is to discover problems and solve them.[3] *Hoshin kanri satisfies this requirement* by applying the Deming cycle of plan, do, check, act (PDCA) to the management and *improvement* of every detail of your business. PDCA is management shorthand for the scientific method:

- ***Plan*** (form a hypothesis and create an experimental design)
- ***Do*** (test the hypothesis)
- ***Check*** (verify the replicability of the experiment)
- ***Act*** (standardize proven hypotheses as part of new work standards)

By applying PDCA systematically, hoshin integrates planning and execution at all levels of the organization. You accomplish this through an elaborate deployment process, called catchball, which we will explore in Chapter 5. The result of the catchball process is to "nest" PDCA cycles, one within the other, as the strategic plan cascades down the management hierarchy.

In Figure I-1, the left side shows us the normal PDCA cycle, in which members of top management make and execute strategy, without engaging those beneath them. Middle managers and the hourly workforce are simply "told what to do." As a result, there is little understanding of—or "buy-in" to—strategic targets, resulting in poor execution in the *Do* stage of PDCA. Moreover, when execution falls short of those targets, top management normally blames middle management and the workforce.

---

3. See Chris Argyris and Donald Shön, *Organizational Learning: A Theory of Action Perspective.* (Reading, Mass: Addison Wesley, 1978). A decade after Bridgestone Tire won the Deming Prize for codifying hoshin kanri, Argyris and Shön defined organizational learning as "the detection and correction of error."

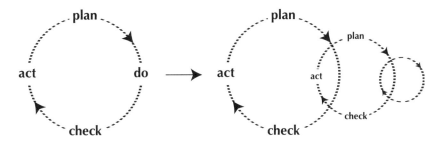

Figure I-1. Nested Deming Cycles

What a difference hoshin kanri makes! On the right, we see a system of nested PDCA cycles, in which top management deploys its strategic plan by engaging middle managers and hourly workers in both the planning and execution of strategy. The result is a powerful new type of organizational *self-control* based on the improved understanding and buy-in of all managers and workers. As you will see throughout this workbook, hoshin kanri requires that every manager—and eventually every single employee—in your company become a licensed, independent practitioner of scientific PDCA methods. To achieve this type of organizational design requires a company to use extensive training and education to develop the requisite methods of self-control.

A self-controlled organization soon becomes a flexible learning organization. Why? Because all of hoshin's PDCA experiments (problem-solving cycles) are nested or linked, so that when you make a change in one cycle it rapidly translates into changes in all others. Once an organization embeds PDCA deeply in its DNA, that organization gains the ability to change its strategic course of action practically at will, because it can act on new information whether it is coming from the shop floor or the boardroom. This is why hoshin kanri emphasizes the need to adopt a well-developed problem-solving methodology.

The major problem-solving methodologies for lean enterprise and six sigma are all distinguished by their use of the scientific method. As Table I-1 illustrates, both PDCA—the problem-solving method Toyota uses—and DMAIC—the six sigma problem-solving methodology—are pocket editions of the scientific method and are fundamentally the same. Table I-1 also compares these to another popular problem-solving methodology, CEDAC (cause-and-effect diagram with the addition of cards), which won the Deming Prize in 1979. Developed by Ryuji Fukuda, CEDAC uses the classic cause-and-effect fishbone diagram with the addition of cards (more recently with the addition of sticky notes) to capture and categorize a team's ideas on a CEDAC board for further employee input. Unlike the usual cause-and-effect analysis, which uses brainstorming sessions to identify and capture the causes of problems, CEDAC is a process of continuous, interactive dialogue between members in a creative problem-solving environment. In such an environment, you can capture a greater variety of ideas from differing perspectives, expanding the team's ability to consider all potential causes.

WHO CAN USE THIS WORKBOOK

The goal of this workbook is to aid any team in implementing hoshin kanri in both mature and less mature lean organizations. Of course, your company's timetable for implementing hoshin kanri depends on the organization's level of experience with lean thinking, six sigma, hoshin kanri, and the requisite tools. Although geared as an implementation primer to accommodate the less mature lean companies, this workbook will be most valuable for those companies that have implemented or are in the process of implementing lean and/or

Table I-1. Equivalence of PDCA, DMAIC and CEDAC Problem-Solving Methodologies

PDCA	DMAIC	CEDAC®
PLAN Plan an organizational change or a product, service, problem solution, or process improvement.	**Define** • Define the problem.	1. Carefully define the problem.
	Measure • Select CTQ characteristics. • Define performance standards. • Validate measurement system.	2. Establish measures of improvement. 3. Establish targets for improvement and charter the team.
	Analyze • Establish product capability. • Define performance objectives. • Identify variation sources.	4. Gather data and systematically analyze information. 5. Generate and prioritize improvement ideas.
DO Do the activity planned, conduct an experiment, or pilot the organizational change.	**Implement** • Screen potential causes. • Discover variable relationship. • Establish operating tolerances.	6. Test solutions under controlled conditions.
CHECK Check the results or effects of the change; study the quantitative and qualitative data collected on the effects of the change.	**Control** • Validate measurement system. • Determine process capability. • Implement process control.	7. Establish the repeatability of the new procedure and establish standards.
ACT Act on lessons learned. Make decision on large-scale production or implementation, abandonment, or activity, or repeating the PDCA cycle steps for continued improvement.		8. Deploy new standards to related processes & problems. 9. Ensure adherence to standards.

six sigma and want to integrate their total value streams. Finally, readers can simply use this workbook and team exercises to create an implementation model to educate themselves and their employees in hoshin kanri process. If you take this approach, you would want to keep your teams small. At a minimum, this workbook will help any lean or six-sigma practitioner understand what hoshin kanri can accomplish, and the tools, processes, and commitments needed to implement it effectively. Though the workbook provides definitions and discussion around the principles of lean and six sigma, as well as the many tools associated with them, it assumes the reader has some working knowledge of these systems and tools.

What's Inside

The workbook is laid out in the PDCA format, following the step-by-step logic of the hoshin process along with the appropriate team exercises. Throughout, the workbook provides many examples of forms and tools, and discusses basic concepts the team will need to complete the team exercises and implement a viable hoshin strategy. The workbook includes a companion CD with the necessary blank forms, documents, and instructions, so that the various teams can complete their hoshin assignments (some of which can be filled in electronically). The Cybernautx case study ties together the PDCA experiments and principles throughout, showing how it deployed and used hoshin to integrate all its business functions and the supply chain. We've also aligned the Cybernautx case study so that it can assist teams in their exercises to deploy and implement their own hoshin kanri.

Chapter 1 covers the basics of hoshin kanri, which include the fundamentals of the X-matrix and chartering teams (see Tables 1-3 and 1-4). In this chapter you'll learn about the first team you will charter, the "hoshin team," which is usually a management team in charge of an aspect of the company. The hoshin team has overall responsibility for the strategic planning and implementation process and designs and guides the first three experiments: (1) long-term strategy, (2) midterm strategy, and (3) the annual hoshin. This team should also represent stakeholders of the business unit to which the hoshin or strategy will be deployed. You will also learn about chartering three other types of teams—*tactical*, *operational*, and *action*—that will eventually carry out the *seven experiments* of hoshin kanri strategy (Table 1-2), using the team exercises in this workbook.

Chapter 2 provides the hoshin team with six tools to scan its company's market conditions to solidify its mission, vision, and long-term strategy and begin populating the X-matrix for the PDCA process. Chapters 3 and 4 cover the *Plan* cycle of PDCA. In Chapter 3, the hoshin team will design a *midterm* strategy and in Chapter 4, an *annual* hoshin, identifying tactical improvement projects to communicate to all the relevant teams to implement.

Beginning in Chapter 5, through a process called *catchball*, the hoshin team will deploy the strategy by engaging the implementing teams, each of which will create a team charter and populate an X matrix. The hoshin team will work out a deployment path with the various teams to identify the starting and ending points of the hoshin process, both vertically (from top to bottom) and horizontally (across business functions and, perhaps, supply chain members). It also decides which hoshin documents to use at each step. Below are the teams responsible for carrying out the next three experiments of the hoshin system—Experiment 4, tactical teams and initiatives; Experiment 5, operational teams and projects; and Experiments 6 and 7, action teams and major improvements or *kaikaku*, and continuously improving daily work, or *kaizen*:

- *Tactical teams:* Responsible for the sweeping improvement initiatives that support the hoshin team's strategy, as well as for developing particular competitive capabilities
- *Operational teams:* Responsible for improving individual improvement projects and processes that make up each tactical initiative
- *Action teams:* Responsible for implementing particular focused improvement activities (*kaikaku* and kaizen) to standardized work

Chapter 5 completes the *Plan* and deployment process of hoshin kanri. Chapter 6 covers the *Do* cycle, in which the teams go over and finalize project plans, use roadmaps, make detailed schedules and determine their approach to developing leaders who can apply reliable PDCA methods (scientific thinking) to train and engage your action teams. Applying scientific thinking and developing organizational learning is the whole point to hoshin kanri. Chapter 7 covers the *Check* cycle and makes sure you create a lean thinking environment to keep your seven experiments on course. Here your teams will learn about conducting monthly progress reports, regular review meetings, and annual reviews.

Chapter 8 continues your *Check* cycle, and is dedicated to one of the six tools introduced in Chapter 2, *the president's diagnosis*. The president's diagnosis provides vital input in strategic planning because it highlights your progress in developing the many internal capabilities required to become a lean enterprise. Furthermore, you are introduced to a PDCA interpretation of lean DNA, and a new, comprehensive system of diagnostic categories and supporting criteria—expressed in the form of *progress tables*—to diagnose all elements of an integrated lean enterprise. This whole system is called *the transformation ruler*. Not only can you use the president's diagnosis and transformation ruler to establish the state of your own competitive resources and capabilities, and those of your suppliers, you can also use this as a system for systematically checking the development of those resources, working hand-in-hand with hoshin kanri to coach and mentor your entire organization in correctly developing its lean resources.

Chapter 9 addresses the *Act* cycle, showing you how to institutionalize the hoshin system itself, together with major new methodologies such as lean, six sigma, and supply chain management. The key to understanding the *Act* cycle of hoshin kanri lies in the concept of standardized work, the bedrock of both lean and six sigma. While many companies have documented standards, adherence to those standards is normally poor. The first step toward institutionalizing any process improvement is to adhere to the new standards that define it. Chapter 9 explains three distinct levels of process standardization: (1) companywide standardization of cross-functional and supply chain business processes, (2) standardization of functional business processes, and (3) standardization of the subprocesses and individual tasks of daily work.

Chapter 9 also looks more closely into standardized work, the seventh experiment of hoshin kanri: continuous improvement or kaizen. While adhering to standards may be enough to ensure the institutionalization of particular improvements, it is not enough to institutionalize the system of hoshin kanri. Hoshin is not about standing still; it is about using the scientific method to adapt to competitive challenges. From the point of view of hoshin kanri, standardized work merely provides a framework of controlled conditions necessary for scientific investigation. Of course, standardized work ensures high quality, but only to the extent of current knowledge. Kaizen, the attitude of continuous improvement—or, as the tagline of Toyota's luxury mark has it, "The relentless pursuit of perfection,"—is nothing other than the scientific spirit, the restless spirit in search of new knowledge. Finally, Chapter 9 reveals the foundation of lean culture in hoshin kanri's unique system of teachable moments, that is, the moments in which leaders become teachers, coaches, and mentors of organizational values, philosophy, and methods.

Caveat

Hoshin is a life-changing technology, particularly if you're a manager schooled in the command and control operating systems of old-fashioned mass production. Like capitalism itself, hoshin, lean, and six sigma are all optimistic about human beings and their ability to solve problems both independently and cooperatively. If you don't subscribe to this brand of optimism, you may end up building a beautiful set of X-matrices and team charters, but you won't tap the potential of hoshin, or become a lean organization. As managers go through this workbook, they should stay focused on the sources of competitive advantage as well as on respecting their fellow human beings. Do this, and I believe you will successfully implement hoshin kanri.

CHAPTER ONE

Hoshin Kanri Basics—Nested Experiments, X-Matrix, and Chartering Teams

In this chapter, we will explore the basics of hoshin kanri. Table 1-1 shows the hoshin kanri road map—Scan, Plan, Do, Check, and Act—that the various teams will follow as they use the team exercises to implement hoshin. As mentioned in the introduction, the workbook follows the Plan, Do, Check, Act (PDCA) cycle, along with the step-by-step progression of the hoshin process. *Scan* represents some of the preplan work the hoshin team must perform before moving into the PDCA cycle of hoshin kanri. *Plan* includes designing a business strategy or experiment, chartering teams, and assigning responsibilities to the four planning and implementation teams. *Do* develops leaders and implements the plan through project management and training. *Check* conducts periodic reviews. And *Act* makes hoshin kanri part of your business culture through standardization and continuous improvement.

The hoshin kanri road map also directs the practitioner to charter a series of teams, each of which are responsible for one or more of the seven experiments of strategy described below. The first team you will charter is the "hoshin team." The hoshin team is usually a management team in charge of a business unit: an entire company, division, brand, product line, department, physical site, or value stream. For the purpose of this workbook, the management team is the hoshin management team or hoshin team. Later in this chapter, you will choose the members for the hoshin team.

For the Cybernautx case study that illustrates the hoshin process, we chose a hoshin management team in charge of an entire value stream. The fact is you can choose any starting point that fits your circumstance. For example, the hoshin team might be the partners of a private equity firm, forming a strategy for increasing the value of its many holdings. Or it might be, as in my book *Implementing a Lean Management System*, a plant manager and her direct reports, forming a plan for implementing TPM. Or it might be a departmental manager and his direct reports, forming a strategy for departmental improvement. Wherever you choose to begin the hoshin process, the hoshin management team should represent stakeholders of the business unit to which the hoshin or strategy will be deployed. Normally this means that the team should be cross-functional or, in the case of the value stream illustrated in the Cybernautx case study, interorganizational (that is, with members drawn from different companies).

Before chartering a team, the company will need to scan the environment to define a problem or challenge for strategy to address. The hoshin team can perform the scan or you can delegate it to functional experts. (For this workbook, the hoshin team will perform the scan.) Once you have performed the scan, the hoshin team designs a strategy with the X-matrix so the company can turn its business strategy into an experimental design, consisting of the seven hoshin experiments, to address the problem or challenge. In designing a

Table 1-1. Hoshin Kanri Road Map

hoshin kanri

plan

Define a problem or challenge and design an experiment to address it

scan	Design strategy with the X-matrix	Charter successful teams through policy deployment
	Fashion business strategy as an experimental design by analyzing the business as a complex system, identifying truly critical factors and their interaction effects.	Engage the entire workforce in conducting the experiment by formally chartering departments and teams at every level in the organization.

Value stream managers

Hoshin team

Middle managers

| 1 Define the elements of strategic intent • mission & vision • long-term strategy 2 Scan environment with 6 smart tools 1. Porter matrix 2. Product/market matrix 3. Market/technology matrix 4. Value stram P&L statement 5. Value stream maps 6. The president's diagnosis | Build a midterm strategy and the annual hoshin 1 Identify 3- to 5-year breakthrough opportunities 2 Forecast financial results 3 Determine measures of process improvement 4 Study interdependencies 5 Identify 6- to 12-month tactics 6 Establish annual targets for process and results 7 Study new interdependencies Play catchball, rounds 1, & 5 | **Tactical teams** Play catchball rounds 1, 2, & 5 1 Prepare for the meeting 2 Introduce the hoshin 3 Discuss the plan 4 Charter tactical teams 5 Study the plan 6 Complete and confirm the tactical plans | **Operational teams** Play catchball rounds 2, 3, & 4 1 Prepare for the meeting 2 Introduce the tactical project plan 3 Discuss the operations plan 4 Charter operations teams 5 Study the plan 6 Complete and confirm the operations plan |

Supervisors & team leaders

Inclusion in planning phase optional; not recommended for companies just starting to implement hoshin kanri

Play catchball rounds 2, 3, & 4

1 Prepare for the meeting
2 Introduce the operations plans
3 Discuss the plan
4 Charter action teams
5 Study the plan
6 Complete and confirm action plans

Staff & hourly associates

Included in implementation but not in the planning

road map

do	check	act
Conduct the experiment under controlled conditions	validate the experiment	institutionalize lean thinking
Transform the mass production organization through training	Check progress in real time	Promote standardized work
Standardized work provides controlled conditions for execution of the experiment. Otherwise, promote adherence through intensive training in productivity and quality methods before initiating continuous improvement.	Empower your workforce of scientists to check results and make adjustments in real time. Manage exceptions through your business operating system.	Make new knowledge part of standardized work through PDCA embedded in daily operations. Coach and mentor to develop leaders at every level.

Action teams	Hoshin team	Action teams	
1 Finalize project plans 2 Apply PDCA methods 3 Eliminate waste/reduce variability 4 Manage internal and external customer connections visually and unambiguously 5 Use scientific methods and tools	Develop leaders who can teach • apprenticeship • kaizen blitz • train-the-trainer • quasi-apprenticeship • six sigma *Note*: Teams at all levels participate in leadership development, but responsibility lies with the hoshin team leader. *Becoming lean cannot be delegated.*	1 Manage visually • OPC • Visual project • Visual hoshin 2 Conduct smart review meetings • Daily 5-minute meeting • Daily management review • Weekly • Monthly • Quarterly • Annual 3 Conduct the president's diagnosis • Self diagnose • Prepare for the president's diagnosis • Site visits • Analyze and score development • Recognize achievement	1 Promote adherence to standardized work 2 Develop leaders and make succession plans 3 Train, coach, and mentor 4 Repeat the hoshin cycle

strategy, the hoshin team will define the elements of strategic intent, which includes identifying the first of seven hoshin experiments discussed below.

THE SEVEN EXPERIMENTS OF HOSHIN KANRI

Because no one can know the outcome of a strategy in advance, especially a dynamic strategy that involves improving the way you do business, *strategy is like a scientific hypothesis*. You have to implement it to find out what will happen. In this scientific sense, your plans become "experiments" where, under the controlled conditions of *standardized work*, the hoshin process involves every manager and employee in *testing* your company's hypothesis about its strategy.

The experiments of hoshin are carried out by a network of teams that eventually include top management, middle management, and ultimately, in the *Do* stage of the hoshin process, the entire workforce. Each PDCA experiment in the hoshin system has a different purpose, depending upon its duration and relation to the organization's overall goals. In general, the longer the cycle, the higher the level of responsibility in the management hierarchy. Furthermore, the hoshin kanri process never ends. Strategic improvement cycles repeat once a year. Companies that are just beginning their lean or six sigma transformations may take up to 18 months to complete the first cycle. Others operating at faster "clockspeeds" may repeat the cycle twice a year to accelerate organization learning.

Table 1-2 defines the four types of hoshin teams and hoshin's seven types of PDCA cycles or experiments, which are nested one within the other. The four teams and basic responsibilities are as follows:

1. The *hoshin team* has the overall responsibility for the strategic planning and implementation process and designs and guides the first three experiments: (1) long-term strategy, (2) midterm strategy, and (3) annual hoshin. These three experiments normally focus on the improvement of companywide business processes that require cross-functional coordination or coordination between the company and its suppliers and customers.

2. The *tactical teams*, chartered by the hoshin team, design and guide the fourth hoshin experiment: tactical initiatives to develop particular competitive capabilities. Tactical initiatives normally focus on the improvement of functional business processes, i.e., the process of marketing, engineering, manufacturing, etc., but also address any important elements of cross-functional coordination required for successful implementation.

3. The *operational teams*, chartered by the tactical teams, design and guide the fifth hoshin experiment: operational projects to improve particular products and processes. Operational projects also focus on the improvement of functional business processes and address the cross-functional coordination required for successful implementation.

4. The *action teams*, chartered by the operational teams, conduct the sixth and seventh hoshin experiments. The sixth experiment is to implement periodic improvements of relatively large magnitude—called *kaikaku*; and the seventh experiment is to implement continuous, incremental improvements—called *kaizen*.

In a mature lean enterprise, these four teams ultimately include every manager at every level of the organization, and by extension every employee. In fact, you can define a lean enterprise as a network of hoshin teams. The seven experiments of hoshin represent the actual work that the teams need to do in order to implement the experimental design of business strategy to resolve emerging problems or challenges (see Figure 1-1).

Table 1-2. The 4 Teams and the 7 Experiments

4 Teams		7 Experiments		
1	**Hoshin Team**	1	Long-term strategy	A general plan of action that aims over a very long period of time—5 to 100 years—to make major changes or adjustments in the mission and/or vision of the business.
		2	Midterm strategy	A partially complete plan of action including financial targets and measures of process improvement that aims over 3 to 5 years to develop capabilities and align the trajectory of business operations with the long-term strategy.
		3	Annual hoshin	A highly concrete plan of action that aims over the next 6 to 18 months to develop competitive capabilities and align the trajectory of business operations in accordance with the midterm strategy.
2	**Tactical Teams**	4	Tactics	Concrete initiatives of 6 to 18 months, defined by the annual hoshin, undertaken to develop specific new capabilities by applying new technologies and methodologies to general business processes.
3	**Operational Teams**	5	Operations	Concrete projects of 3 to 6 months, defined by the annual hoshin, undertaken to apply new technologies and methodologies to standardized processes of specific business functions.
4	**Action Teams**	6	Kaikaku	Concrete projects of 1 week to 3 months, usually defined after the deployment of the annual hoshin, undertaken to apply new tools and techniques in standardized daily work.
		7	Kaizen	Problem-solving in more or less real time to address defects, errors, and abnormalities that arise in the course of standardized daily work, as well as improvements resulting from employee suggestions.

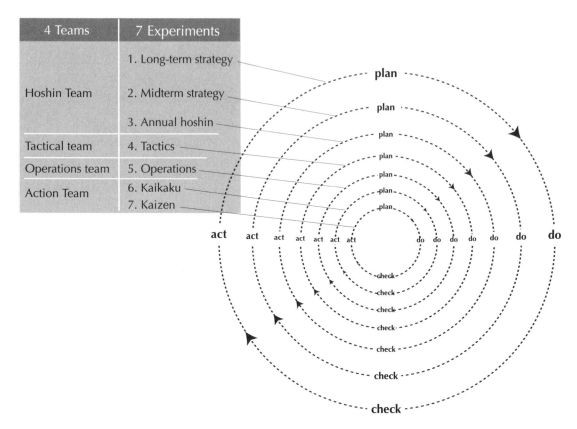

4 Teams	7 Experiments
Hoshin Team	1. Long-term strategy
	2. Midterm strategy
	3. Annual hoshin
Tactical team	4. Tactics
Operations team	5. Operations
Action Team	6. Kaikaku
	7. Kaizen

Figure 1-1. The 4 Teams and the 7 Experiments

As we explained above, the hoshin team takes responsibility for the first three experiments of the hoshin system. Once in the *Plan* stage, the hoshin team will help form and hand off responsibility for the last four experiments to the other three types of teams that will have their own set of duties within each Plan, Do, Check, Act cycle. There will be several tactical teams—roughly one for every member on the hoshin team, even more operational teams, and an even larger number of action teams. By the end of the *Plan* phase, you may engage every manager in the hoshin process. Ultimately, in the *Do* phase of the hoshin process with its action teams, you will engage the entire workforce at every level in the organization.

DESIGN OF STRATEGY—ANATOMY OF AN X-MATRIX

A strategic plan is a detailed, *documented* course of action. Most companies already have missions, visions, and long-term strategies. So, this workbook concentrates on helping the hoshin team document its *midterm* strategy, *annual hoshin*, and tactical improvement projects (Experiments 2, 3, and 4 respectively) with the X-matrix. Hoshin kanri requires management teams at various levels within an organization to cooperate in designing the experiments for strategy, tactics, and operations. The *design of strategy* strives to optimize overall system performance by identifying the factors critical to the company's success and the interdependencies or linkages among them.

The hoshin team guides the process of strategy design, and records the results on a memorandum called an *X-matrix*. (We will discuss this in Chapter 3 and 4.) As Table 1-3 shows, the X-matrix has the unique advantage of visualizing the design of strategy on one piece of paper. It is essentially a memorandum on which you record the decisions—and supporting discussions—needed to articulate and execute an effective strategy. The X-matrix is on one side of the document and easy-to-follow instructions appear on the back. The instructions in each part of the workbook refer to your X-matrix and related team charters. (The instructions for the X-matrix are included on a separate page on the companion CD.)

Table 1-3. Anatomy of an X-matrix

The prime mover on the matrix is strategy, recorded to the left of the "X" in the middle of the matrix. Strategies are high-priority and companywide improvement strategies or "breakthroughs" for the current period and the following 2 to 3 years.

Strategy gives rise to tactics, recorded at the top of the matrix. Tactics are tactical improvement projects for the current period initiatives and projects for the current period (6 to 18 months).

Tactics require measures of process improvement, recorded to the right of the "X." Establish improvement-friendly measures that indicate the development of business processes and relationships critical to the business model.

One of the most important features about the X-matrix is that it records important relationships among individuals, teams, departments, and your suppliers.

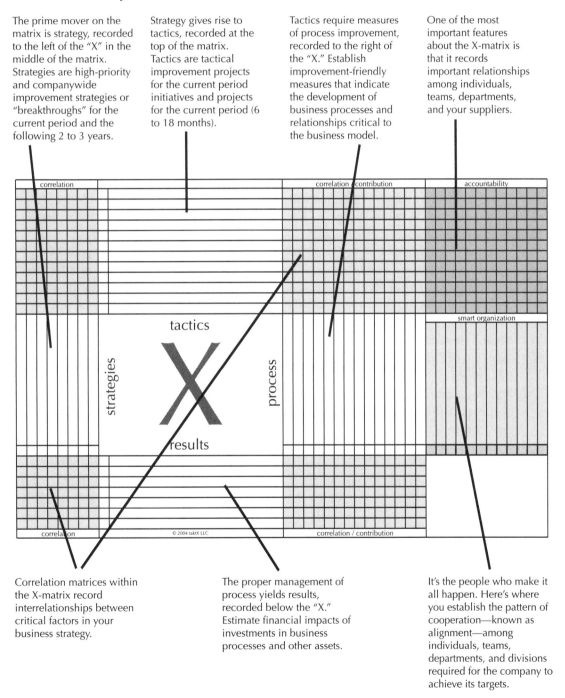

Correlation matrices within the X-matrix record interrelationships between critical factors in your business strategy.

The proper management of process yields results, recorded below the "X." Estimate financial impacts of investments in business processes and other assets.

It's the people who make it all happen. Here's where you establish the pattern of cooperation—known as alignment—among individuals, teams, departments, and divisions required for the company to achieve its targets.

> **Hoshin Team Exercise:** Before choosing members for your hoshin team, review the Hoshin Kanri Road Map and the purpose of the four teams and seven experiments. From the CD companion, print out the X-matrix and instructions (CD Form 1-2). Review the instructions. Become familiar with the format. Once management determines who is on the hoshin team, the team will begin using the X-matrix to record breakthrough objectives, and later to help build its midterm strategy and *annual hoshin* (Chapter 3). Later, various tactical and operational team leaders and their teams will continue to revise and populate this X-matrix. Normally, the team leader does the prework or delegates it to another team member.

THE A3: BUSINESS MEMORANDUM OF THE 21ST CENTURY

When I teach the X-matrix to my clients, I often refer to it as "the business memo of the 21st century." That is only part of the story. Many companies now support strategic planning and problem solving with a unique suite of documents that have come to be known as A3s because in Japan they are printed on one side of a sheet of European A3 size paper (equivalent to American tabloid [11″ x 17″] paper). The A3 is a technical writing format designed for communicating the story of continuous improvement succinctly, visually, and in a standardized way. Printed on tabloid paper, as I encourage my clients to do, the X-matrix itself becomes an A3. But there are others, too.

Toyota, the originator of the A3 format, actually employs several different types of what we may call "classic" A3 story forms, including a team charter proposal, an information report, problem solving report, and status report A3. Most of Toyota's A3 forms (at least those that have been published) contain nine typical elements critical to good project management.

1. Theme (thesis at the top of the form stating the problem or challenge)
2. Problem statement (including an initial current state) defining the motive of the project
3. Target statement (oor future state) defining the scope of the project
4. A scientific process (PDCA, i.e., scientific) process of investigating the problem
5. Systematic analysis (5 whys, cost benefit, cause-and-effect diagram, design of experiments, etc.)
6. Proposed solution (including any cross-functional coordination of resources)
7. Implementation timeline (including the action, responsible parties, and deliverable date of the action)
8. Graphic illustrations to convey information at-a-glance.
9. Date and reporting unit or owner at the bottom of the form (the individual or team responsible for this particular A3).

The A3 format sharpens thinking, forcing managers to know their audience and flow their stories logically so they can succinctly document what they have to say to fit on one page. Quality and productivity guru, Ryuji Fukuda, and other pragmatically minded Japanese consultants also have recommended this practice.

This workbook presents six different types of A3 documents (see Table 1-4). Four are based on Toyota's original four A3 forms, a fifth A3 is based on Fukuda's X-matrix [see Fukuda's *Building Organizational Fitness* (Productivity Press); see also my *Implementing A Lean Management System* (Productivity Press)], and a sixth A3 is based the summary status reports found in my *Implementing a Lean Management System* (Productivity Press). Each A3 form has corresponding how-to instructions that you can print on the back of a blank A3 when using the forms for the first time.

Toyota's and Fukuda's all-on-one page documents rely heavily on the *graphic illustrations* (instead of textual descriptions) of processes, such as value stream maps, which condense information into visual form to facilitate quick comprehension when communicating with others. In addition to value stream maps, you will find many illustrations throughout this workbook (fishbone diagrams, interrelationship diagrams, simple bar charts, milestone charts, radar charts, etc.) that you can incorporate into your own A3s. The graphic presentation of complex information is not a trivial subject. As such, it is beyond the scope of this workbook. People who are serious about visual communication should visit the website of Yale University Professor Edward Tufte at *http://www.edwardtufte.com* for a list of his wonderfully illustrated books plus pages of useful resources.

Presentation Tip: In some companies, PowerPoint and the ubiquitous LCD projector have almost entirely displaced the important practice of technical writing. Some managers actually manage to combine all the information found on an A3 onto a single presentation slide for review meetings. You should resist this apparently universal urge. *Do not convert A3's into presentation slides!* The A3 is perfectly useful as a *handout*, but it is "death by PowerPoint." Good presentations emphasize simple pictures and graphics that people, even those unfamiliar with the problem or issue, can easily grasp at a glance. Avoid text—especially text "builds," and use big fonts when text is required. See Tufte's web site for more information and discussion about the proper, limited role of presentation software in the management process.

Not only is the A3 highly visual, its one-page format is highly portable, so it facilitates "managing by walking around," a practice that encourages managers to discuss progress towards company goals frequently, face-to-face with their direct reports as well as their superiors. Some managers punch holes in their A3s and insert them into 3-ring binders, or carry their A3s in their back pocket. Some managers have so much to do that they use both sides of the A3 form. The A3 will never be as good as "managing by walking around," but it should be the next best thing.

Practitioners sometimes discuss the A3 form as if it were a scientific process. It is, however, *purely a format for encouraging good technical writing about scientific investigation and project management*. Toyota favors using the PDCA process in its investigations, and we have standardized more or less on PDCA throughout this workbook. In writing A3 reports about hoshin projects or problems, however, a company can use *any* world class problem-solving process as a framework for scientific investigation. Generally speaking, all the A3s discussed in this workbook are consistent with PDCA, CEDAC, six sigma's DMAIC, and any other methodology based on scientific principles of hypothesis testing. As Table I-1 (in the Introduction to this workbook) demonstrates, the similarities between these methods are more striking than the differences. If your company has already adopted one of these problem-solving processes as a standard, there is no need to change to another process to use the A3 format. Instead, you should revise the terminology in the A3 reports as necessary to reflect the standard method that you use. This is one of beauties of the A3 format. It is extremely flexible, and, as it spreads to other types of businesses and industries, such as healthcare, it can be easily adapted to suit any need.

The six A3s presented in this workbook are designed as an integrated set to promote good technical writing and, more importantly, to support organizational learning about the processes of hoshin kanri and companywide problem solving. Below is a short description of

Table 1-4. Hoshin Kanri A3 Starter Set

Document	Description	Example
A3-i	**Intelligence report** Designed to build consensus about changes in the conditions of demand and supply before building the A3-X. Used in the "scan" phase of the hoshin process.	
A3-X	**X-matrix** Designed to bundle several A3-Ts together, explore interdependencies, and relate them all to bottom line results. Used in the "plan" phase of the hoshin process.	
A3-T	**Team charter** Proposal to conduct a strategic, tactical, or operational hoshin experiment; A3-Ts appear as "tactics" in the A3-X. Used in the "plan" phase of the hoshin process.	

Table 1-4. Hoshin Kanri A3 Starter Set, *continued*

Document	Description	Example
A3-SR	**Status report** Monthly, quantitative progress report on a PDCA investigation linked to specific A3-Ts and A3-Ps. Used in the "check" phase of the hoshin process.	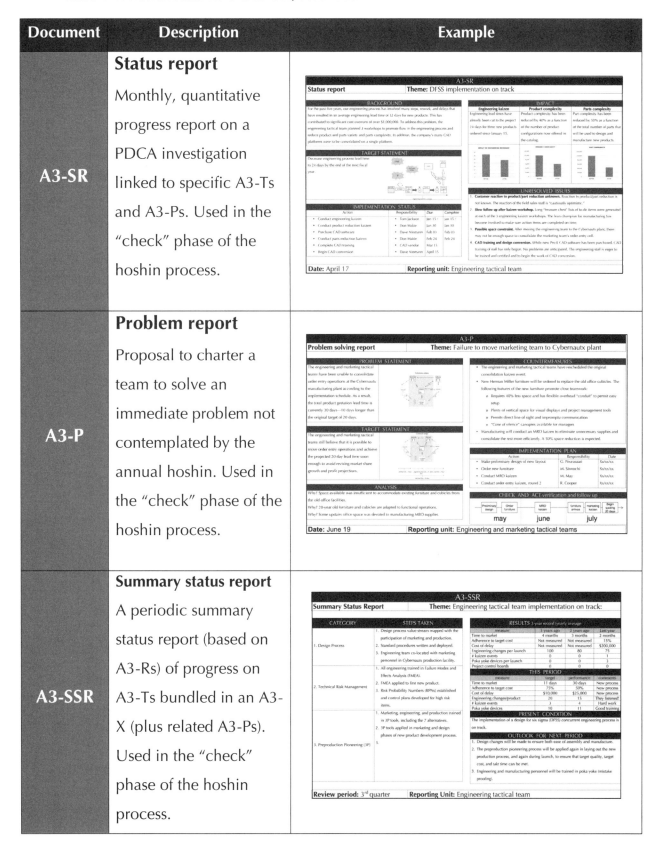
A3-P	**Problem report** Proposal to charter a team to solve an immediate problem not contemplated by the annual hoshin. Used in the "check" phase of the hoshin process.	
A3-SSR	**Summary status report** A periodic summary status report (based on A3-Rs) of progress on A3-Ts bundled in an A3-X (plus related A3-Ps). Used in the "check" phase of the hoshin process.	

each A3, roughly in the order they are used to manage the hoshin process, along with references to the figures in the workbook and the templates on the CD companion. Instructions for printing A3 documents on the companion CD and a "tip" are on page 13.

A3-i: Competitive Information Report

See Figure 2-4 and companion CD Form 1-1. The A3-i is a free form but concise report on important developments in the competitive environment. You can use the form at any point during the hoshin process to raise awareness about changing business conditions that should be reflected in your strategy. The form is processed during the scan phase of the hoshin process (see Chapter 2).

A3-X: The X-matrix

See Table 1-2 and Companion CD Form 1-2. This A3 form supports the hoshin process for planning the mid-term strategy and annual hoshin, and deploying the annual hoshin to tactical and operational teams. You use this form to build and deploy the company's mid-term strategy and annual hoshin (see Chapters 3, 4, and 5). The A3-X is actually an A3 of A3s, because it links all of your many A3-Ts (see below) into a single, grand experiment focused on realizing strategic intent. Managers who carry A3-Xs are responsible for coordinating and monitoring the projects listed in the "tactics" section of the X-matrix, each of which refers to its own A3-T.

A3-T: The Team Charter

See Figure 1-5 and companion CD Form 1-4. The A3-T patterns after the "classic" proposal A3 that supports action planning at all levels of the organization. In this workbook, we use it to support action planning in the hoshin process of catchball. Managers who carry A3-Ts or team charter A3s are responsible for the execution of a project or initiative listed as a tactic on the A3-X or X-matrix of their team leader. Managers can print their related A3-Xs and A3-Ts back-to-back for convenience. Managers who are responsible for managing more than one project may carry more than one team charter A3-T or print them back-to-back and carry the A3-X separately.

A3-SR: The Status Report

See Figure 7-5 and companion CD Form 1-4. The A3-SR or status report A3 is designed as a monthly report for managers to summarize progress made on an individual project defined by an A3-T or an A3-P, and to list obstacles encountered in implementation and plans on how to overcome them. To improve acceptance of the A3 writing method by new practitioners, some organizations incorporate reporting elements of the A3-SR into their A3-Ts and A3-Ps. After the method of hoshin planning and disciplined project management and problem solving have been accepted, however, it is a good idea to switch to more complete progress reports. This encourages the habit of careful reflection, which is one of the requirements of an effective "check" phase in the hoshin kanri cycle (see Chapter 7).

A3-SSR: The Summary Status Report

See Figure 7-6 and companion CD Form 1-5. The A3-SSR or summary status report A3 is designed as a periodic (monthly, bi-monthly, or quarterly) report for managers to summarize progress made in multiple hoshin projects listed as tactics on an A3-X. You should use this form during the check phase of the hoshin process (see Chapter 7). You can print the A3-SSR back-to-back with the A3-X to which it is related.

A3-P: The Problem Solving Report

See Figure 7-7 and companion CD Form 1-6. This is another "classic" A3, one that supports problem solving at all levels of the organization. The format is almost identical to that of the A3-T. You can use this form at any point during the hoshin process, but it is probably most useful during the check phase (see Chapter 7). This is when you may need to address failures to meet critical milestones associated with an A3-T linked to the annual hoshin, or address unanticipated problems not contemplated by the annual hoshin, such as the failure of an existing product or process that no-one thought was in trouble.

Hoshin Tip: Don't adopt it; adapt it! In the 1980s, when Americans were making the pilgrimage to Japan to learn about Toyota, a friend of mine once asked a Toyota manager why his company was willing to permit foreigners to visit its best plants and even to take photographs. "It doesn't really matter," said the manager. "Everything you see will be different by the time you get home, anyway." So, consider this workbook's suite of A3s as a starter set. You should plan to adapt these documents to your company's own culture and conditions, based upon your own PDCA learning process. Never attempt to copy Toyota or imitate "best practices," because when you think you've pinned down Toyota or "best practices," they will have changed.

Tip on Printing Forms off the CD Companion: The documents included on the CD Companion have been formatted as Adobe pdf (portable document format) files so that they may be printed from practically any computer on practically any printer. We recommend that you print the documents using Adobe Reader, which is available as a free download on the web at *www.adobe.com*. Once you have installed Adobe Reader, you can easily print all of the documents on the CD Companion. Please note, however, that the documents have been formatted for various sizes of paper, including US letter (8½″ × 11″), US legal (11″ × 14″), and in some cases tabloid size paper (11″ × 17″). When you print, use Adobe Reader's "page setup" function (available from the pull-down "file" menu) to verify the size for which the document you are printing has been formatted. Also check that your printer is capable of printing that paper size and is loaded with the correct paper. If your printer is not capable of printing tabloid size paper, you must do two things to shrink tabloid-size documents to letter-size: 1) change the paper size setting in the "page setup" window to "US letter" and 2) choose "Reduce to Printer Margins" in the "page scaling" function, which appears halfway down the "print" window (in Adobe Reader 7). Note that letter- and tabloid-size pages are proportional to one another, but not to legal-size pages.

Preparing for the Hoshin Process

The focus in a lean enterprise, and the focus of the hoshin process, is the empowerment of frontline decision makers who add value to your products and services. Perhaps the best way to visualize this is the circular organization chart (see Figure 1-2). At the center of the chart are the value-adding employees who actually shape the final product or service for the external customer.

The point to the circular organization chart is that every business function at every level of the organization must support the value-adder, or else the customer won't be satisfied and the company won't make money.

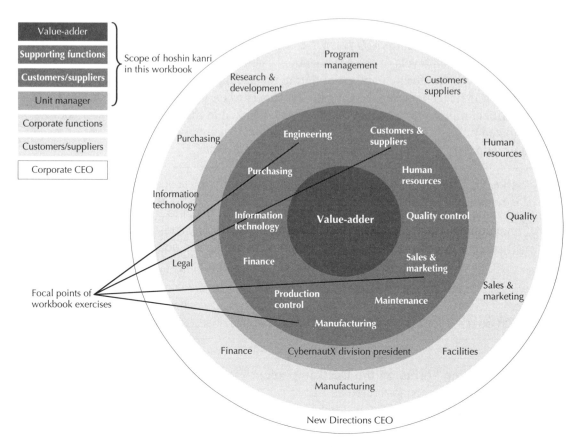

Figure 1-2. Circular Organization Chart

Hoshin Team Exercise: An excellent way to prepare for the hoshin process and decide the members for the hoshin, tactical, and operational teams, is to build a circular organization chart. (In the next exercise, you will select the appropriate members for this hoshin team.) You must gear the hoshin process to supporting actions teams and, ultimately, the value-adding employees on the front line. Below are seven steps for building a circular organization chart for your implementation of hoshin kanri.

1. *Identify the business unit for which you will plan and implement strategy.* Is it a brand? A product or product line? A manufacturing facility or technical center? The circular organization chart here has been drawn for the business unit in our case study, the Cybernautx Division of New Directions, Inc. Cybernautx manages a single value stream.

2. *Identify the leader of the business unit you have chosen.* This person should be the hoshin team leader. At the very least, the hoshin team leader should report directly to the business unit leader. In the case of Cybernautx, the hoshin team leader is the value stream manager, who is also the president of the Cybernautx Division.

3. *Identify the value-adding work that your strategy will support within the business unit you have chosen*. Is it physical work on the manufacturing shop floor? Is it the administrative work of marketing or engineering? Place the value-adding operation you identify at the center of your chart. In the example, the value-adding work is the work of manufacturing associates who assemble Cybernautx's products. Alternatively, if the focus of the case study were on engineering alone, the value adders in the circular organization chart would be the engineering staff members.

4. *Identify the individuals who supervise this value-adding work*. They may be known by many different titles: supervisors, project managers, team leaders, group leaders, or may be other individuals who manage the activities of groups of value-adding employees. At this point, you must begin to think beyond the management hierarchy and include informal leaders of value-adding activities. These individuals should become members of the hoshin action teams. The number of action team leaders will determine the number of action teams you will create through the hoshin process. Be sure to make a list of action teams, including leaders and members.

5. *Ask the following question: "Who, at the next level in the management hierarchy, should support the value adder, by providing tools, material, or information?"* Another way to look at this is to ask: *"If I were an hourly associate or staff member, whom would my supervisor or project leader have to ask for tools, material, or information in order to change how I do things?"* You will probably identify a number of areas or business functions and maybe some informal leaders that need to be involved to make things go smoothly. The leaders—formal or informal—of these areas or functions should be members of operational teams and leaders of action teams. Make a list of operational teams, including leaders and members.

6. *Ask, "Who, at the next level in the management hierarchy, should support the operational team leaders, by providing tools, material, or information?"* You will probably identify a number of corporate functions, the leaders of which are often members of tactical teams. Once again, be sure to identify informal as well as formal leaders. Both types of leaders must be involved in the hoshin process for it to work well.

7. *Assign tactical team leaders*. The tactical team leaders are by definition members of the hoshin team, because they report to the leader of the business unit that is the subject of the hoshin exercise.

You may identify more than four levels of teams in your organization. In this case, plan on having two levels of tactical and/or operational teams. If your organizational structure is complex, you may also build more than one circular organization chart. The point is to understand who must be involved in supporting the empowerment of frontline value-adding work, be it in the form of assembly, fabrication, providing services, or crafting documents. These are the same business units and individuals that should participate in the hoshin process. Once you have identified and grouped them into teams, you may create whatever terminology you need to keep the levels and relationships between these teams straight for all participants in the hoshin process.

CHARTERING TEAMS WITH THE A3-T

The basic document of the hoshin process is the team charter, which is summarized on an A3-T team charter proposal form (see Tables 1-4 and 1-5). Essentially, a team charter is a binding contract between the company and members of a team to undertake a project to achieve certain targets by applying certain means. Through the hoshin process, the company (and ultimately the hoshin team) formally charters teams throughout the organization to experiment with the company's business processes. In fact, hoshin kanri is about writing team charters—lots and lots of team charters, contracts for every experiment in the hoshin system, and at least one for every department, every cross-functional team, and (eventually) every key supplier in the company's value stream.

Hoshin kanri is also about planning projects, which means every team charter in the hoshin system establishes an improvement project, with a work breakdown, schedule, and budget. Table 1-5 describes the anatomy of a classic A3-T or team charter, with a graphic example of the actual form that you will use. (The instructions for the A3-T are included on a separate page on the companion CD.)

The chartering process is fully consistent with the leading problem-solving methodologies, including PDCA, 8-Ds, CEDAC®, (cause-and-effect diagram with the addition of cards), DMAIC (Define, Measure, Analyze, Improve, Control), and Toyota's A3 format, so your teams will have all the necessary information to conduct truly scientific experiments on the processes you want to improve.

A Community of Scientists—Cross-Functional Management

Lean enterprises and six sigma organizations distinguish themselves from traditional enterprises and organizations in that they have communities of practically minded scientists with a shared vision, a vision that transcends organizational boundaries. Lean and six sigma recognize that technologies and markets have become so complex that in order for customers to be happy and businesses to make money, everyone involved in producing and consuming a product *must share information throughout a product's lifecycle*. Complex systems give birth to chronic problems, caused by a host of small, interacting causes that are difficult to identify and analyze. To find the root causes of such problems, both research and corrective action must be interdisciplinary. Therefore, you must make problem-solving teams *cross-functional* and supply chain management teams *interorganizational*. Through hoshin, your teams cross boundaries—any boundaries that interrupt the flow of information vital to solving problems in real time—and take lessons learned forward through strategic planning.

Toyota, one of the first companies to practice the new concept of cross-functional management (also called matrix management), introduced the well-known cross-functional management chart. Table 1-6 shows how Toyota linked quality, production control, and cost management activities. Hoshin is how Toyota and other practitioners of cross-functional management successfully charter and manage cross-functional teams.

The cross-functional chart is more of an organizational value stream map representing all players in the order in which they become engaged in a process, for example, in a new product launch. As this workbook is more about helping organizations continue their transition from the charter of mass production to the charter of lean enterprise, we will not delve into building cross-functional problem-solving teams and interorganizational supply-chain management teams. For a good example of how to do this, see the value stream maps in *The Complete Lean Enterprise* by Beau Keyte and Drew Locher, as well as other resources in the Appendix listed under value stream mapping.

Table 1-5. Anatomy of a "Classic" A3 Team Charter Proposal

PDCA methodology: The A3 technical writing format incorporates PDCA problem-solving methodology.

Plan. Completing the A3-T requires the author to create a problem statement that defines the problem, a target statement that defines the scope of improvement, and an analysis that articulates the root cause of the problem.

Do. The A3-T articulates proposed actions and specify an implementation plan that addresses the root cause of the problem.

Check and Act. The A3-T establishes a timeline for verifying implementation and ensuring follow up to ensure adherence to new standards.

Improvement Theme: List the team's improvement theme, which will often be derived from the annual hoshin.

Problem statement: Include a problem or gap statement that describes the reason why improvement is required. The problem statement includes an exact timeframe and one or more measures of the gap.

Target Statement: Enter a complete sentence or short paragraph that incorporates the team's main targets. You may want to summarize your targets by listing your value stream profit target.

Proposed Action: Enter suggested tactics for achieving the targets you've set in the target statement. You may already have listed these on the problem statements you developed for your mid-term strategies.

Implementation plan: Specify actions, parties responsible for implementation, and projected completion dates.

Analysis: Succinctly describe the root cause analysis that supports your proposed action.

Check and Act: Create a visual timeline to facilitate verification of implementation and follow up to ensure adherence to new standards.

Note on visual management: A3 documents are part of your visual management system for self-managed team activity (see Chapter 7 on the "check" phase of the hoshin process). For example, you may establish a project management board and post your A3-T. The board should also contain charts for each of your major target values as well as a draft schedule or Gantt chart. The management board will be a focal point of the deployment process, as well as for reviewing and taking corrective action that is needed to execute the hoshin. As part of your visual management system, you can also create a web page on your company's web site to mirror the information on your management board.

Table 1-6. Example of Toyota's Cross-functional Management Chart

Company activities / Office Function	Product planning	Product design	Product preparation	Purchasing	Manufacturing	Sales	
	Engineering plan / Product plan	Design / Test	Production plan / Production engineering	Purchasing control / Purchasing	Corporate / Finance	Domestic / Overseas	
Quality	⊙	⊙	⊙	⊙	⊙	⊙	→
Cost	⊙	○	⊙	⊙	○	○	→
Engineering	○	⊙	○	△	△	○	→
Production	△	○	⊙	△	○	⊙	→
Sales	⊙	○	△	△	△	⊙	→
Personal-clerical	○	○	○	○	⊙	○	→

Cross-function control

↓ ↓ ↓ ↓ ↓ ↓

Departmental or function control

△ no relation   ○ some relation   ⊙ strong relation

Hoshin Team Exercise: Print out the blank A3-T with the instructions from the companion CD, CD Form 1-3. Construct the team charter with an eye to the hoshin team becoming a dedicated cross-functional and, eventually, interorganizational team. Choose and expand your hoshin team to six to twelve managers. Remember, the hoshin team should represent stakeholders of the business unit to which the hoshin or strategy will be deployed.

Then have the members review the circular organization chart. The purpose of reviewing the circular organization chart is not so much to change the composition of the team as to prepare those managers chosen for the team to accept the new paradigm of lean thinking. They are there to solve complex problems together and to develop leaders of lean, that is to say, to utilize and to teach the PDCA thinking processes executed ultimately by the value adders at the center of the circle. The circular organization chart comes as close to representing the choreography of cross-functional management as possible.

To implement the first three experiments and begin adopting hoshin as the company's next operating businesses system, the hoshin team will need to dedicate a minimum of six to eight weeks to these activities:

- *Scanning the environment.* This is research that the team should complete before anything else. It is also an activity the team should be doing all year long.

- *Designing a midterm strategy.* The hoshin team should spend one solid week building the midterm strategy and discussing the intricacies of process measures and financial results.
- *Designing the annual hoshin.* This requires an additional week to populate the A3-X, and, as most of the hoshin team members are tactical team leaders, to establish tactical teams. Deploying the hoshin to the other teams will take roughly one week per level of deployment, plus one more week to hold the final hoshin team meeting—another four weeks in total. The process may take more time if the organization has many sites in different states or countries, and the involvement of suppliers will require even more time.

THE *MIS*USE OF HOSHIN KANRI

As this chapter demonstrates, hoshin kanri has many uses, and because of this, you can easily misuse it. One widespread misuse frequently occurs in six sigma. Six sigma programs use hoshin tools under the heading of "breakthrough strategy," which frequently focuses on large, short-term cost reductions, not necessarily on the development of the intangible resources required for future competitiveness. Typically, projects become worthy of the title "breakthrough" only if they can deliver at least $250,000 in bottom-line cost savings. Traditional accounting rules may complicate the focus on cost savings. For example, we know of one six sigma company in which a substantial increase in capacity in a production unit could not be counted as a six sigma "savings." As a cost center, the production unit did not formally have authority to sell its extra production. Thus, the rules of accounting did not permit the production unit to "take credit" for creating extra capacity, even when the capacity was needed. The moral of this story is that, when applied inappropriately, hoshin kanri can destroy competitive capability rather than create it.

To avoid misusing hoshin, a company must work hard to achieve a systems perspective, that is, to understand your strategic intent—mission, vision, and long-term strategy. This is one of the purposes of the hoshin *Plan* cycle, where you define a problem of designing a strategy. Only when you know your strategic intent are you in a position to make good business judgments in picking your improvement projects.

CYBERNAUTX CASE STUDY DEFINED

To illustrate how the hoshin process works and how the various documents in the hoshin system are used, we have developed a case study about a fictional company named Cybernautx. Throughout this workbook, the Cybernautx case study will help the teams to use hoshin planning to create, deploy, implement, and monitor a successful strategic plan to manage profit proactively.

Cybernautx Case Study Defined

Cybernautx is a division of New Directions, Inc., producer of electronic navigation equipment and other high-tech applications. Cybernautx is an engineer-to-order outfit that produces electronic guidance systems for the aerospace industry. It plans to integrate its design for six sigma and lean manufacturing programs to create a truly lean value stream. From the voice of the customer to product concept, through prototype, launch, and production, Cybernautx must improve all its processes and link them together, in order to compete against new competitors emerging in India and China. Cybernautx even gets one of its key suppliers, Nonesuch Casting, involved in the project.

In my earlier book on hoshin kanri, *Implementing a Lean Management System*, I developed a case study based on my experience with Nissan Casting (Australia). The company in the case study was named *Nonesuch Casting*. Nonesuch returns in the Cybernautx case study as a supplier of cast aluminum casings for Cybernautx's high tech aerospace guidance equipment. Nonesuch has previously used hoshin kanri to implement total productive maintenance, an important element of lean manufacturing.

Readers familiar with my earlier book will notice that where lean manufacturing is concerned, Nonesuch hasn't progressed far beyond where we left them in 1996. Although Nonesuch was on the path of virtue, a corporate reorganization placed a pal of fellow Australian Jacques Nasser in charge of the company. Nasser became CEO of Ford Motor Company in 1998, and promoted six sigma at Ford with great fanfare, some say at the expense of Ford's valiant attempt to implement lean manufacturing. Under Nasser's influence, both Ford's and Nonesuch's commitment to lean manufacturing weakened.

While Nonesuch trained lots of black belts and made important improvements in the area of quality—it lost its focus on material flow. Ironically, Cybernautx originally chose Nonesuch as a supplier based on its superb quality. But now Cybernautx is focused on building a lean supply chain. So Cybernautx will now use hoshin kanri to *integrate* lean and six sigma in a new, lean six sigma program, in which Nonesuch will play a supporting role.

Finally, this case study is as simple as can be, but no simpler. Boiled down to basics, hoshin kanri *is* simple. Applied to a complex organizational culture, it can be daunting to a beginner. But once you understand how to manage hoshin kanri for a single value stream, the application to multiple value streams is straightforward. At each step in the hoshin process, we will use the documents and planning tools in this workbook to show you how Cybernautx and Nonesuch did it.

CHAPTER TWO

Scan: Checking Market Conditions

In most continuous processes like hoshin kanri, knowing where to begin is always a challenge. Hoshin, however, requires a well-defined set of inputs, so we'll start with these. Once the team has been through the hoshin process, many of these inputs will be natural outputs of the annual review described in Chapters 7 and 8. Right now, let's look at hoshin Experiment 1, the *Scan* section in the hoshin kanri road map (Table 1-1). The hoshin team must perform some of this in the preplan work before moving into the Plan, Do, Check, Act (PDCA) cycle of hoshin kanri.

THE FIRST HOSHIN EXPERIMENT: DEVELOPING THE ELEMENTS OF STRATEGIC INTENT

The first thing the hoshin team needs to develop is a well-defined idea of the company's strategic intent. These elements include mission, vision, and long-term strategy and define the first of the seven experiments of hoshin kanri. Establishing the elements of strategic intent is well beyond the scope of this workbook. Excellent resources for this are the classic *Harvard Business Review* article by Gary Hamel and C.K. Prahalad, "Strategic Intent (HBR Classic)," *Harvard Business Review*, July 2005, and Robert S. Kaplan's and David P. Norton's *Strategy Maps: Converting Intangible Assets into Tangible Outcomes* (Harvard Business School Press, 2003). Most likely, your company has most of the elements in place anyway. Nonetheless, the hoshin team needs to perform a short review of each of these elements:

- *Mission.* Your mission is your reason to be. It takes stock of your resources and capabilities and defines the types of products and services you will provide, and to what types of customers you'll provide them.
- *Vision.* Your vision is an ideal picture of just how good you expect to be at what you do. Vision is an important standard for measuring strategic gaps you want to close through the hoshin process. A vision statement, like a mission statement, is essential in creating organizational focus.
- *Long-term strategy.* Strategy defines how you will fulfill your mission and achieve your vision. Your long-term strategy takes into account your competitors and what you intend to do about them. Normally what you do is something *different*, that is, you have to differentiate yourself from your competitors, either by competing in different market segments, pricing your product lower (or higher), or providing unique functions and features. A long-term strategy simply explains in more precise terms those segments, prices, and features you will provide, and when, how, and why. Importantly, the long-term strategy also explains how you will develop or acquire the resources and capabilities needed to be different. For example, what will it take to

become a low-cost producer? What will it take to become a producer of high-end luxury goods? And so forth.

From the standpoint of hoshin kanri, the elements of strategic intent provide only a baseline. This is an important point. Strategic intent is a baseline because *change* happens, making strategic intent a kind of speedometer that measures how fast the company responds to change, e.g., developing or acquiring and deploying the resources needed to compete effectively. When the conditions of supply and demand shift, making your products or even your capabilities less valuable than you estimated, hoshin kanri helps the company to keep moving toward its goal, which may mean moving the goal if necessary, even if the company has to go all the way back to zero and reinvent its reason for being.

> **Hoshin Team Exercise:** You must have a clear understanding of your strategic intent to scan your environment thoroughly. Review the company's strategic intent. Are the mission, vision, and long-term strategy aligned, up to date, coherent, or even well written? Does the team agree on the strategic intent, or interpret it in the same way? Disagreements about the markets in which you want to participate, the products you should provide your customers, or the relative strength of your competitors could indicate that it's time to revisit the foundation of your company's business. If revisiting the basic documents of strategy doesn't seem warranted, then your environmental scan should give you the necessary information to make incremental adjustments in your midterm strategy and annual hoshin in response to any changes in your business environment.

SIX TOOLS FOR CHECKING THE ENVIRONMENT

When change happens in business, as in everyday life, it's a good idea to look both ways before crossing the proverbial road. In business, this means that you should thoroughly understand the conditions of supply and demand. In particular, you should have a clear idea of how your competitive resources or capabilities stack up against those of your competitors. This means knowing your competitors and their capabilities, as well as all the important technological trends and social and ecological conditions of production and distribution. It also means knowing your customers and the social and technological trends that influence how they live and what they want to buy.

In this chapter, the hoshin team will learn about and perform exercises using six tools designed to support midterm strategic planning and the planning of your *annual hoshin* (covered in Chapter 3.) Together, these six tools will give you a rich perspective on your markets and competitive resources. They are:

1. Porter matrix
2. Product/market matrix
3. Market/technology matrix
4. Value stream profit and loss (P&L) statement
5. Value stream maps
6. The president's diagnosis

If your company has not performed an environmental scan, it's essential that the hoshin team go through the exercises for at least five of these six tools to determine what works best for them in understanding their company, their markets, and their competition. The purpose of these six tools is to address seven environmental trends affecting strategy that we will use later in prioritizing potential breakthroughs that can put your company ahead of the competition. These are trends in competitive positioning among business firms operating in the same market segment, trends in customer requirements, trends in technological and business process innovation, trends in human resource development, trends in government regulation (local, national, and international), and trends in the financial requirements of shareholders. See Table 2-1, which shows the strength of the relationships between these trends and the six environmental scanning tools.[1]

Table 2-1. Relationship between Scanning Tools and Environmental Trends

Environmental scanning tool	Competitive positioning	Customer requirement	Technology	Business process	Human resources	Government regulation	Finance
Porter matrix	◉	○	△	△	△	△	○
Product/market matrix	○	◉	△	△	△	△	◉
Market/technology matrix	○	◉	◉	◉	△	△	○
Value stream profit and loss statement	△	○	△	◉	△	△	◉
Value stream maps	△	○	○	○	◉	△	○
The president's diagnosis	○	△	○	◉	◉	○	○

△ weak relationship   ○ important relationship   ◉ strong relationship

---

Planning Note: The tools, some of which are on the CD companion, will be used as training aids, aide-memoires, and memoranda in the rough-and-tumble planning sessions that you will facilitate with much arm waving in front of large sheets of butcher paper. We highly encourage that the team translates all these tools to the wall using sticky notes. This way, instead of team members slavishly staring at their computers they will be actively engaged in the planning process.

Tool 1: Porter Matrix

The Porter matrix is a tool for analyzing how you and your competitors have positioned yourselves in your industry. The concept is exceedingly simple. As Cybernautx's Porter matrix shows (Figure 2-1), the left-hand axis of the matrix measures the degree of market segmentation from narrow (at the bottom of the matrix) to broad (at the top). The horizontal

---

1. Alternatively, you may use the four "perspectives" of the so-called "balanced scorecard." The four perspectives are those of the financial community, the customer, internal/business processes, and the perspective of learning and growth.

axis measures the degree of product differentiation from low (on the left) to high (on the right). It is assumed that product cost rises as a function of differentiation. Below is an analysis of Cybernautx's strategy.

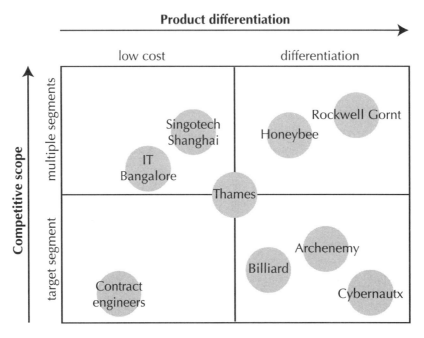

Figure 2-1. Cybernautx's Porter Matrix

Analysis of Cybernautx's Porter Matrix

Cybernautx's Porter matrix shows that it is pursuing a strategy of focused differentiation centered on focused the aerospace market, as opposed to serving multiple markets. Moreover, it strongly differentiates its product by engineering to order for its customers. Cybernautx has several competitors that have less focused and differentiated strategies. Two new competitors appeared on the Cybernautx Porter matrix for the first time this year, one based in Bangalore, India, and another in Shanghai, China. Because of their lower cost structures, they are able to offer products in other markets where high margins are harder to sustain.

Hoshin Team Exercise: From the CD Companion, print out the Porter Matrix Form (CD Form 2-1) and build a Porter matrix by doing the following:

1. Place the name of each competitor on a sticky-note and place it on a flip chart.

2. Locate low-cost producers with a wide market segment in the upper left-hand cell of the matrix. *Examples*: Coca-Cola, Ford, Whirlpool.

3. Locate low-cost producers in a targeted market segment in the lower left-hand cell of the matrix. *Examples*: Local lemonade stand, Proton/Saga (small Malaysian-built car), Mabe (maker of small refrigerators for the Mexican market).

4. Locate differentiated producer with a wide market segment in the upper right-hand cell of the matrix. *Examples*: Johnnie Walker Black Label (blended scotch), Mercedes E-class.

5. Locate differentiated producers in a targeted market segment in the lower right-hand side of the market. *Examples*: Laphroig (single malt scotch), Bentley, Subzero.

6. On flip charts, record the reasons why each company has been positioned the way that it has. Be sure to identify the competitive resources that you might need to change your position.

Caveat: Everyone wants to be a "low-cost producer." This positions a company in one of the two left-hand quadrants of the Porter matrix. Few businesses have the will to focus their product offering so narrowly. To be a low-cost producer means that you must mass-produce a relatively small number of products. As product variety increases, a company's position moves slowly into the right-hand quadrant of the matrix. As variety increases, so does complexity and cost. All too frequently, companies think that they can have it both ways. The result is low margins from high sales of a wide variety of products that can't be made at low cost.

Tool 2: Product/Market Matrix

Most companies have more than one product, so it's important to keep track of what products/services are generating money—and where the money is going. In a joke that turns Pareto's 80/20 rule on its head, Robin Cooper (coinventor of activity-based costing and coauthor of *Target Costing and Value Engineering,* and *Supply Chain Development for the Lean Enterprise*) stated that 20 percent of *his* client's products were losing 200 percent of their profits! Of course, most companies have loss leaders. However, when was the last time your company seriously evaluated which products pay the bills?

The product/market matrix analyzes the relative value of market segments for your products or major product groups. To build a product/market matrix, simply list your major products down the left-hand side of the matrix and your major customers across the top. Then analyze the importance of each market segment—the individual cells beneath your customers' names—by classifying them according to the value of their relative contribution to your bottom line. "H" indicates a relatively high contribution value; "M" indicates a medium contribution; and "L" indicates a relatively low contribution. As you will see below, Cybernautx's product/market matrix shows the product with the best promise.

Analysis of Product/Market Matrix for Cybernautx's Products

Figure 2-2 shows that the most significant market segment is for the electronic guidance systems of Cybernautx, which are in high demand by customers 1, 2, and 4. Cybernautx's midrange products, guidance system components, show considerable promise. This indicates that Cybernautx might want to consider a "mass customization" strategy. Mass customization is a strategy to offer a relatively wide variety of products at a relatively low cost, through the combination of modular design and flexible, lean production. The margin for a mass-customized product is not necessarily as high as for a one-off custom product, but the company makes up the difference in increased volume, as it satisfies more customers with the same resources.

Market Product	Customer 1	Customer 2	Customer 3	Customer 4			
Electronic switches	L	L	L	M			
Guidance system componenets	M	H	L	L			
Electronic guidance systems	H	H	L	H			

Market importance	
Relative value	**Net margin**
H = high end	$250,000,000
M = medium range	$50,000,000
L = low end	$15,000,000

Figure 2-2. Product/Market Matrix for Cybernautx's Products

Hoshin Team Exercise: Print the Product/Market Matrix blank form on the CD companion (CD Form 2-2). As discussed above, list your major products down the left-hand side of the matrix and your major customers across the top. Analyze and then classify the importance of each market segment per the value of its relative contribution to your bottom line using "H" for a high contribution; "M" for a medium contribution and "L" for a low contribution. *Note:* There are more detailed instructions for building a product/market matrix on CD Form 2-2.

The keys to a successful product/market analysis are (a) an excellent understanding of who your customers are and (b) accurate information about product margins. Surprisingly, companies frequently do not know their customers well. Is the customer a distributor, dealer, installer, or contractor? If so, who is the end user? It is important to know, because the end user ultimately decides whether the form, fit, and function of your product meets expectations. At the same time, installers and contractors may require support from you in the form of education and other technical services.

With regard to accurate information, often traditional accounting systems yield very little good information about margins of specific products. This is because traditional accounting spreads indirect costs around like "peanut butter." It is important to invest in "lean" accounting systems that can gauge the relatively intensity of transactions surrounding different products. Some systems, like "order line profitability analysis," described in Johnson's and Abrams' *Profit Beyond Measure* (Free Press, 2002), trace indirect costs down to the individual order line.

Tool 3: Market/Technology Matrix

What breakthrough in your markets or in the world of technology and management methodology would completely change the way you do business? If your competitors are smart, they are already working on the answer to this question. As the analysis of Cybernautx shows, the market/technology matrix will help you get there first.

Analysis of Cybernautx's Market/Technology Matrix

Cybernautx's market/technology matrix shows several important developments (see Figure 2-3). On the demand side, Cybernautx has been focusing on aerospace, but there are significant new applications of cybernetic control devices in everyday items such as automobiles and toys. This means that Cybernautx might need to reconsider its focus on aerospace. On the supply side, the company faces two important developments. First, the soft technologies of lean manufacturing and design for six sigma have now become prerequisites of doing business in aerospace. In response, Cybernautx plans to integrate its existing six sigma, design for six sigma, and lean manufacturing programs into a new lean program. Second, Cybernautx's big customers have been pressuring the company to adopt lean supply chain practices to reduce both cost and lead time. So Cybernautx will also look at lean supply chain management.

Technology / Market		Existing hard and soft technologies	Related hard and soft technologies	New hard and soft technologies
Existing market	**Aerospace**	Cybernetics Lean Manufacturing	Secure, wireless cybertechology Design for six sigma Lean supply chain	Techno-minimalism Indestructible systems Beyond lean?
Related market	**Automotive**	Driver assisted navigation Lean manufacturing	On-board systems repair Design for six sigma Lean supply chain	Affordable redundancy Electronic paper maps Beyond lean
New market	**Toys**	Self-regulating toys Lean manufacturing	Self-repairing toys Self-reliant pets? Design for six sigma Lean supply chain	Self-replicating toys Beyond lean

Figure 2-3. Cybernautx's Market/Technology Matrix

Hoshin Team Exercise: To build your company's market/technology matrix, print CD Form 2-3 and follow these steps to analyze your existing, related, and future markets. An *existing market* is a market segment that you currently serve. A *related market* is a market that already uses goods and services in some way similar to those that you provide. A *future market* is a market that has not been penetrated by products or services similar to yours, but which might be.

- Sections 1a–3a (of Figure 2-3 and CD Form 2-3). Describe customer trends in existing (1a), related (2a), and new (3a) markets. What do existing customers want in terms of functionality, service, cost, and delivery? What is their attitude toward risk?

- Sections 1b–3b. Describe trends in innovation and identify technologies that you currently possess that you use to serve existing (1b), related (2b), and new (3b) market segments. Be sure to think in terms of both hard and soft technology. Hard technology needs no explanation. Soft technology includes management techniques and other social or organizational innovations that might have an impact on productivity or quality. Lean manufacturing and six sigma are good examples of soft technology.

- Sections 1c–3c. Describe trends in innovation and identify hard and soft technologies related to those that you currently possess and which you might use to serve existing (1c), related (2c), and new (3c) market segments more effectively.

- Sections 1d–3d. Describe trends in innovation and identify hard and soft technologies that are new or "on the horizon" that you might acquire or develop to serve exiting (1d), related (2d), and new (3d) market segments more effectively.

Have patience in building your market/technology matrix. Thinking about the future is like staring at the horizon. The "tipping points" on that horizon may not be obvious. Meanwhile, history has made a mockery of many famous businesspersons who thought they knew where their markets and technologies were going. As Harry Warner said after the release of *The Jazz Singer*, the first talking picture, "Who the hell wants to hear actors talk?" If you've been successful in the past, it may be difficult for you to see the future, even if it's right under your nose. Moreover, the more successful you have been, the more difficult it is likely to be. Xerox invented the graphic user interface, but it took industry outsiders, Steven Jobs and Steven Wozniak, the founders of Apple Computer, to understand its potential. The Swiss watch industry was undone by a Swiss invention—the quartz watch, which the Swiss dismissed and then showed publicly. Seiko took one look; the rest is history.

Tool 4: Value Stream P&L Statement

Gone are the days when consultants or managers could sell total quality or lean manufacturing with sheer enthusiasm. Technology decisions today, especially decisions to adopt new management technologies such as lean manufacturing or six sigma, are driven more and more by cost. Cash flow is what big investors look for when valuing a business. So does Toyota. Cash flow is a value-free measure of your capability to generate a continuing stream of value for your customers.

One of the best tools available for thinking about profitability is the value stream profit and loss (P&L) statement, which focuses on the raw profitability of a particular product or a product family. The *value stream* P&L states everything in terms that translate process improvements into dollars and cents (see Table 2-2). Value stream accounting ignores the difference between direct and indirect labor and treats waste in administration the same as waste on the shop floor.

Table 2-2. Anatomy of a Value Stream P&L

	Dollar sales	$50,000,000
Development costs are costs of research and development related to specific new products. Development costs are sometimes broken out in a separate value stream profit and loss statement.	Development costs	($1,400,000)
	Material costs	($40,000,000)
Conversion costs include the costs of all direct and indirect labor, as well as rent, depreciation, energy, etc.	Conversion costs	($8,000,000)
	Value stream profit	$600,000
Value stream profit includes no administration or overhead costs that are not directly connected to the value stream. Divisional or corporate P&Ls that contain more than one value stream reflect administrative and overhead costs and inventory changes.		

Table 2-3 captures Cybernautx's value stream P&L. Here we use the value stream P&L to illustrate how to integrate *hoshin* with budgeting and financial management. This is not a textbook on value stream profitability accounting, per se, and because of its complexity, there

Table 2-3. Cybernautx's Baseline Multiyear Value Stream P&L

	This year	Next year	Year 2	Year 3	Year 4
Market size (units)	100,000	100,000	100,000	100,000	100,000
Average sales price	$5,000	$5,000	$5,000	$5,000	$5,000
Market share	10.0%	10.0%	10.0%	10.0%	10.0%
Unit sales	10,000	10,000	10,000	10,000	10,000
Dollar sales	$50,000,000	$50,000,000	$50,000,000	$50,000,000	$50,000,000
Development costs	$1,400,000	$1,400,000	$1,400,000	$1,400,000	$1,400,000
Material costs	$40,000,000	$38,000,000	$36,100,000	$34,295,000	$32,580,250
Conversion costs	$8,000,000	$7,600,000	$7,220,000	$6,859,000	$6,516,050
Value stream profit	$600,000	$3,000,000	$5,280,000	$7,446,000	$9,503,700
Annual return on sales	1.2%	6.0%	10.6%	14.9%	19.0%

Cumulative sales	$250,000,000
Cumulative development costs	7,000,000
Cumulative material costs	180,975,250
Cumulative coversion costs	36,195,050
Cumultative VSP	$25,829,700
Average percent return on sales	10.3%

will be no team exercise. For more information on value stream accounting, see the Appendix, under Value Stream Profitability Accounting. A good place to start is Brian Maskell and Bruce Baggaley, *Practical Lean Accounting* (New York: Productivity Press, 2004).

Analysis of Cybernautx's Value Stream P&L

As illustrated in Table 2-3, Cybernautx has prepared a multiyear analysis of its value stream profitability for the next four years. For the sake of simplicity, the analysis assumes that there is a static market for electronic guidance systems of 100,000 units per year. Cybernautx's share of the market is fixed at 10 percent because of perceived resource constraints. Also, no pressure on prices is expected because of the continuous introduction of new models. Cybernautx assumes that through its lean program, engineering and manufacturing will be able to reduce both materials and conversion costs at a rate of 5 percent per year over the next four years. All of this adds up to an average return on sales of about 10.3 percent, which Cybernautx's CFO reasons is sufficient to keep Wall Street and the company's shareholders happy. For now.

Why Use a New Accounting System?

Value stream profitability accounting captures the spirit of the Japanese practice of profit management, also known as target costing, which is part of the famous Toyota Production System. Lean companies apply target costing during the design stage of the product lifecycle. It is a strategic cost management process, concentrating the integrated efforts of all related departments of a company such as marketing, engineering, production, and accounting, as well as related suppliers, for reducing total costs of products, services, and capital equipment at the planning and design stages. You can look at target costing as a *lean product development* accounting tool. Closely related to target costing is the practice of kaizen costing, a technique to manage the cost of existing products. The objective of kaizen costing is to reduce a product's cost by making production processes more efficient in order to ensure that each product earns an adequate profit across its life. You can look at kaizen costing as a *lean production* accounting practice that involves cost reduction activities to achieve a target cost for each product and cost reduction activities for each period. Achieving target costs and kaizen cost targets are prerequisites to achieving targeted profits.

Profit management, target costing, and kaizen costing turn the old practice of cost-plus on its head. Cost-plus is a pricing technique that begins with a producer's costs, C, tacks on a desirable profit margin, Π, and charges price P:

$$C + \Pi = P$$

The assumption hidden in this practice is that the buyer will be willing to pay price P. Cost-plus thinking has been normal in government contracts. It has also influenced the point of view of many industries, notably industries in which large companies have plenty of market power. Profit management begins with very different assumptions. The buyer, not the seller, is assumed to have the power. So there is no point in setting a price, P, because the market will set it anyway. Profit management begins instead with the producer's target profit, Π, which we may assume is set by the company's investors. The target profit is then deducted from the market price, P, to yield a target cost, C.

$$P - \Pi = C$$

To ensure that the target profit will be made, target cost drives the budgeting process as well as the annual hoshin and process improvements in all functions, including marketing, product development, and manufacturing. Profit management employs hoshin kanri to integrate target costs and kaizen cost targets—and the means to achieve profit targets—into a company's strategic plan. Budgeting is subrogated to strategy and not, as is often the case, vice versa. Through hoshin kanri, all business functions are coordinated to ensure that cost, and hence profit, targets are met reliably.

Tool 5: Value Stream Maps

One of the most powerful techniques for understanding your current state is the value stream map. Value stream mapping, a technique developed within the Toyota Motor Company, has become extremely popular since the publication of John Shook and Mike Rother's groundbreaking workbook, *Learning to See* (Brookline, MA: Lean Enterprise Institute, 1998). Originally, companies applied the technique to manufacturing operations but it has now been adapted and applied to a wide variety of situations, including administrative processes, new product development, and the entire value stream.

Value stream mapping is one of the first activities a company needs to do before beginning its lean journey and is an important tool for identifying breakthrough opportunities in the hoshin planning stage (discussed in the next chapter). Not only does value stream mapping help identify the company's value stream for each product and/or product family, it also shows its current state and the waste of its many non-value-adding activities, and develops a future state to eliminate these wastes. This workbook does not go into the intricacies of mapping your value stream(s) and as a result, if your company has not already applied this technique and/or the readers are not familiar with the mapping concept, you will need to refer to other books and resources to do the mapping (see "Value Stream Mapping" in the Recommended Reading).

For the purposes of this workbook, I have set up a team exercise to do a value stream map, creating a value-stream management team and selecting a value stream manager/leader. (*Note*: The value stream manager or leader is the same as the hoshin team leader.) However, this activity is not mandatory as this workbook uses value stream mapping as a "scanning" tool to help the team determine the company's market conditions and customers. So if you do not do this exercise, it will not affect your ability to apply or implement hoshin kanri.

In the next section, we will use the Cybernautx case study to take you through their value stream mapping process, which will show you its importance and power. This begins with Cybernautx's current state (see Figure 2-4). *Note*: to simplify matters, none of these value stream maps contain the purchasing cycle.

Cybernautx's Lean Value Stream P&L

Cybernautx is enthusiastic about value stream mapping. In fact, Cybernautx has used the technique to map its entire product lifecycle. We call this a total lean value stream map because it incorporates flows of information and material through marketing and engineering (the focal points of design for six sigma) and the manufacturing supply chain (the focal point of lean manufacturing). The map provides an aerial view of Cybernautx at the moment of maximum organizational exertion: conceiving and delivering a new product to a customer. To build the fact pattern for our case study, we present each of three individual current state maps, one for the order entry process, one for engineering, and one for the manufacturing supply chain, in Figures 2-5, 2-6, and 2-7.

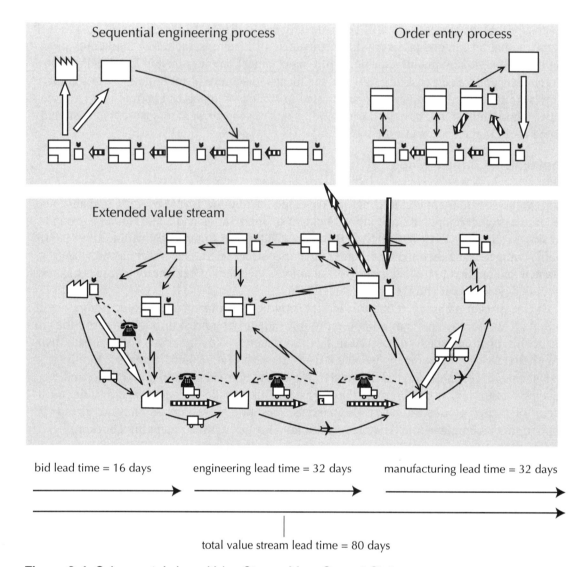

Sequential engineering process

Order entry process

Extended value stream

bid lead time = 16 days   engineering lead time = 32 days   manufacturing lead time = 32 days

total value stream lead time = 80 days

Figure 2-4. Cybernautx's Lean Value Stream Map: Current State

Cybernautx's Order Entry Process Map: Current State

Figure 2-5 shows the current state map of Cybernautx's messy order entry process, which the marketing tactical team created. (You will learn about tactical teams in Chapter 4 and 5.) Sales and marketing occupy one office, and finance occupies another, in the same building. The processing of a request for quote (RFQ) involves multiple computer systems (the client, finance, sales & marketing, engineering, and manufacturing), much walking to and from offices, many telephone calls, faxes, emails, trips (walking) to the engineering office across the street, trips (by car) to the plant, and sometimes trips (by plane) to the customer. The total lead time for the order entry process is currently 16 days.

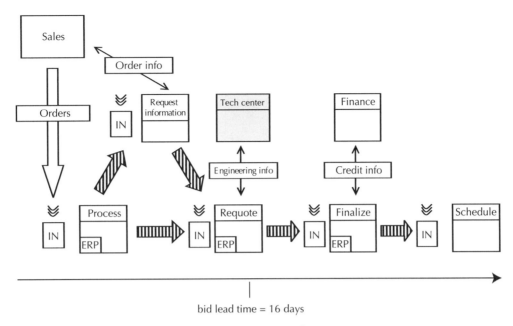

Figure 2-5. Cybernautx's Bid Process Map: Current State

Cybernautx's Engineering Process Map: Current State

The engineering tactical team also developed a current state map for Cybernautx's engineering process (see Figure 2-6). It looks very similar to marketing's order entry process map because all the same players and IT systems are involved. But it's actually more complicated. There is still a lot of walking around and driving back and forth to the plant, and many more plane trips. Engineering sometimes flies to the customer to confirm designs; if the designs are wrong, sometimes marketing gets on the plane to make sure they understand customer requirements. By the time the product is being prototyped, manufacturing may have to travel, too, if there is a quality problem. The whole process takes an average of 32 days from start to finish.

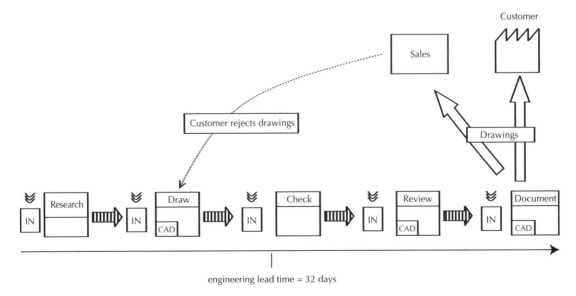

Figure 2-6. Cybernautx's Engineeering Process Map: Current State

Cybernautx's Manufacturing Supply Chain Map: Current State

Cybernautx's lean manufacturing tactical team made a value stream map of its entire supply chain, called an *extended* value stream map that shows a typical pattern of mass production (see Figure 2-7). Within the factory, Cybernautx's manufacturing lead time (including time spent in raw material, work-in-process [WIP], and finished goods) is 30 days plus 2 days for delivery. There are 14 days of parts and materials stored in the warehouse. In addition, a great deal of inventory is stored throughout the value stream. Cybernautx's main supplier, Nonesuch Castings, has a manufacturing lead time of 30 days. Other suppliers add an additional 60 days to the whole process. So the total lead time in the value chain is 136 days! To complicate the whole mess, there are multiple computers and information systems, lots of paperwork, frequent phone calls, and shipments by truck and train. Occasionally, parts have to be flown in from the suppliers, and products have to be flown to the customer—at highway robber prices!

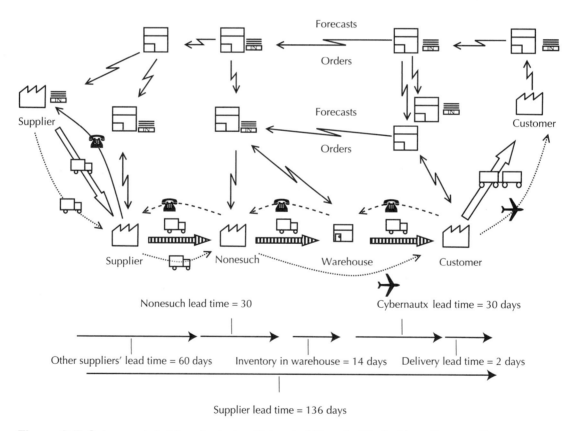

Figure 2-7. Cybernautx's Manufacturing Extended Supply Chain Map: Current State

Cybernautx's Lean Value Stream Map (Ideal State)

Cybernautx's ideal state lean value stream streamlines the flows of information and material through marketing and engineering as well manufacturing (see Figure 2-8). Cybernautx envisions the process beginning with the *voice of the customer (QFD)*, represented by a "house of quality" on the left-hand side of the picture. An efficient engineering center or "cell" located on the Cybernautx campus would handle the processes of bidding and designing the product. The engineering center would contain a cross-functional team of marketing, engineering, and manufacturing experts, as well as representatives from the customer and supply base.

The Cybernautx campus would also contain a lean production facility and a "supplier mall," which would house the lean facilities of Cybernautx's key suppliers, anchored by Nonesuch Casting. Everything would operate on a pull system. Certain inputs, such as steel, common parts, and specialty items, might be trucked, shipped, or flown in from outside suppliers located in various parts of the world. (The timing of these shipments would depend upon a variety of factors, including manufacturing lead time and the cost of shipping.) Ideally, deliveries of final goods to the customer would also operate on a pull system, depending upon the volume and regularity of customer demand.

The Cybernautx campus is obviously a long-term goal. Cybernautx's marketing, engineering, and lean manufacturing teams will use the lean value stream map throughout the rest of the *Plan* cycle of PDCA to highlight opportunities for improvement. Theoretically, the whole product creation process should take no more than 5 days; start to finish—with some allowances for exotic materials that might have to be special-ordered for particular applications from suppliers not based on-campus.

Hoshin Team Exercise: If you have value stream maps relating to the problem or challenge, review them. If not, develop a value stream map or maps relating to the problem or challenge that the team defined and is designing an experiment to address. Once you understand value stream mapping, this should take no more than a few days to do. Many value stream mapping methods are available. All use standard icons that illustrate basic components of the lean value stream. You will find a guide to these icons on the companion CD (CD Form 2-4). The use of icons greatly enhances teamwork and improves the effectiveness of communication of the sometimes-counterintuitive concepts of lean enterprise, for example, the inverse relationship of time and quality.

All value-stream mapping methods follow the same basic pattern, which is outlined below.

---

1. Map the current state of the process by identifying:
    a. The customer of the value stream and important data about customer requirements
    b. Process steps (or internal customers) and important data about each step (or internal customer)
    c. Suppliers and important data about supplier capabilities
    d. Inventories
        i. Inventories of raw materials, WIP, and finished goods—in the case of manufacturing; or

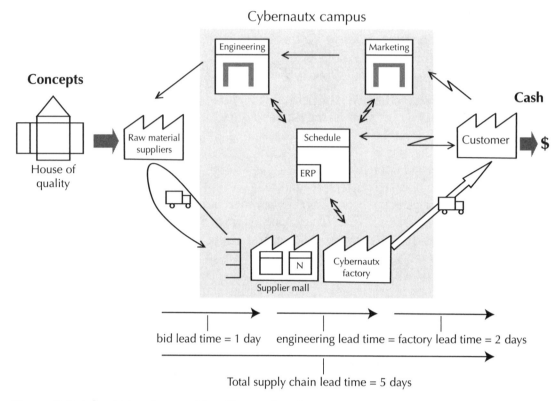

Figure 2-8. Lean Value Stream Map (Future State)

      ii. Inventories of information or decisions in process—in the case of administrative processes such as sales and product development

   e. Scheduling systems and forecasts

   f. The methods by which products and information flow through the process

      i. Are products—be they physical or information products—"pushed" by centralized computer signals geared to a forecast?

      ii. Are products "pulled" through the process by demand signals generated by the next process step, ultimately by actual consumption by the end user?

      iii. Is information transmitted electronically or manually?

   g. The time it takes the product to travel from a state of raw material or raw information until the product is consumed by the end user. Time is sorted visually into two categories:

      i. Value-added time, i.e., the time actually spent transforming material or information to meet customer requirements

      ii. Non-value-added time, i.e., the time spent in activities that do not add value. Normally, non-value-added time is classified under seven categories. Table 2-4 shows the seven original "deadly" wastes, and four more, interpreted from the perspectives of material and information, "hidden wastes."

2. Once the current state map is done, construct an "ideal state" map using lean concepts. An ideal state map normally assumes that you have eliminated all eleven non-value-adding wastes, or reduced them to an absolute minimum. The purpose of building an ideal state map is threefold. First, the ideal state provides a starting point for "backwards planning," a time-tested technique for strategic planning. In other words, the ideal state is a starting point for imagining the future. Second, the team can

Table 2-4. Eleven Wastes of In-Process Material and Information

Categories		Examples	
	Definitions	**Material wastes**	**Information wastes**
Toyota's 7 deadly wastes	**1. Excess production** Producing more, sooner, or faster than is required by the next process	Producing unnecessary materials, parts, components, or products before they are needed.	Printing or processing reports, emails, or other information products before they are needed. Overdissemination of reports, etc.
	2. Waiting Time delays, process idle time	Late delivery of raw material or work in process. Searching for schedules, tools, and gauges. Waiting for equipment to be fixed.	Searching for information. Waiting for information system response. Waiting for approvals from superiors.
	3. Conveyance Unnecessary handling or transportation; multiple handling	Multiple handling, delay in material handling, unnecessary handling or transportation.	Transferring data files between incompatible computer systems or software packages. Over-dissemination of reports, etc.
	4. Overprocessing Unnecessary processing, steps, or work elements/procedures	Longer than necessary heat treatment. Too many coats of paint. Unnecessary inspections.	Reentering data, extra copies; reformatting or excessive/custom formatting. Unnecessary reviews. Longer than necessary reports, etc.
	5. Inventory Producing, holding or purchasing unnecessary inventory	Producing, holding or purchasing unnecessary raw material, work in process, finished goods or MRO.	Decisions in process. Outdated, obsolete information in file cabinets or stored in databases.
	6. Movement Excessive handling, unnecessary steps, nonergonomic motion	Lifting more than 35 pounds; excessive walking to retrieve tools that can be stored at the point of use.	Repetitive stress injuries resulting from poor keyboard design. Excessive walking to and from remote printers.
	7. Processing failures Rework, correction of errors, quality problems, equipment problems	Processing defects, human errors, equipment failures, and equipment downtime.	Order-entry errors. Design errors and engineering change orders. Invoice errors. Information system downtime.
4 hidden wastes	**8. Administration** Excess time and labor in direct, indirect, and overhead labor	Excessive paperwork trails in quality. Excessive parts tracking. Tracking direct labor. Inefficient inspection procedures.	Unnecessary or inefficient reporting or review procedures.
	9. Technology Overuse of technology when simplicity will do	High-speed equipment that runs faster than takt time.	Computerized data collection systems on the shop floor with no defined need. Excessive use of the Internet in product development instead of co-locating team members.
	10. Creativity Restricting creativity through lack of empowerment	Decisions made by supervisors without input from hourly associates.	Decisions made by project leaders without input from team members.
	11. Space Failure to use layout as a factor to reduce other classes of waste	Space devoted to shelves for inventory. Machines separated in different departments or buildings that can be moved into JIT cells.	Continued use of obsolete cubicles in laying out the office. Conference room walls devoted to pretty pictures instead of problem-solving charts.

literally see the palpable improvements in lead time, inventory, quality, staffing, capital investment, and quality that make lean enterprise so powerful. Third, it dislodges even stubborn holdouts on the team from old patterns of thinking about their business and their respective roles in it.

3. Construct interim state maps that represent short to midterm steps from the current state to the ideal state. Rome wasn't built in a day, and neither was a lean value stream. Interim state maps bring the ideal state into the realm of the possible.

Value Stream Map Note: You will be using your value stream maps in the next chapter to compare your ideal and interim state maps side-by-side with your current state maps to highlight the eleven wastes in each of your business processes and target them for elimination.

Tool 6: The President's Diagnosis

The president's diagnosis is a powerful method of review originally developed in Japan. It is an integral part of the hoshin kanri business system. The president's diagnosis is the mother of all quality and productivity prizes and is an absolutely vital input in strategic planning, because it highlights your progress in developing the many internal capabilities required to become a lean enterprise.

The diagnosis begins with a set of criteria for judging the development of resources, capabilities, or other intangible assets that you have identified as important to holding your own in the markets in which you compete. If you use the Shingo Prize or Baldrige Award or other criteria in your own company today, you may be practicing the president's diagnosis already. The version of the president's diagnosis presented in this workbook is built around a *transformation ruler* that measures your organization's progress in eleven dimensions (control points) of organizational fitness in the four phases of PDCA. Table 2-5 provides an overview of the transformation ruler. We will return to discuss an expanded version of the transformation ruler and the president's diagnosis in Chapter 8. For now, you can get an idea of the control points from Table 2-6, which shows the Cybernautx Diagnostic Framework, with a further discussion below of its comparative analysis of resource development. (If you would like a definition of the control points in this workbook's version of diagnostic framework, you can look ahead to Table 8-3.)

The diagnostic framework is an overview of the process by which a company moves from a culture of mass production to a culture of lean enterprise in every one of its business functions. The text under the *Scan* column of the transformation ruler (at the top of the framework) describes for each control point the state that many small companies find themselves in today, in which there is often little awareness of the need to adopt lean enterprise methodologies. The text under the *Act* column describes a state of maturity for a lean enterprise. The text under the columns *Plan*, *Do*, and *Check* describes states for the control points that developing organizations will pass through as they become truly lean.

Table 2-5. Overview of the Transformation Ruler

	1	2	3	4	5
	mass	the transformation ruler			lean
	scan	plan	do	check	act
Overview	If you have some awareness of the need to change and have undertaken a formal environmental scan, but have no formal plan to improve, you are in the "scan" phase for the category or subcategory that you are diagnosing.	If you have (a) completed a formal environmental scan, (b) have both a longterm and mid-term strategy, and (c) have deployed an annual hoshin using the catchball process, but you haven't developed leaders and or successfully completed initiatives or projects linked to your plan, you are still in the "plan" phase for the category or subcategory you are diagnosing.	If you have developed and certified leaders, and successfully completed initiatives and projects linked to your annual hoshin, but have not (a) followed up with systematic visual controls, (b) adopted hoshin kanri as your business operating system, or (c) completed at least one formal president's diagnosis, then you are are still in the "do" phase.	If you have (a) adopted hoshin kanri as your business operating system; (b) implemented systematic visual controls and (c) completed a president's diagnosis, but have not formally trained everyone in PDCA or integrated leadership certification into succession planning, then you are still in the "check" phase.	Hoshin kanri is your only business operating system; you are inventing new PDCA methods specialized to your industry and conditions; your facilities are showplaces of visual management; every single employee is a practicing PDCA scientist; leadership development and certification are an integral part of your succession planning.

Table 2-6. Diagnostic Framework of the President's Diagnosis

Diagnostic Framework

	1 mass scan	2 plan	3 do	4 check	5 lean act
Business operating system		S	C	A	
Finance and accounting system			S C A		
Human resource system		S	C A		
Supply chain system			S C A		
Information system			S C A		
Quality system			S C A		
Sales and marketing system		S	C A		
Engineering system			S A		
Manufacturing operations system			S C	C	
Maintenance system			S C A	A	
Materials and logistics system			S C A		

C = Cybernautx   A = Archenemy   S = Shanghai

Cybernautx Comparative Analysis of Resource Development

As part of its environmental scan, Cybernautx performed a diagnosis of its capabilities and those of the suppliers listed on its Porter matrix. Hard data were not available, but the hoshin team did its best to gather enough competitive intelligence to estimate competitors' development in each of the eleven control points of the diagnostic framework for the companies Archenemy and Shanghai. The diagnosis and resulting radar diagram indicates that, compared to Archenemy and Shanghai, Cybernautx's development has been relatively even (see Figure 2-9). The company shows outstanding strength in product development, but it lags behind its competitor Archenemy in manufacturing capability. And while Asian competitor Shanghai lags in systems thinking, product development, and marketing, it shows surprising strength in all other areas. Cybernautx will use this information to identify where it can achieve breakthroughs in competitiveness through investments in lean projects.

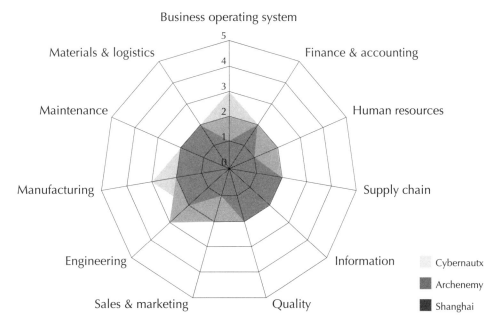

Figure 2-9. Cybernautx's Comparative Analysis of Resource Development with Archenemy and Shanghai

Hoshin Team Exercise: Jump ahead to read Chapter 8 and use the transformation ruler on the companion CD (CD Forms 8-1 through 8-14) to conduct a president's diagnosis. You probably will be surprised at the quality of discussion generated within your team as they struggle to reach a consensus about the level of development within each of your business functions. The president's diagnosis will also give the team a sense of movement in time as your company progresses through the phases of transformation.

I strongly recommend that you diagnose the lean capabilities of your major competitors, too. Although you may not have concrete information about them, you probably know more than you realize. The president's diagnosis is an excellent way to compile the hoshin team's tacit knowledge of the competition and compare it to what you've discovered about yourself. This exercise will also focus the team on "the enemy," and motivate them to complete the often tiresome planning process.

USE THE A3-i TO DOCUMENT AN ENVIRONMENTAL SCAN

You should use the A3-i format introduced in Chapter 1 (see Table 1-4) to document your scan of conditions in your markets and industries (see Figure 2-10 and CD Form 1-1). The A3-i goes beyond simple observation and analysis to reach conclusions about the impact of change and how the company should adapt to it. Actually, the A3-i would normally be circulated in advance of finalizing the scan, to build consensus among the company's leaders about the meaning of developments and trends in the competitive environment. The A3-i report might go through several revisions and clarifications before being adopted as definitive of the company's official position.

Having performed a scan, the hoshin team is ready to move to the *Plan* phase of the PDCA cycle, and hoshin Experiments 2 and 3, designing a midterm strategy and annual strategy, shown in Chapter 3 and 4. In Chapter 4, the hoshin team also assigns the tactical team members. In Chapter 5, the hoshin team begins Experiment 4 by involving the other three hoshin teams in a deployment process called *catchball*, so named because there is a good deal of back and forth negotiating in the four major rounds of building tactical and operational A3-Ts and A3-Xs (team charters and X-matrices). The hoshin team will also engage in the first and last rounds of the catchball process.

Competitive information report | **Theme:** Erosion of global competitive position

OBSERVATION

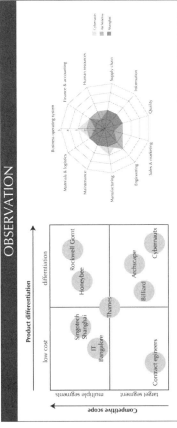

ANALYSIS

Porter analysis. Cybernautx's Porter matrix shows that it is pursuing a strategy of focused differentiation centered on the aerospace market, as opposed to serving multiple markets. Moreover, it strongly differentiates its product by engineering to order for its customers. In its targeted market segments, Cybernautx faces at least one close competitor, Archenemy. Two new competitors appeared on the market this year, one based in Bangalore, India, and another in Shanghai, China. Because of their lower cost structure, they are able to offer products in markets where high margins are harder to sustain.

Radar analysis. Hard data were not available, but the lean team did its best to gather enough competitive intelligence to estimate competitors' development in each of the eleven control points of

ANALYSIS (continued)

the diagnostic framework for the companies Archenemy and Shanghai. The radar diagram indicates that, compared to Archenemy and Shanghai, Cybernautx's development has been relatively even (see Figure 2-9). The company shows outstanding strength in product development, but it lags behind its competitor Archenemy in its business operating system as well as in manufacturing capability. And while Asian competitor Shanghai lags in systems thinking, product development, and marketing, it shows surprising strength in all other areas. Globalization has created a situation in which the cost of educating and compensating talented engineers is falling in developing countries, especially India and China, while it is rising in developed countries like the United States.

IMPLICATIONS FOR THE BUSINESS

1. Companies based in developing countries show surprising levels of organizational development, particularly in low-end engineering and mass production. The pool of talented foreign engineers is large, however, and Cybernautx's high end business may be at risk in the future if developing country companies continue to adapt, as they certainly will.

2. Developed country competitors are building new capabilities in areas that have historically been weak for Cybernautx (manufacturing, supply chain). They may use these advanced capabilities to lay a foundation for an assault on Cybernautx's engineering superiority.

3. Products without significant intellectual property (patents and/or trade secrets) are likely to become uncompetitive. Cybernautx must strengthen advanced engineering capabilities that are relatively difficult to replicate. It must also build manufacturing and other capabilities to meet rising customer expectations that its competitors may be better qualified to meet.

Date: June 16, 2006 | **Reporting unit:** Hoshin team

Figure 2-10. Hoshin Team A3-i Competitive Intelligence Report

CHAPTER THREE

PLAN: Design a Midterm Strategy

This chapter covers hoshin Experiment 2, in which the hoshin team begins to build the midterm strategy and annual hoshin. Midterm strategy governs the second of the seven experiments of the hoshin system. It has a 3- to 5-year planning horizon with a set of break-through objectives that link the company's strategic intent to multi-annual objectives of normal operations. The team chooses breakthrough objectives to eliminate specific gaps between the company's vision (the ideal state of the company's value stream map) and its current capabilities. The team will measure gaps in terms of deviations from benchmark values for competitive resources such as brand equity, patents, and other intellectual property, as well as business processes such as lean manufacturing and six sigma.

REVISIT THE ENVIRONMENTAL SCAN

To produce reliable knowledge, good scientists always attempt to challenge their hypotheses, so as Plan, Do, Check, Act (PDCA) scientists, team members need to revisit the planning assumptions they made and the data collected during the environmental scan in Chapter 2 and to identify strategic gaps in seven distinct areas that affect strategy: the positioning and repositioning of competitors within market segments, evolving customer requirements, trends in technology and new business processes, trends in human resource development, trends in government regulations, and financial trends. Has anything surprising happened that points to the need for the hoshin team to return to the environmental scan and revisit the "hard" data it collected and look for new data to challenge it?

One way the PDCA scientists should prepare for challenging their hypotheses is to keep a journal of events pertaining to their industry and markets. Teaching business at the University of Vermont years ago, I asked my students to subscribe to one or more reputable business publications—such as *The Economist*, *The Wall Street Journal*, *The Christian Science Monitor*, *Business Week*, *U.S. News and World Report*, or *The New York Times*—and to keep a personal journal of their observations, thoughts, and feelings about the future of the U.S. and global economy. What are the leading publications in your industry? Do you routinely consider alternative points of view? Do you have a Steven Jobs in your industry? How would you know? Here are some basic rules for keeping a journal:

1. ***Choose the right time and place for journaling.*** Quiet and comfort will help the process.
2. ***Choose the right journaling tools to encourage reflection and creative thinking.*** Use whatever works for you: computer, sketchbook, or notebook. Keep a favorite pen or colored pencils close at hand. Other useful items include scissors for clipping articles and glue or tape for fixing clippings, photos, and other materials into your notebook.
3. ***Be regular.*** Commit yourself to making a certain number of entries a week, and try to sit down at the same time each day.

4. *Keep it informal and messy.* Don't bother to write complete sentences, and don't stop to correct spelling errors or to make things neat and pretty. Keep the reflective process moving ahead.

5. *Be creative.* There are many strategies to overcome the proverbial writer's block. When your head is full of ideas, try to focus on one. Consider telling a story. Or ask and answer interesting questions, such as "Why is it that our customers prefer the competitor's product?" Periodically take a break from solving business puzzles to reflect on positive information and experiences. Make sense of new information, events, and ideas that may challenge, surprise, or confuse you. Consider alternative theories or perspectives by asking "What if" in the safety of your journal. Don't forget to keep track of how your theories or perspectives have changed.

6. *Share your perspectives.* Use your journal to create a list of observations or questions for the hoshin review meetings described in Chapter 7. Use the A3-i competitive information report to build consensus for your views.

For general information about keeping a journal, see Joan Neubauer's *The Complete Idiot's Guide to Journaling* (Alpha, 2000). Journaling is a well-tested form of self-education, favored by Leonardo da Vinci and many others of note. Other, more recent titles on the subject of keeping a journal focus on spirituality and scrapbooking, but will nevertheless contain useful information about setting up and keeping any type of journal.

Hoshin Team Exercise: The team needs to look for recent or emerging data that don't support the planning assumptions it made when it originally scanned the competitive environment. For example, have competitors unexpectedly announced new products? Have recent political developments increased the risk of planned investments at home or abroad?

As mentioned above, all good PDCA scientists (and business leaders) should be vigilantly scanning the news for new developments that may affect their companies, especially as it concerns the basic economic trends in supply and demand. Hoshin team members should look at these conditions of supply:

- trends in product and production technology
- trends in basic and higher education
- international trends affecting foreign investments and the flow of capital and labor across borders

Conditions of demand include:

- the growth rate of your own economy
- the growth of the economies of countries to which your company may export products

The team should also review service call information about existing products and services, as well as emerging information about product and process failures from design and manufacturing reviews in new product introductions. In addition, you can begin to impose some structure to your findings, opinions, and revelations. For example, you might tab or highlight your journal entries to correspond to things your competitors are up to, trends in customer requirements, new inventions and technologies, developments on Wall Street, trends in human resource development, and so forth. Not only will this structure help you later when you translate vision into a concrete strategy, it can even spur creativity.

IDENTIFY BREAKTHROUGH OPPORTUNITIES USING VALUE STREAM MAPPING

In addition to using the six tools in your environment scan to support midterm strategic planning and the planning of your annual hoshin, the team can use the value stream map tool to identify specific midterm opportunities by highlighting the gaps between the current state and your hypothesized future or intermediate states. Normally the current state—especially for the entire value stream—is full of opportunities that will take years to realize. If you've been running kaizen events in your company, you probably have a long list already. If there are too many opportunities from which to choose, create one or more intermediate state maps. Then compare your intermediate maps to the ideal state map.

Cybernautx Interim Future State Value Stream Map

To envision how far Cybernautx should go during the next three years, the Cybernautx hoshin team constructed an interim value-stream map (see Figure 3-1). Naturally, Cybernautx's interim value stream map is less idealistic than its future state vision. The interim map assumes in the next three years that the company will not be able to relocate its marketing and engineering staff. The supplier mall in its future state map (Figure 2-8) is also not in the picture. But the interim map does show that Cybernautx expects marketing, engineering, and manufacturing to implement lean principles, concepts, and practices. It also shows that key suppliers should also make the move to a lean process. Finally, the whole supply chain should begin to operate as a pull system, linked by kanban to the customer. As a result of these planned improvements, the hoshin team estimates a 50 percent reduction in lead times in all phases of product development and delivery. The exciting news is that Cybernautx might reduce total development lead-time cycle from order entry to delivery from 80 days to 40 days.

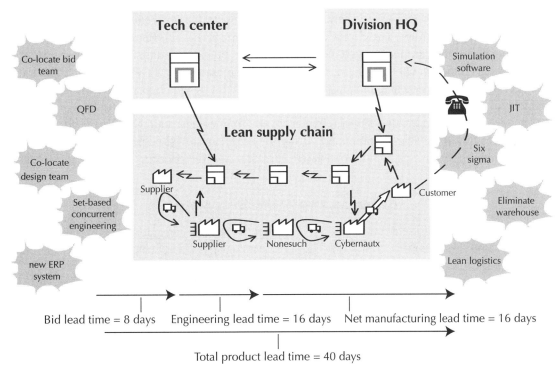

Figure 3-1. Cybernautx Midterm Interim Future State Product Life Cycle Map

Hoshin Team Exercise: Compare your ideal state lean value stream maps side-by-side with the current state maps that you created when you did your environmental scan. Place *kaizen bursts* prominently on the maps to generate ideas and record important improvement opportunities. Ask the team members which of these improvements are possible to accomplish in two to three years. Then construct fairly aggressive interim value stream maps that graphically illustrate a new state of affairs midway between your current state and your ideal state.

Alternatively, hoshin team members, who are aften department heads and cross-functional team leaders, should have prepared interim value stream maps in advance of the midterm strategy meeting. In either case, assemble all the value stream maps—current, interim, and ideal state—and place them on the walls of your meeting room. If possible, make this display a permanent installation to be used as a reference for hoshin team meetings through all phases of the hoshin process. As you make your improvement ideas real, be sure to keep your current state maps up to date.

USE A3-TS TO DOCUMENT POTENTIAL BREAKTHROUGHS

Document the potential breakthrough strategies that you discover with A3-T team charter proposals (see Tables 1-4 and 1-5 and CD Form 1-3). Create a separate A3-T for each breakthrough you identify. You will incorporate these A3-Ts into your mid-term strategy, annual hoshin (see Chapter 4), or your tactical, operational, or action plans (see Chapter 5). Any remaining A3-Ts will be filed in your idea bank (see Figure 3-10). Figure 3-2 shows an example of an A3-T that proposes a 50 percent reduction in Cybernautx's total product lead time, from the current 80 days to a projected 40 days in the next three years.

PRIORITIZE BREAKTHROUGH OPPORTUNITIES

The prioritization matrix is an excellent tool for focusing strategy on only the most promising breakthrough opportunities. The choice of decision criteria is critical. Returning to Cybernautx, they have chosen the competitive gap index based on the president's diagnosis (see Figure 2-9), customer satisfaction, technological innovation, lean business processes, employee satisfaction, and environmental impact, and total cost reduction as criteria by which to sort out the company's many breakthrough opportunities (see Figure 3-3). These criteria correspond one-for-one to the seven types of business trends addressed by the six environmental scanning tools (see Table 2-2). This ensures that the research completed during the scan, and revisited prior to brainstorming breakthrough opportunities, will be translated faithfully into the decision process.

Cybernautx's Prioritization Matrix

In addition to the kaizen bursts on its value stream maps, Cybernautx generated a long list of other promising "breakthrough" opportunities. (Some companies brainstorm hundreds of opportunities!) Each opportunity represents a gap between the company's vision and its current state with respect to competitive positioning, customer requirements, advances in technology and business processes, human resource development, government regulation, and finances, as measured by the Porter Matrix, the market/technology matrix, and other tools of strategic planning. The team listed all of these opportunities in its prioritization matrix and assigned scores for each of them using the seven criteria listed at the top of the matrix.

A3-T

Proposed team charter | **Theme:** Eliminate DIP and WIP in throughout the supply chain

PROBLEM STATEMENT

For the past five years, the total product lead time has averaged 80 days from first customer contact to final delivery of the product. Archscape can deliver a similar product in only 60 days. Our long lead time not only adds cost, but also places us at a competitive disadvantage.

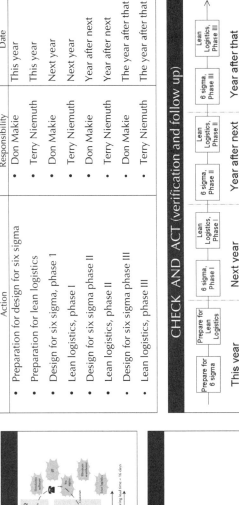

TARGET STATEMENT

Decrease the total product lead time (from order to delivery) to 40 days over the next three years.

ANALYSIS

What is taking so long to design, build, and ship products?

- Waste Number 1: Decisions in process throughout the supply chain
- Waste Number 2: Defective and reworked decisions
- Waste Number 3: Work in process.

Root cause: Misunderstood and miscommunicated customer requirements.

Date: July 15 | **Reporting Unit:** Hoshin team

PROPOSED ACTION

Implement Design for Six Sigma to reduce internal decisions in process:

- Implement QFD and set-based concurrent engineering
- Implement a new ERP system; purchase design and production simulation software
- Co-locate a design team and an order entry team

Implement lean logistics to eliminate work in process throughout the supply chain:

- Work with suppliers to adopt lean logistics and eliminate the warehouse
- Put our internal JIT implementation on fast forward

IMPLEMENTATION PLAN

Action	Responsibility	Date
• Preparation for design for six sigma	• Don Makie	This year
• Preparation for lean logistics	• Terry Niemuth	This year
• Design for six sigma, phase 1	• Don Makie	Next year
• Lean logistics, phase I	• Terry Niemuth	Next year
• Design for six sigma phase II	• Don Makie	Year after next
• Lean logistics, phase II	• Terry Niemuth	Year after next
• Design for six sigma phase III	• Don Makie	The year after that
• Lean logistics, phase III	• Terry Niemuth	The year after that

CHECK AND ACT (verification and follow up)

Prepare for 6 sigma	6 sigma, Phase I	Lean Logistics, Phase I	6 sigma, Phase II	Lean Logistics, Phase II	6 sigma, Phase III	Lean Logistics, Phase III
Prepare for Lean Logistics						
This year	Next year		Year after next		Year after that	

Hoshin team

Figure 3-2. Hoshin Team A3-T Team Charter

Identified Breakthrough Opportunities	Criteria for Breakthrough Opportunities							
	Competitive gap index	Customer satisfaction	Technological innovation	Lean business process	Employee satisfaction	Environmental impact	Total; cost reduction	Total score
Make better products JIT at target cost	3	3	3	3	3	3	3	2187
Design and engineer without delays	3	3	3	3	3	3	3	2187
Integrate the total enterprise	3	3	3	3	2	3	3	1458
Know what the global customer is thinking	3	3	3	3	3	2	2	972
Implement new ERP system	2	3	2	3	3	2	2	432
Hire new marketing consultants	2	3	3	3	2	2	2	432
Buy new simulation software	2	2	2	3	3	2	2	288
Company jet	1	1	1	2	2	1	1	8
Build new HQ	1	2	1	1	1	2	1	4

Scoring

0 = no impact
1 = minor impact
2 = medium impact
3 = major impact

To calculate a score for each item, simply multiply all the scores in that row and enter the product at the end of the row in the column "total score".

Figure 3-3. Cybernautx's Prioritization Matrix

Hoshin Team Exercise: Print out the prioritization matrix and instructions from the companion CD Form 3-1. On flip charts, list breakthrough opportunities the team has identified either as kaizen bursts on their value stream maps or other ideas. Then list these opportunities on the left-hand side of a prioritization matrix. Across the top of the matrix, evaluate and list the criteria for your breakthrough opportunities. On the right-hand side of the matrix, calculate a total score. Sort the matrix to highlight opportunities with the highest scores.

In choosing evaluative criteria, keep your company's mission and vision clearly in mind. Above all, stay focused on what adds value for the customer. We suggest using the seven criteria in Table 2-2, which appear again in Figure 3-3, modified to meet Cybernautx's planning requirements. If you have used the six environmental scanning tools in Chapter 2 and updated your scan as recommended at the beginning of this chapter, you will have excellent information about most of these criteria. Weighting the criteria is optional, but recommended only if you have many potential breakthroughs to prioritize. If you choose to weight the criteria, try using the "paired comparison" technique outlined on CD Form 3-2.

In applying the criteria, ask yourself how well (relatively speaking) each potential breakthrough that you have identified might address the challenges presented by changes in each criterion: changes in what your competitors are doing, changes in what customers want, changes in what Wall Street expects from you, and so forth. Always remember that the point of the hoshin exercise is to develop capabilities that directly add value to products and services, or that support adding value. All other capabilities, however attractive, are purely waste. The point of prioritization is to "deselect" non-value-adding initiatives and projects. In the process, you are likely to euthanize a number of sacred cows and pet projects. Be understanding and politically savvy, by all means, but encourage the team to be as ruthless as necessary. Pay particular attention to the Porter matrix the hoshin team constructed during its environmental scan. Have you identified breakthroughs that will support your market position or move you into a more competitive position?

ANALYZE PROMISING OPPORTUNITIES

Before committing to a strategic course of action, the hoshin team must imagine how implementing promising breakthroughs identified on the prioritization matrix will deliver the desired strategic effects indicated by the company's vision, mission, and long-term strategy. This is accomplished by developing A3-Ts that document rough project plans—one for each breakthrough. Two quality tools are used at this stage in the planning process:

- A standard problem-solving methodology, such as such as CEDAC® (Cause-and-Effect Diagram with the Addition of Cards) or DMAIC (Define, Measure, Analyze, Improve, and Control in Six Sigma) clarifies the exact nature of each promising breakthrough identified on the prioritization matrix and how it can contribute to improving the company's competitiveness.
- A simple "block flow" diagram, or implementation roadmap, clarifies basic steps and resources that will be involved in implementing the breakthrough.

Writing a problem statement is the first step in defining the scope of strategic improvement for a given breakthrough. Below, Cybernautx has used the CEDAC process to write a problem statement that clearly defines the problem that the breakthrough entitled "Design and engineer without delays" (see Figure 3-3) is intended to solve.

Cybernautx's Problem Statement for "Design and engineer without delays"

During Cybernautx's new product launches in the last five years, significant delays typically occurred in all phases of the process, and often in missed deliveries and significant cost overruns. During the past twelve months, our major customer was seriously inconvenienced and cost overruns amounted to $1,000,000.

Hoshin Team Exercise: Choose a standard problem-solving methodology to use, such as CEDAC or DMAIC. Then for each breakthrough opportunity that the team has listed, use the chosen problem-solving methodology to write a problem statement and determine a measure and target of improvement.

Referring to the prioritization matrix, each hoshin team member should identify a high-priority breakthrough opportunity that falls within his or her area of responsibility. For that opportunity, each member should individually identify several "problem effects," i.e., major conditions that need improvement. A problem effect is also referred to as a "problem" or "unsatisfactory situation." For example, these effects might include poor sales or a lower than average response on direct marketing efforts, long lead times in engineering, quality problems in manufacturing, and so on, that the hoshin team highlighted on the documents from the environmental scan. Team members should quantify their problem effects by providing valid, concrete information about the problems.

Team members should translate this information into the language of the company's profit plan—lost dollars, work hours, production, etc. Also, team members should state specific timeframes using such words as "since," "during," "from ____ to ____" and so on. Underline the seriousness of the problem by including a point of comparison. Compare the problem effect with what it was a month ago, a year ago, or with that of a different shift or different location. Compare it against a company or industry standard, or against the performance of a competitor. Once team members have clarified what the problem is, have them write a problem effect statement to clarify and communicate the problem effects. A problem effect statement is a full sentence that quantifies the problem effect, states the specific time frame in which the problem has occurred, and contains a comparative or reference value. It's short, easy to read, and clearly defines why this is a problem.

When you are satisfied with your problem statement, enter it into your A3-T.

Cybernautx Analysis of the Problem

Cybernautx then used the root cause analysis to understand how the problem in the launch process occurs, brainstorm improvement ideas. Next the team used sticky notes to construct a simple block flow diagram or roadmap for implementing design for six sigma to "Design and engineer without delays." Figures 3-4 and 3-5 show these three activities.

Hoshin Team Exercise: Have team members use root cause analysis to understand how their problems occur. A simple fishbone diagram will often suffice for this part of the exercise. Once team members have developed a good understanding of their problems, have them brainstorm improvement ideas. Then use sticky notes to construct block flow diagrams or implementation roadmaps to illustrate how solutions would be put into effect.

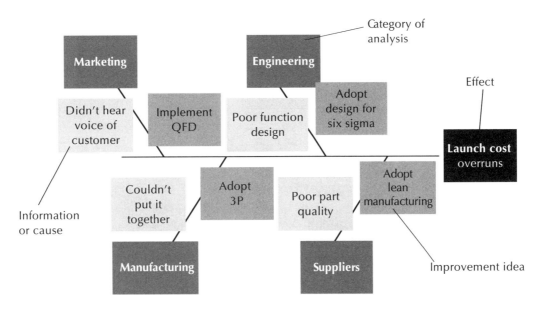

Figure 3-4. Cybernautx Cause-and-Effect Diagram of Cost Overruns

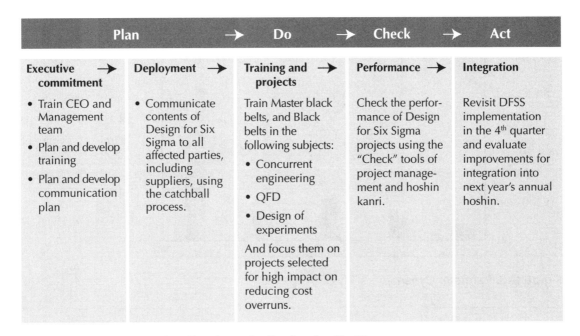

Figure 3-5. Implementation Roadmap for Design for Six Sigma

Root Cause Analysis Tip: To analyze problems more thoroughly, follow your implementation roadmap with tree diagrams to improve the logic of the analysis and to translate the breakthrough into specific operational requirements. Three to four levels of detail ought to be enough.

Using a prioritization matrix may often indicate a handful—three to five—of dominant opportunities that can become the focal points of the midterm strategy. If not, the team must prioritize again by carefully analyzing the most promising opportunities with high scores on the prioritization matrix. At this stage, three additional tools are useful:

- a Pareto diagram clarifies the relative frequency of the problems associated with potential breakthroughs;
- FMEA (failure modes and effects analysis) clarifies potential risks involved and acts as a check on the effectiveness of a breakthrough idea;
- an interrelationship diagram clarifies how subsets of breakthroughs work together to achieve the desired results.

Cybernautx Uses Additional Tools to Facilitate Prioritization

Cybernautx conducted a Pareto analysis (see Figure 3-6) to understand the frequency of the problems or opportunities that the breakthroughs address. This analysis revealed that cost overruns during the launch process were the most serious, considered in terms of frequency. The team then isolated important risks in implementing Design for Six Sigma to improve the launch process through FMEA (failure modes and effects analysis)[1] (see Figure 3-7). Cybernautx conducted FMEA analysis on additional breakthroughs as well.

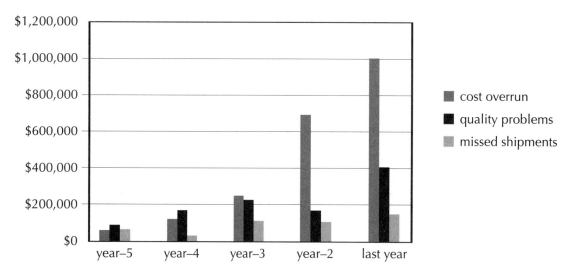

Figure 3-6. Pareto of Cybernautx's Major Problems

Hoshin Team Exercise: Each team member should conduct a Pareto analysis to understand the frequency of the problems or opportunities that his or her breakthroughs address for the problems described above. If particular breakthroughs require more analysis, ask the team to do a FMEA (failure modes and effects analysis) to isolate important risk probabilities for potential failures for those breakthroughs. Some breakthroughs may be riskier and more difficult to manage than others.

---

1. FMEA, or failure modes and effects analysis, was first developed in the automotive industry to isolate risks associated with new product designs and production processes. The method isolates "risk probabilities," that is, the probabilities that certain types of product or process failures may occur with calamitous effects to customers as well as the company. High-risk failures are addressed through preventive actions.

item number	process function / requirement	potential failure mode	potential effects of failure	severity	potential causes or mechanisms	occurrence	process controls / prevention	detection	R.P.N.
1	Voice of the customer	wrong requirements	wrong functions	9	marketing, engineering	5	QFD, phase gates	6	270
2	Design of functions	poor design	bad quality	5	engineering, IT	8	concurrent engineering	3	120
3	Design of systems	poor design	bad quality, hi cost	6	engineering, IT	9	concurrent engineering	8	432
4	Design of subsystems	poor design, supplier	bad quality, hi cost	3	engineering, IT	3	supplier development	3	27
5	Design of parts	supplier	bad quality, hi cost	5	suppliers, IT	2	supplier development	5	50
6	Manufacturing	poor DFM	bad quality, hi cost	8	en'g, manufacturing	5	preproduction planning, JIT	3	120

R.P.N. = Risk Probability Number = Severity x Occurrence x Detection

Figure 3-7. Risks Involved with Making the Breakthrough with FMEA

Hoshin Planning Tool: In the context of strategic planning, you can apply FMEA to business processes, such as the launch process for a new product launch, or to entire initiatives to isolate risks and address them through preventive actions, as in the case of the hoshin plan, where you incorporate them into the design of strategy.

Cybernautx Constructs an Interrelationship Diagram

At the end of the preceding analysis, the Cybernautx hoshin team had a short list of seven alternatives from which to choose. To see which of these alternatives might work best together, the team constructed an interrelationship diagram. Based upon the number of inputs and outputs on the diagram, "Make better products JIT at target cost" and "Design and engineer without delays" quickly rose to the top of the list, followed closely by "Integrate the supply chain." (See Figure 3-8.) the hoshin team decided to select three breakthroughs and to "deselect" the remaining alternatives. They reasoned that the other top contenders, "Adopt QFD" and "Implement 3P" could be integrated into initiatives for design for six sigma and lean manufacturing.

Hoshin Team Exercise: The team should have reduced their list of breakthrough opportunities to a manageable number, probably around twenty or less, by using a prioritization matrix. The number may have reduced even further through Pareto analysis and FMEA. If the team has more than five alternative breakthroughs remaining at this point, understanding the breakthroughs *as a system* the team should further reduce the number. For this purpose, your interrelationship diagram is very helpful. An interrelationship diagram reveals the interdependencies of the breakthroughs on your short list of opportunities. The candidates with the strongest interdependence (shown by the number of inputs and outputs on the diagram) will reinforce each other. Thus, they are probably better candidates than others on the list that don't work so well as a system.

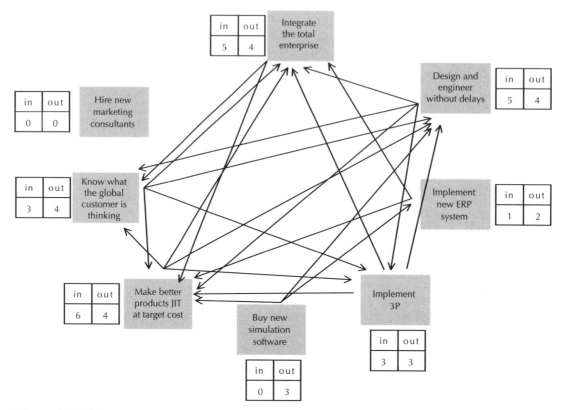

Figure 3-8. Cybernautx's Interrelationship Diagram of Major Opportunities

RECORD BREAKTHROUGH OBJECTIVES ON THE A3-X

Once you analyze all your improvement ideas, you'll have a stack of three to five A3-Ts (consisting of a problem statement, cause-and-effect diagram, and implementation roadmap), one for each breakthrough on your prioritized list. In Chapter 4, you will learn how to use these A3-Ts to create team charters for the annual hoshin. Now it's time to return to the X-matrix introduced in Chapter 1. Recall that the A3-X (X-matrix) is a memorandum that the team uses for identifying the factors critical to the company's success and the interdependencies or linkages among these factors organized around the quadrants labeled strategies, tactics, process, and results. Before you can write team charters and finalize project plans, you must *design the experiments* of strategy, tactics, and process or operations. This *design of strategy* during the plan stage is for the purposes of optimizing overall system performance and achieving good financial results.

The strategies you record to the left of the "X," communicate in broad terms how the company's position is shifting and creates a context for discussing the future. Figure 3-9 shows Cybernautx's strategies. If it sounds like a musical composition, bear in mind that you're teaching an elephant to dance.

Lean Tip: K.I.S.S. (Keep it Simple, Stupid). Keep the number of breakthroughs on the midterm strategy and hoshin small, between three and five. Strongly resist the temptation to do more. Otherwise, the number of improvement projects you must manage will spin out of control. In fact, the number of improvement projects under management will grow more or less exponentially, with each level in your management hierarchy representing a separate "dimension" mathematically speaking.

For the sake of argument, let's assume you are a plant manager with three levels reporting to you. You identify five projects for each of your direct reports. Each of your four departments has five area managers reporting to a department head. Moreover, each area manager manages ten supervisors. Let's say that you identify 20 break-through opportunities, 5 for each of 4 departments. These $4 \times 5 = 20$ breakthrough projects at the plant manager level could grow into $(4 \times 5) \times (5 \times 10) \times (10 \times 5) =$ 50,000 projects! If you identify only two breakthroughs for each direct report, the number of projects is still large: $(4 \times 2) \times (5 \times 2) \times (10 \times 2) = 1,600$ projects. If you keep the number to only one breakthrough for each direct report, the number is a much more manageable $4 \times 5 \times 10 = 200$ projects. If in this example we were to consider the possibility of *additional*, cross-functional teams, the need to keep the number of breakthroughs to a minimum becomes absolutely clear.

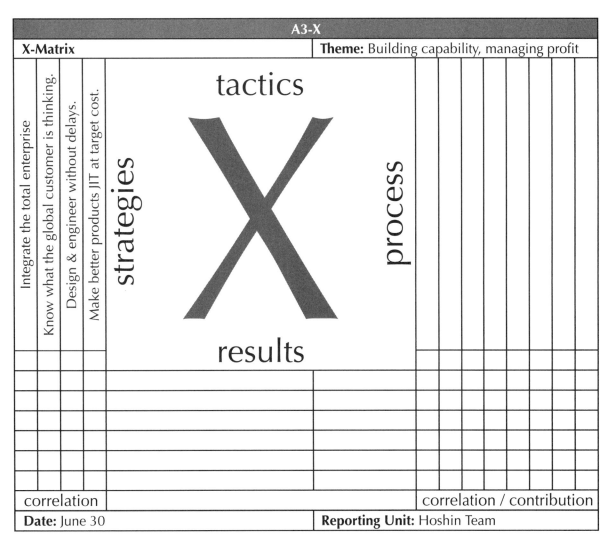

Figure 3-9. Record Breakthrough Strategies on the A3-X

Hoshin Team Exercise: Please refer to Table 1-2. Return to the A3-X (X-matrix) in Excel format from the companion CD that you reviewed in Chapter 1 (CD Form 1-2). Also review the nature of the seven experiments in Table 1-2. From here on, the team will be developing hoshin Experiment 2, midterm strategy, and hoshin Experiment 3, the annual hoshin.

For this exercise, identify your breakthrough objectives and *midterm hoshin* improvement strategies and record them on the A3-X (CD Form 1-2), under the quadrant, strategies. It's important to keep everything in the memo on one page so the team should only record the key points on the face of the document. Record more detailed information or comments on separate sheets of paper.

To access the comment function of Excel, highlight the spreadsheet "cell" to which you wish to add a comment, then draw down the "insert" menu and choose "comment." When you've finished writing your comment, the cell on which you have commented will contain a small red triangle in the upper right-hand corner. To view the comment, drag the cursor over the red triangle and the comment will reappear. To add information or edit the comment, highlight the cell, draw the insert menu, and choose "edit comment." To view all comments, draw down the "view" menu and choose "comments."

Store Extra Ideas in an Idea Bank

You can hand off your "deselected" opportunities documented on A3-Ts to your team members for consideration as improvement strategies or tactics in the next phase of the planning process. Or team members can treat them as continuous improvement opportunities to be fixed immediately as part of daily work. If the team doesn't intend to implement these breakthrough projects right away, they can store them in an online idea bank. Cybernautx has used the criteria from its president's diagnosis as a classification system for storing breakthrough ideas (see Figure 3-10).

FORECAST RESULTS ON THE A3-X

The best way to think of the results section at the bottom of the A3-X is as a value stream profit and loss statement (value stream P&L). Value stream profit and loss statements analyze the raw profitability of particular product families by associating product revenues with costs that are directly related to the design and production of those products. Your chief financial officer or controller—who will certainly be on the hoshin team—can help you determine this, if you don't have a value stream manager. A multiyear value stream profitability analysis is the best way to put decisions about investments in new technologies—hard and soft—into the correct perspective for midterm strategy. The numbers in Cybernautx's midterm strategy are drawn from the multiyear analysis in the figure below (see Figure 3-11).

In planning for improved results, value stream profitability accounting focuses on three basic questions:

1. Will new business from existing or new customers, markets, or products increase or decrease value stream profit?
2. Can the company increase capacity to support new business that will generate more cash?
3. Can the company free resources to cut costs so that existing business will generate more cash?

	People	Material	Machine	Method	Measure	Information
Management	CEO to take primary responsibility			Morning meetings for office staff	Conduct the president's diagnosis	Construct an idea bank
Finance & Accounting						
Human Resource Development	Get Keith involved in initial cleaning			Train the Trainer		
Supply Chain Management		Supplier quality to variable		Establish co-makership program		
Information Management		Books from Productivity Press		Implement new ERP system		
Quality Assurance	More employee involvement			Apply poka yoke method		
Marketing & Sales	Take Mark to visit the customer		Use the Internet to stay in touch	Hire consultant		What are our customers thinking?
Engineering Operations		New alloys for lighter, stronger parts		Engineering office on the shop floor	What is our time to market	Study set-based concurrent engineering
Manufac- turing Operations			Install quick-change fasteners	Implement 3P	Gather OEE data on an hourly basis	
Maintenance Operations						
Materials Management						

Figure 3-10. Idea Bank Classification System

Lean Tip: Investing in a value stream profitability (VSP) accounting system will greatly improve this step in the hoshin process. Without VSP accounting, you may have difficulty linking your existing budgeting process to improvement planning. The hallmark of VSP accounting is the ability to trace both direct and indirect costs of goods and services to

A3-X															
X-Matrix					**Theme:** Building capability, managing profit										

The X-Matrix shows:
- Integrate the total enterprise.
- Know what the global customer is thinking.
- Design & engineer without delays.
- Make better products JIT at target cost.

tactics

strategies / process

results

○	⊙	⊙	○	Revenue		$50,000,000									
○	△	⊙	○		Development cost	$1,400,000									
○	△	○	⊙		Material cost	$38,000,000									
○	○	○	⊙		Conversion cost	$7,600,000									
⊙	⊙	⊙	⊙	Value stream profit		$3,000,000									
correlation							correlation / contribution								
Date: June 30					**Reporting Unit:** Hoshin Team										

Figure 3-11. Record Results on the A3-X

individual value streams and even to individual orders in as close to real time as possible. In effect, all costs become direct costs. Real-time accounting has the potential to reveal cause-and-effect relationships between processes and results in short order and with little ambiguity. Traditional accounting systems spread indirect costs over products without a clear understanding of the cause-and-effect relationships between the activities that generate indirect costs and the products and services such activities in fact support. Activity-based costing can successfully allocate indirect costs to products based on cause-and-effect relationships, but may require more resources that it is worth. Recently, several promising new approaches have been developed that are consistent with hoshin kanri and require relatively few accounting resources to support. (See the Appendix, under value stream profitability accounting for resources.)

You can use the value stream framework in marketing, new product development, and manufacturing operations. In the case of marketing, the main issue is revenue. In the case of new product development, answers to the first question bear directly to the company's ability to meet the target cost of a new product. In the case of manufacturing, the questions bear on the company's ability to meet cost reduction (or "kaizen cost") targets set for existing products.

Forecast Results Tip: Organizations need not limit themselves to documenting financial results. You can also document critical capabilities and other intangible assets that will be developed because of breakthrough projects. Certainly, in not-for-profit organizations and privately held for-profit businesses, nonfinancial results are often of equal or greater importance than making money. For example, a health care organization might target the improvement of specific measures of public health in the population that it serves.

Hoshin Team Exercise: Continue using the A3-X in Excel format, and use value stream profitability accounting or an equivalent mechanism to record the company's multiyear analysis about investments in new technologies—hard and soft—into the correct perspective for midterm strategy. In planning for your improved results, make sure the team asks the three basic questions above. Enter your results on your A3-X in the results quadrant.

If your company is not doing well, then your mission will automatically be clear: become profitable as soon as possible! But if your company is already doing well, perhaps very well, then think about going from "good to great." In the wake of their business being acquired by an equity fund, one of the hoshin teams I recently facilitated discovered that their business unit had a gross margin of only 5 percent! They planned to increase that margin aggressively to 25 percent or more in three years and then decided to increase that margin from 5 to 15 percent in the first year, from 15 to 20 percent in the second year, and from 20 to 25 percent in the third year. This pattern of financial improvement gave the team absolute clarity in choosing tactics to develop capabilities in sales, marketing, engineering, and manufacturing to yield these results.

MEASURE PROCESS IMPROVEMENT

Next the team must closely link its value stream profit improvement targets to measures of process improvement, because you can't improve results without improving the processes that define your competitive capabilities. Effective measurables have several important characteristics.

- They measure the development of competitive capabilities—the intangible assets that do not appear on your balance sheet
- They reflect growing customer expectations in quality, cost, delivery, innovation, and other customer needs
- They help to prevent problems by alerting us to conditions that contribute to problems
- They help eliminate non-value-adding wastes and reduce variability
- They work with each other as a system to achieve complex goals
- They are leading indicators of improvement in financial results
- They do not distort real costs

Table 3-1 shows some excellent measurables, which also appear in the Cybernautx matrices because they translate easily into dollars on the value stream P&L.

Table 3-1. Effective Measurables for Process Improvement

Brand equity	Measures the strength of customer understanding and loyalty to your value proposition. Focuses your company on building customer perception and the reality behind that perception.
Market share	Measures the percentage of the total market segment that you have targeted which is actually served by your company.
Number of new patents	Measures innovation in terms of the number of inventions patented by your company.
Time to market	Measures the lead time from the initial concept to the launch of a new product.
Sales dollar/ employee	Measures how efficiently you use your people—managers as well as hourly associates. Also avoids the pitfalls of direct labor utilization, which emphasizes running machines, which results in overproduction and unnecessarily high inventories of work in process and finished goods.
Sales dollar/ machine hour	Measures how effectively you use your capital equipment—particularly useful in capital intensive businesses. Like the measure above, it avoids the pitfalls of direct labor utilization.
PPM	Defined as defective parts per million parts produced. Measures quality in a refined way. $6\sigma = 3.4$ ppm.
Inventory turns	Inventory turns are defined as the ratio of your average standard cost of goods sold to your average inventory. Measures the rate at which material (or information) flows through your business processes. Another way to look at inventory turns is to think of it as the rate at which you can convert raw material into cash—assuming, of course, that you have synchronized your production to actual customer demand.
Overall supplier effectiveness	Overall supplier effectiveness measures the reliability of your suppliers. Mathematically it is the multiple of supplier quality, cost, and delivery performance. $OSE = Q \times C \times D$.
Employee satisfaction	Measures employee job and career satisfaction. Usually based upon an annual survey.

Of course, you can choose alternative measurables. The *Balanced Scorecard* and the *Lean Manufacturing Measurables* are two influential and recommended sets of measurables that focus the organization on metrics that matter as well as financial results (see Table 3-2). The Balanced Scorecard measurables have the advantage of having everything that six sigma requires, including metrics for such areas as customer satisfaction, internal processes, and learning and growth. The advantage of the Lean Manufacturing Measurables is that you can directly link them to the concerns of lean manufacturing, as well as easily stratify them down to the level of daily work.

Lean Tip: Avoid these three measurables.

1. *Direct labor utilization.* Focusing on direct labor utilization causes you to overproduce in order to demonstrate that you kept your people busy, even when customers aren't buying your product! Focus on total people (direct and indirect) per sales dollar instead.

2. *ROI on kaizen events*. This causes you to cut spending on training (as if your accountant needed an excuse!) and spend it instead on machines that run faster than you need. Focus on the process, not the results.

3. *Plantwide OEE (overall equipment effectiveness)*. Focusing on OEE for the plant causes false comparisons of one plant to another. Focus OEE on constraint equipment instead.

Table 3-2. Balanced Scorecard and Lean Manufacturing Process Improvement Measurables

Balanced Scorecard Measurables	Lean Manufacturing Measurables
Market share Brand recognition Customer retention Customer acquisition Customer satisfaction Customer profitability % sales from new products % sales from proprietary products New product introduction v. competitors' Manufacturing process capabilities Time to develop next-gen products Brand management Parts per million quality (ppm) Yield Waste Scrap Rework Returns % processes under statistical control Employee satisfaction Employee retention Employee productivity Published successful suggestions Benefits achieved through suggestions	Dock to dock • Alternatively a measure of total lead time or total inventory (raw material + WIP + finished goods) Overall equipment effectiveness • The famous measure of process reliability First time through • The probability that a given unit will make it through your processes without a scratch Build to schedule • A tough plantwide measure intended to enforce the FIFO sequencing of parts and products known as "flow"

Source: Kaplan and Norton, *The Balanced Scorecard*, Harvard Business School Press.

The key to profit management is in measuring and managing intangibles. In fact, when you consider a lean company like Toyota has a market capitalization that is greater than that of all its major non-Japanese competitors combined, it's clear that Toyota's competitive dominance is built upon its investment in the intangible assets of lean manufacturing (process improvements) and its close relationships with its key suppliers.

Hoshin Team Exercise: Brainstorm improvement measures. The team should adopt a set of smart measurables that satisfy the points above. You will be using these in your next exercise. As you move forward in the hoshin kanri roadmap (PDCA) and into the annual hoshin, you will define and hand these measurables off to other teams. Ask the hoshin team members to reflect on the problem statements in the A3-Ts that they began to develop earlier (see above). How will your team members know that their respective problems are being solved? Each team member should select an improvement measure and answer three questions:

1. What will you measure? _____

2. How will you measure this? _____

3. How often will you measure (and plot) this? _____

What?	How?	How Often?

Team members should put the improvement measurement or measurements they select into a phrase that starts with "as measured by," and include "by tracking, recording, logging," etc. An improvement measure is the yardstick we use to determine if the problem is getting better or worse. Therefore, team members should be especially creative; and should not spare time, effort, or cost on these discussions and necessary preparations. As you think about how to measure, think about who can or will do the measuring.

STUDY THE INTERDEPENDENCY BETWEEN STRATEGIES, TACTICS, PROCESS, AND RESULTS

Understanding how systems work takes more time and effort than you might think. In the case of hoshin kanri, this effort revolves around team members discussing and determining the interdependencies of the five different correlation-combinations below and ranking them on their X-matrix:

1. Strategies and results
2. Process and results
3. Strategies and tactics
4. Tactics and process
5. Different teams, departments, and business organizations

In building a midterm strategy, the team's focus is on determining and ranking the correlations for the first two combinations: between strategies and financial results, and between process improvements and financial results. The team will determine the correlations for the other three combinations later, when it builds the annual hoshin in Chapter 4. In-depth discussion of interdependencies in business systems will reward the team not only with a common vision, but also with a common understanding of the mechanics of transformation and success. These discussions take some time and *are not optional*, because they are essential to building a common understanding of how your business operating system actually functions in terms of cause and effect.

The usual way of determining links between neighboring elements of the A3-X is to use rank-order correlations in the manner of *quality function deployment (QFD)*.[2] If there is no important correlation at all between the two elements that you're analyzing, make no entry in the correlation/combination section of the A3-X otherwise:

Enter △ (or "1") if the level of correlation is weak, but strong enough to take note.

Enter ○ (or "2") if the level of correlation is not very strong, but still important.

Enter ⊙ (or "3") if the level of correlation is strong.

Study the Interdependency Between the Strategies and Results and Determine Correlation

How strongly are the strategies you have chosen going to increase revenue? Reduce costs? The study of these interdependencies will confirm the team's understanding of how strategy is expected to have the intended effect on the bottom line. Proceed pairwise; that is, discuss the relationship of each strategy you have listed to each line item in your value stream P&L and record the level of correlation: weak, not very strong, or strong. In addition, be realistic about the combined effect that you expect your strategies will have on the bottom line. Have you identified the right strategies?

Study the Interdependency Between the Process Improvements and Results and Determine Correlation

Most managers learn to manage numbers to maximize profits, not everyday business realities, yet profit is an *effect* resulting from business conditions, not a *cause*. It is an effect of the right strategies and tactics, executed in real time. Managing the business's revenue and cost numbers leads directly to accepting business and cutting costs without reference to impact on business systems, including impact on shareholders and customers, not to mention the environment. For example, to improve revenue, sales representatives may be encouraged (through incentives) to accept low margin business that makes negative profit, or that complicates production scheduling (in lieu of production flexibility). Controllers may cut costs across the board, without realizing that deferred maintenance causes unplanned downtime or that lack of cross-training limits production flexibility.

The analysis of the interdependencies between process improvements and results is akin to analyzing the interdependencies between measures and target values in a *Taguchi design of experiments*.[3] A look at Cybernautx, Figure 3-12, shows the measures of process improvement in the right quadrant of the A3-X and the interdependencies with financial results in the correlation area.

As you did for strategies and results, you can determine rank-order correlation links between results and process improvements in the manner of quality function deployment.

---

2. QFD is a team strategy to transform the voice of the customer into measurable design targets (specifications) and major quality assurance points that are deployed throughout the production stage. It broadly means deployment of quality through deployment of quality functions.

3. Taguchi design is a technique used in the early stages of manufacturing to investigate problems as well as optimize the basic design parameters and check the effect of variations in manufacturing settings you are likely to encounter in production. The purpose of this is to deal with production issues before they cause trouble and expense and to ensure quality. The Taguchi approach is to develop a design that produces good quality despite the inevitable variables in the manufacturing process.

A3-X															
X-Matrix							**Theme:** Building capability, managing profit								

The X-matrix shows the following labels arranged around the central X:
- **tactics** (top)
- **strategies** (left)
- **process** (right)
- **results** (bottom)

Strategies columns (left side, top to bottom labels): Integrate the total enterprise. / Know what the global customer is dreaming. / Design & engineer without drawings. / Make perfect products JIT at target cost.

Process columns (right side): Build brand equity from 1 to 3. / Preserve market share. / Increase the number of new patents. / Reduce time to market to 7 days. / Increase inventory turns from 5 to 50. / Improve overall supplier effectiveness to 75%. / Improve employee satisfaction.

○	⊙	⊙	○	Revenue		⊙	⊙	⊙	⊙	○	○	○	
○	△	⊙	○	Development cost	Reduce 5% per year	△	△	○	○	△	⊙	○	
○	△	○	⊙	Material cost	Reduce 5% per year	△	△	○	○	○	○	○	
○	○	○	⊙	Conversion cost	Reduce 5% per year	△	△	○	○	⊙	○	○	
⊙	⊙	⊙	⊙	Value stream profit	Improve by 10.3% per year	⊙	⊙	⊙	⊙	○	○	○	

correlation			correlation / contribution	
Date: June 30			**Reporting Unit:** Hoshin Team	

Figure 3-12. Interdependency Between Process Improvements and Results

Alternatively, the team may wish to establish economic relationships between process improvements and results through long-term research. For example, Westinghouse's nuclear fuel reprocessing division established that for every 50 percent reduction in lead time (both in manufacturing and in engineering) it experienced a 10 to 15 percent reduction in cost. (Other Westinghouse divisions established their own relationships based on separate studies.) Obviously, this can be extremely powerful in strategic planning, where it's often difficult to know where to allocate resources. In fact, we have used the Westinghouse rule of thumb in the Cybernautx case study.[4]

Hoshin Team Exercise: On your A3-X, identify the combination-correlation areas for strategies and results, and for process and results. These areas are located to the left and right of the results quadrant at the bottom of the matrix. Have a team discussion around the correlation of the first combination above, strategies and results, and then process and results. Determine the levels of correlation and enter them in the A3-X.

---

4. See Jack Fooks, *Profiles for Performance* (Reading, MA: Addison Wesley, 1993).

Each cell in each correlation matrix represents a discussion about the relationship of one of the elements on the A3-X to another element. Discussion proceeds pairwise until the team discusses and records all correlations and their relative intensities. The team can capture comments on the causal links between A3-X elements using Excel's comment function. In this way, the team builds a rich understanding of the critical interdependencies within the company's business model. Obviously, given the number of correlations, discussions can be exhaustive. One way to enliven discussion is to print the A3-X in large sections on a plotter. Assemble the sections on a free wall and use sticky notes to record correlations directly on the matrix. This gets people out of their seats and stimulates conversation. If your team does not have the luxury of time, the hoshin team leader may develop these correlations after the team meeting and publish them for comment. It is better, however, to develop correlations as a team. In fact, only the detailed understanding of the complexities of business yielded by this type of exercise can prevent the very problems that team members normally give as an excuse for having to cut the planning meeting short!

Comparing the Midterm Hoshin A3-X with the Balanced Scorecard

Looking back at Table 3-2, note the close similarity between Cybernautx's midterm strategy and the "balanced scorecard" of Robert S. Kaplan and David P. Norton. The real contribution of Kaplan and Norton's book *The Strategy-Focused Organization* (Boston: Harvard Business School Press, 2001) is not scorecards that balance process and results. These existed in hoshin-practicing companies like Toyota and Komatsu more than 30 years before Kaplan and Norton "invented" them. Kaplan and Norton's real contribution was to connect balanced scorecards to the literature on resource-based competition to address the growing role of intangible assets in corporate strategy. And for this we thank them. But as we will see in the section on the *Act* phase of PDCA, there has been a failure to connect the scorecard to standardized work and continuous improvement on the front line of process control.

Hoshin Team Exercise: Look for "interaction effects" that are worth the trouble to track. The team discussion should proceed "pairwise" and the team should use the Excel comment function to note and record significant relationships (interdependence) between process improvements and financial results on the right side of your A3-X.

Then, as the team did in the exercise for strategies-results, determine the rank of correlations in the manner of quality function deployment for and process-results and fill in the symbols (links) in the correlation area for the results-process quadrant.

Having completed the exercises for the first two of five correlation-combinations, you now have your midterm hoshin goals. In the next chapter, the hoshin team will complete the last three correlation-combinations, strategies and tactics, tactics and process, and different departments and business organizations for its annual hoshin.

CHAPTER FOUR

PLAN: Design the Annual Hoshin

Experiment 3, the third of the 7 experiments of the hoshin system, is designing the annual hoshin. Geared to the development of competitive resources, the annual hoshin is similar to the midterm strategy. Though it contains the same basic strategies, results, and process improvement measures as the midterm strategy, the annual hoshin has a relatively short-term focus of 6 to 18 months. You also fully develop it in terms of tactical projects and teams. So if you have been thorough in establishing a midterm strategy, establishing the annual hoshin will be relatively easy. You have already answered the philosophical questions. All that remains is to deal with the practical reality. To establish your annual hoshin, follow these steps:

1. Identify opportunities for the next 6 to 18 months.
2. Prioritize, analyze, choose, and record high-impact opportunities.
3. Establish contribution targets for results.
4. Establish annual targets for process improvement.
5. Study interdependence.
6. Assign teams for each tactic and provide accountability.

To establish annual improvement tactics, you'll follow much the same process you used to identify your midterm goals in the last chapter. The hoshin team will focus on the gap between the company's current state and its midterm strategic objectives. Then it will choose the right short-term tactics to place on the A3-X, linking them to the team's breakthrough strategies and measures of improvement.

> **Hoshin Team Exercises for Chapter 4:** Because the team is following the sequence of the previous chapter to continue to populate its A3-X, each section in this chapter is an exercise for the hoshin team. The heading is your action item and you can refer to back to Chapter 3 for tools you'll need to fill in the tactics and process sections on your A3-X. When you complete this chapter, your A3-X will look like Figure 4-2 at the end of this chapter.

IDENTIFY OPPORTUNITIES AND DEVELOP TACTICS FOR THE NEXT 6 TO 18 MONTHS

A tactic is an improvement initiative or project that an assigned team of ten or so people can complete in a twelve-month period. To establish tactics, the team needs to revisit A3-Ts for the project plans—one each for each breakthrough on your prioritized list—that it defined in its midterm improvement strategies.

As you progress along the road to becoming a lean enterprise, you will probably have a clear idea of where you stand and what needs to happen next. You will have plenty of improvement ideas. The difficulty will be in prioritizing all of them. If you're just beginning the journey, you may want review each of the long-term implementation roadmaps that the team constructed in Chapter 3 and then look at the next step listed in it. That step may be a good candidate for one of your company's annual tactics. For example, if last year you began to conduct JIT workshops on the shop floor, it may be time this year to implement pull systems and kanban (see Figure 4-1).

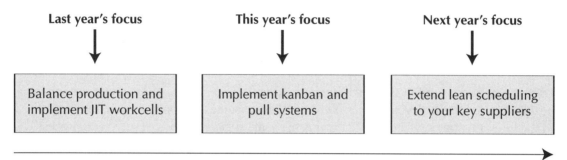

Figure 4-1. Lean Manufacturing Implementation Roadmap (Detail)

To identify additional opportunities, the hoshin team needs to build and compare additional value stream maps for specific business processes such as marketing, engineering, and manufacturing. In addition, retrieve from the idea bank of A3-Ts (project plans) the team identified in Chapter 3 the A3-Ts that didn't qualify as midterm strategies. If it has been a year or more since the company has looked seriously at breakthrough objectives, the team can brainstorm and prioritize more opportunities. *But keep the focus on what the company can accomplish in the next 6 to 18 months.*

The market/technology matrix (CD Form 2-3) you used in Chapter 3 to identify breakthrough opportunities is another technique the team can use for identifying tactical opportunities for the annual hoshin. Every business unit in your organization has its own internal as well as external markets, as well as its own perspective on the hard and soft technologies that create possibilities for new products and new production processes. Use the market-technology matrix to raise the question in every department. Ask: *"What change in technology or methodology would fundamentally change the way our business function does business with our internal customers?"* For example, have there been important new developments in the fields of marketing? Engineering? Manufacturing? Accounting? How might these new developments be applied to support the company's strategy?

PRIORITIZE AND ANALYZE OPPORTUNITIES

Once the team has created a list of opportunities, it should follow the same process it used to narrow the field of midterm breakthroughs in Chapter 3. Print out a new prioritization matrix from the companion CD Form 3-1, put promising opportunities in a prioritization matrix, and analyze each opportunity thoroughly. Then select three to five things to do and record them in the "tactics" quadrant of your A3-X. These are your improvement tactics.

Lean Tip: Be careful not to overload the A3-X for the annual hoshin with too many tactics. Each tactic should strongly correlate with at least one of the strategies on the midterm strategic plan. In the fourth experiment of the hoshin process, operations, there will be opportunity for more improvement ideas, frequently related to specific business functions. In this, the third experiment of hoshin, it is important to spell out which of the business functions plays a starring role, and which of the functions plays a supporting role.

Cybernautx's Hoshin Team Leader's List of Promising Improvement Tactics

In proposing tactics, the Cybernautx hoshin team leader listed the following:

1. Implement design for six sigma by creating a customer-focused marketing process.
2. Implement design for six sigma by streamlining the engineering process.
3. Take lean manufacturing to key suppliers.
4. Engage key suppliers in building a lean supply chain.
5. Close the gap on emerging technologies
6. Support lean enterprise in finance, HR, and IT.

ESTABLISH CONTRIBUTION TARGETS FOR RESULTS

To establish improvement targets for financial results, the team needs to work backward from its midterm financial expectations. If your team has constructed a multiyear financial forecast, this is a straightforward exercise. Otherwise, you must now determine how much your company's revenues and profit must grow, and perhaps how much your company's costs must shrink, in the coming fiscal year. The team will place these financial improvement targets on the results quadrant of the A3-X.

Cybernautx's Results from Its A3-X (Figure 3-10)

Here are the financial targets for Cybernautx, which has simply transposed the value stream profit and loss statement for the next twelve months from its multiyear profitability analysis (see Figure 2-2) directly onto its A3-X.

Revenue	$50,000,000
Development cost	$1,400,000
Material cost	$38,000,000
Conversion cost	**$7,600,000**
Value stream profit	$3,000,000

ESTABLISH TARGETS FOR PROCESS IMPROVEMENT

In setting targets for process improvement, ask your team to plan backward from the financial improvements you have recorded in the results quadrant of the A3-X. To reiterate a point we made in Chapter 3, financial results are an effect, the cause being the process improvements that your team is now engaged in planning. Improvement targets are often called "stretch" targets, because they're meant to stretch the company's capabilities, yet the company has a high probability of reaching the targets set. This means the team must base stretch targets on educated and reasoned guesses, not hunches, about implementing process improvements. Don't be afraid to set ambitious targets, such as six sigma quality, lead times collapsed by 98 percent, changeovers under three minutes, inventory turns over 100 percent per year. These all are possible, given time.

The team needs to be prepared to address, one-by-one, the issues that managers and employees discover as they begin to investigate the root causes of poor performance behind these processes. To help the team think in terms of developing capability, ask the following questions: "How strong do we need to be in order to achieve the results we expect?" "How agile?" "How big?" "How creative?" "How different?" Once again, place the emphasis on building competitive capability—on the regimen of training for competition—not on the results. Once the team identifies its process improvement targets, place them on the process quadrant of the A3-X.[1]

Lean Tip: Despite what your stock analyst may tell you (if your company is publicly traded), cost cutting is *not* a process improvement because it does not stretch your capabilities. More often, it destroys them. Cost reduction in the sense of lean enterprise and six sigma (properly understood) is the *result* of appropriate process improvements.

Estimating the Financial Impact of Lead-Time Reduction

The best way to set improvement targets is to acquire a detailed understanding of the economics of your own business and industry; but the economics of lean enterprise is still its infancy. Because few—if any—economic models of lean enterprise have been developed, estimating the impact of process improvements on cost and profit can be a significant challenge. For purposes of illustrating how targets of process improvement might be related to targets for financial results, we have used a simple rule of thumb developed at Westinghouse for estimating the impact of lead-time reduction on cost improvement. The Westinghouse nuclear fuel division determined that for every 50 percent reduction in lead time, it could expect a 10 to 15 percent reduction in conversion costs (including the costs of operating the equipment and running the factory, too). In the Cybernautx case study, we've assumed a similar 5:1 ratio of lead-time reduction to cost improvement. For example, a 50 percent reduction in lead time translates into a 10 percent cost reduction, a 10 percent reduction in lead time translates into 2 percent cost reduction, and so forth. The following targets were entered (among others):

- 50 percent reduction in order entry lead time
- 50 percent reduction in engineering lead time
- 50 percent reduction in manufacturing lead time

---

1. For those companies that utilize the approach to planning and implementing lean management and production techniques described in *Implementing a Lean Management System* (Productivity Press), and *Corporate Diagnosis* (Productivity Press), improvement objectives may be brainstormed and categorized using the system of keys and control points (categories in this book) described in those books. See the Recommended Reading, under "Hoshin Kanri."

Cybernautx's conversion cost target for the current year is $7,600,000, which is a 5 percent reduction over last year. Thus, to reach its conversion cost, Cybernautx has established a lead-time reduction target of 25 percent.

Establishing economic relationships like these permits you to work backward from what you think you can achieve in terms of process improvement to results, or backward from results you must achieve to the necessary process improvements.

Note that you must develop your own planning rules based upon observation and analysis of your own processes. The two most powerful methods for estimating the impact of process improvements in established lean companies are of course target costing and kaizen costing, both integral parts of classic profit management. It is often very difficult for companies making the transition from mass production to perform these estimates, which are based ideally upon the careful, first-hand study of products and processes by empowered front-line employees.

Lean Tip: As a rule, you should not lay off anyone as the result of an improvement activity. You can use headcount reduction as an improvement target if there is alternative employment within the organization for persons displaced by improvement activity. In a turnaround situation—one in which the very existence of a business is in jeopardy, headcount reduction or even the closing of plants may be an unfortunate necessity.

STUDY INTERDEPENDENCIES BETWEEN TACTICS AND PROCESS AND RESULTS AND DETERMINE CORRELATION

Recall that in Chapter 3 we listed five correlation-combinations for the A3-X. You have already determined the first two, strategies and results, and process and results, when you determined your midterm hoshin goals. In the following sections, the team will complete the next three correlation-combinations for the annual hoshin: strategies and tactics, tactics and process, and process and results. Normally, you cannot know the precise correlations. You may, of course, estimate them using engineering or business economics methods. Nevertheless, the correlations you identify may be nothing more than a set of hypotheses about what makes your business tick. The point is to *test* these hypotheses by executing your strategy, and make adjustments to your business model based on the feedback of performance in the real world.

Like the team did in Chapter 3 in studying the interdependencies between strategies and results, the main thing is to discuss all the factors that might affect the success of your strategy and make contingency plans to deal with the risks you identify. Then use rank-order correlations in the manner of quality function deployment, and populate the correlation boxes in its A3-X for strategies and tactics.

If there is no important correlation at all, make no entry.

Enter △ (or "1") if the level of correlation is weak, but strong enough to take note.

Enter ○ (or "2") if the level of correlation is not very strong, but still important.

Enter ⊙ (or "3") if the level of correlation is strong.

Study Interdependencies Between Strategies and Tactics and Determine Correlation

For the strategies and tactics correlation-combination, the team must be sure that the tactics it chooses support its strategies. Like the discussion about the correlation of results and strategies in Chapter 3, this discussion is straightforward and can be completed in about five minutes.

Study Interdependencies Between Tactics and Process and Determine Correlation

For the tactics and process correlation-combination analysis, the team connects the tactics it chooses to specific measures of process improvement. The team discusses how the measures of process improvement it has chosen will be affected (usually in a positive manner) by each of the tactics it has identified on the A3-X. This discussion will require about thirty minutes or more. Many tactics will affect more than one measure of process improvement, and some tactics may affect the same measures as other tactics. Another important thing to keep in mind when checking this particular correlation is the need for additional measures of process improvement, which should be recorded in the process quadrant of the A3-X. In addition, the team may discover that the tactics chosen do not address all of the measures of process improvement on the midterm strategy. If so, the team should select at least one additional tactic to ensure that you positively affect all measures of process improvement.

Study Interdependencies Between Process and Results and Determine Correlation

In setting process improvement targets, the hoshin team has already examined the impact of process improvement on financial targets. So for the process and results correlation-combination analysis, the team will simply doublecheck its understanding of the economics of business improvement.

ASSIGN TEAMS FOR EACH TACTIC AND PROVIDE ACCOUNTABILITY

The hoshin team has finally come to the point where it's time to begin delegating responsibilities to other teams. Determine the person on the hoshin team responsible for each tactic it has identified on the A3-X and enter the person's "title" in the team member section. Next, with the input of the tactical team leader, assign one or more core team members to each tactical team. Core team members are expected to participate fully on the team. Finally, assign rotating team members. Don't assign too many members. For hoshin, you typically form teams around a core membership of two to three individuals, including the team leader. Other team members' input will be critical to the success of the project, but they may not need to attend all team meetings. In the upper right-hand corner the A3-X, place the appropriate symbol (or number) in the appropriate accountability boxes to designate each team member's role and responsibility.

Make no entry if the person or group will not be participating on the team.

Enter △ (or "1") if participation on the team is not full-time.

Enter ○ (or "2") if the member is expected to attend all team meetings.

Enter ⊙ (or "3") to indicate a team leader.

Figure 4-2 shows Cybernautx's A3-X and first draft of its annual hoshin.

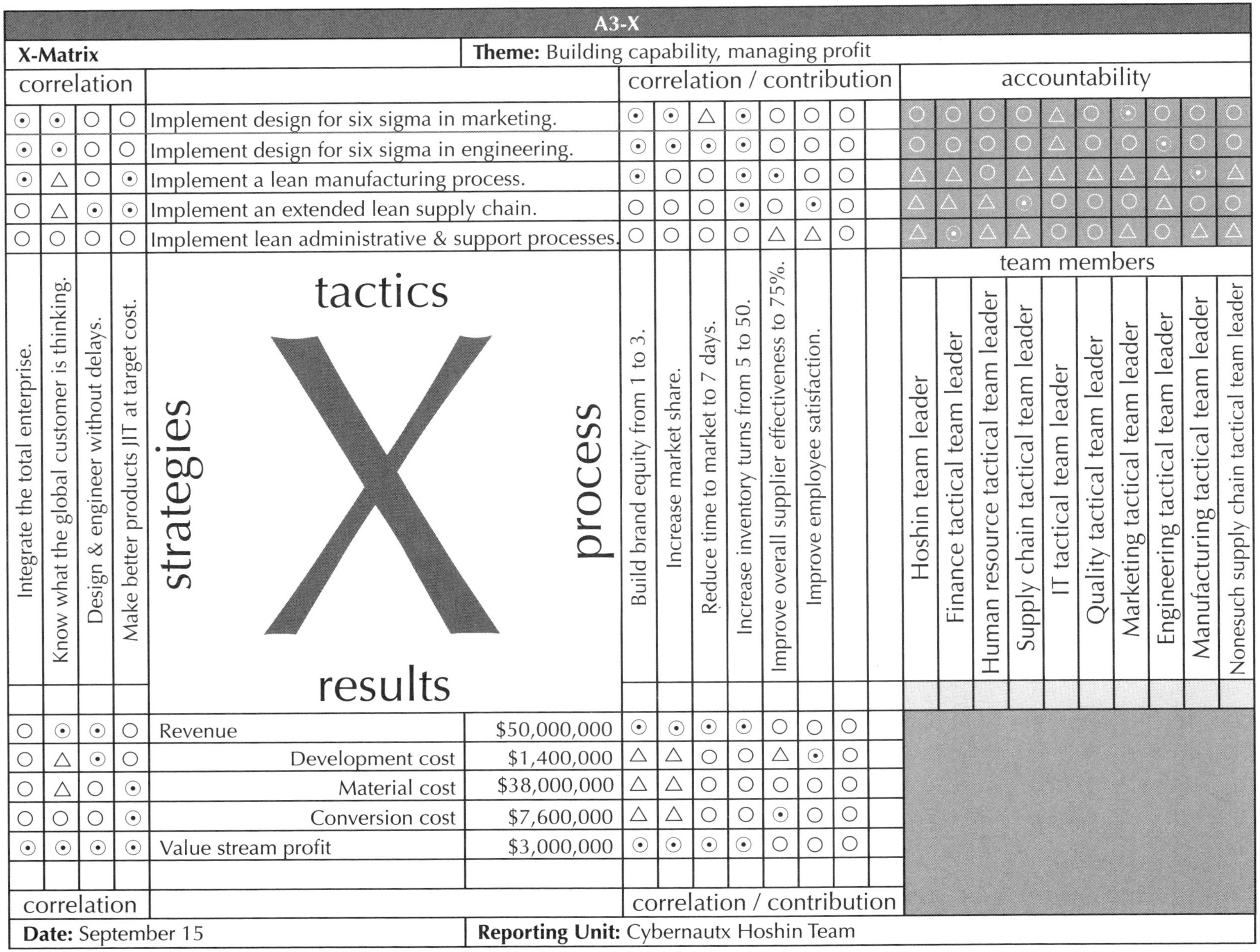

A3-X

X-Matrix

Theme: Building capability, managing profit

accountability — team members

correlation / contribution

correlation

Team members (accountability):
- Hoshin team leader
- Finance tactical team leader
- Human resource tactical team leader
- Supply chain tactical team leader
- IT tactical team leader
- Quality tactical team leader
- Marketing tactical team leader
- Engineering tactical team leader
- Manufacturing tactical team leader
- Nonesuch supply chain tactical team leader

Tactics:
- Implement design for six sigma in marketing.
- Implement design for six sigma in engineering.
- Implement a lean manufacturing process.
- Implement an extended lean supply chain.
- Implement lean administrative & support processes.

Process (correlation / contribution):
- Build brand equity from 1 to 3.
- Increase market share.
- Reduce time to market to 7 days.
- Increase inventory turns from 5 to 50.
- Improve overall supplier effectiveness to 75%.
- Improve employee satisfaction.

Strategies:
- Make better products JIT at target cost.
- Design & engineer without delays.
- Know what the global customer is thinking.
- Integrate the total enterprise.

Results:

Results	Value
Revenue	$50,000,000
Development cost	$1,400,000
Material cost	$38,000,000
Conversion cost	$7,600,000
Value stream profit	$3,000,000

correlation / contribution

correlation

Date: September 15   **Reporting Unit:** Cybernautx Hoshin Team

Figure 4-2. Cybernautx's A3-X and First Draft of the Annual Hoshin

Accountability of the Cybernautx's Hoshin Team

On the first line in the accountability matrix (in the upper right-hand corner of the A3-X), the two ◉ symbols indicate that responsibility for implementing design for six sigma is shared between the marketing and engineering managers (see Figure 4-3) . The ◉ on the next line in the accountability matrix indicates that responsibility for implementing lean manufacturing belongs to the manufacturing manager. Responsibility for the extended lean supply chain belongs to the hoshin manager. Finally, responsibility for implementing lean administrative and support processes (also known as transactional six sigma) belongs to the finance manager.

Note that in this case study, no special lean organization has been created, although it might be. Cybernautx has decided to abolish competing six sigma and lean bureaucracies and to integrate both types of process improvement into its business operating system. The responsibility for integrating lean and six sigma rests with the hoshin team and the hoshin team leader.

	team members			accountability
Hoshin team leader	○	◉		
Finance tactical team leader				
Human resource tactical team leader				
Supply chain tactical team leader			○	
IT tactical team leader			○	◉
Quality tactical team leader			○	◉
Marketing tactical team leader	◉	○		
Engineering tactical team leader	○	○		
Manufacturing tactical team leader	○	○		
Nonesuch supply chain tactical team leader		○		

Figure 4-3. Team Membership and Accountability (detail)

USE A3-TS TO DOCUMENT TACTICAL TEAM CHARTERS

If they have not already done so earlier when building the midterm strategy, your tactical team leaders should now document the tactics listed on the A3-X for your annual hoshin with A3-T team charter proposals (see Tables 1-4 and 1-5 and CD Form 1-3) and update existing A3-Ts with any changes that they have made. There should be a separate A3-T for each tactic on the A3-X. Figure 4-4 shows an example of an A3-T for the tactic named "Implement design for six sigma."

A3-T

Proposed team charter

Theme: Design New Products without Delays

PROBLEM STATEMENT

For the past five years, our engineering process has involved many steps, rework, and delays that have resulted in an average engineering lead time of 32 days for new products. This has contributed to significant cost overruns of over $1,000,000.

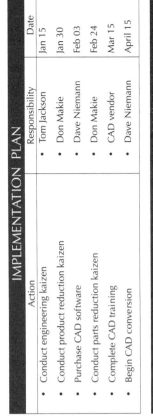

TARGET STATEMENT

Decrease engineering process lead time to 24 days by the end of the next fiscal year.

ANALYSIS

There is still a lot of walking around and driving back and forth to the plant, and many more plane trips. Engineering sometimes flies to the customer to confirm designs; if the designs are wrong, sometimes marketing gets on the plane to make sure they understand customer requirements. By the time the product is being prototyped, manufacturing may have to travel, too, if there is a quality problem. The whole process takes an average of 32 days from start to finish.

PROPOSED ACTION

- Conduct a 5-day kaizen event to implement DFSS (design for six sigma) principles by:
  - Eliminating 50% of the steps in current the engineering process
  - Implementing a batch size of "one" to increase workflow and prevent documents from piling up in inboxes
  - Implementing quality at the source to eliminate errors and rework
  - Linking the order entry process to the engineering process by means of a visual kanban system
- Conduct a 5-day kaizen event to eliminate unnecessary products from the catalog
- Conduct a 5-day kaizen event to eliminate unnecessary parts from remaining products
- Convert designs listed in the catalog to a common CAD platform

IMPLEMENTATION PLAN

Action	Responsibility	Date
Conduct engineering kaizen	Tom Jackson	Jan 15
Conduct product reduction kaizen	Don Makie	Jan 30
Purchase CAD software	Dave Niemann	Feb 03
Conduct parts reduction kaizen	Don Makie	Feb 24
Complete CAD training	CAD vendor	Mar 15
Begin CAD conversion	Dave Niemann	April 15

CHECK AND ACT (verification and follow up)

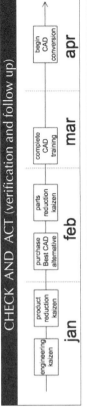

Engineering tactical team

Date: September 1 | **Reporting Unit:** Engineering Tactical Team

Figure 4-4. Engineering Tactical Team A3-T Team Charter

CHAPTER FIVE

PLAN: Align the Organization Through Catchball

Getting people to engage and buy in on the deployment process and deliverables is the key to strategy execution. In this chapter, you will use a process called catchball (hoshin Experiments 4 and 5) to involve your managers in the design of strategy as well as to align the entire organizational structure. Catchball is the process by which team leaders elaborate and communicate the annual hoshin to all the teams in the organization. It is so named because there is a lot of back-and-forth between the parties in negotiating team charters that govern the experiments of the hoshin process. Recall that an X-matrix is a bundle of contracts called team charters, that is, agreements between individuals, teams, departments, and—eventually—your suppliers, to achieve your company's strategic goals.

Hoshin Tip: The concept of "team" under hoshin kanri is very broad. It refers to any group organized around a hoshin team charter to execute the company's strategy, tactics, or operations. For this purpose, natural workgroups can be teams, and areas within departments—if they have an area leader—can be teams. Even departments and divisions can be teams, if they have a hoshin team charter. More importantly, the teams of *hoshin kanri cut across functional and organizational boundaries* as needed to address the control points of the value stream identified through the design of strategy.

In this sense, catchball occurs at all levels and sectors of your organization, both vertically (top down and bottom up) and horizontally (between tactical teams and departments that have a stake in implementation plans). Through catchball, the hoshin team communicates and deploys responsibilities and deliverables to *tactical teams, operational teams,* and *action teams* (see Figure 5-1). The catchball process links all seven experiments of the hoshin process (see Figure 1-1 and Table 1-2) and all levels of the organization to one another through lively discussions about the future of the company and negotiations about targets and means, roles, responsibilities, and the allocation and development of resources.

How your hoshin team designs your catchball process depends upon your current organizational structure. In a small organization, catchball may be a short process, involving only two layers of the management hierarchy and three rounds of catchball. In large organizations, the process can involve additional teams and additional rounds of catchball. For this reason, you must carefully stage-manage catchball, as it can involve a cast of thousands! As we go through the Cybernautx case study, the process involves three layers of the hierarchy and five separate rounds—A, B, C, D, and E—of catchball. In addition to the A3-X built by the hoshin team leader, each member of the hoshin team will construct an A3-X, too.

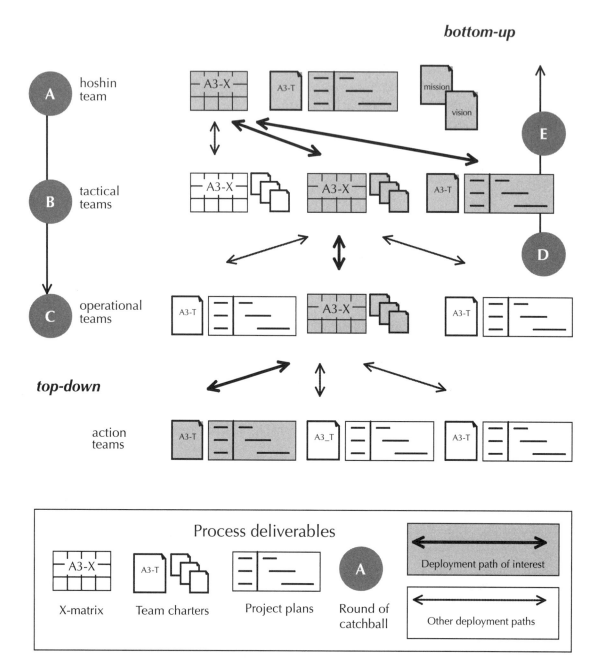

Figure 5-1. Catchball

As you move through the five rounds of the hoshin, tactics, and operations catchball process, keep in mind that:

- Hoshin is a bundle of tactical projects to make process improvements linked to midterm strategy.
- A tactical plan is an A3-X (X-matrix), itself a bundle of operational team charters and projects to make process improvements linked to the hoshin.
- An operational plan is an A3-X, itself a bundle of action team charters and projects linked to tactics.

- Every A3-T (team charter) contains by reference a project plan. In other words, the project is what the team is chartered to do. So you can think of team charters and project plans as interchangeable, and *all* plans in a hoshin system as *project* plans.
- All hoshin projects are aimed at process improvement to develop competitive capabilities.

You might say that as your organization becomes leaner, your deployment becomes more *chromatic*, with catchball being the half tone in between each level of the organization. The danger in the beginning is that if all you know is the mass-thinking pentatonic scale, it is easy to misinterpret what you hear in between each level.

Catchball Tip: If you're using hoshin kanri for the first time, keep it simple. Involve your functional managers in the construction of the annual hoshin (see Chapter 4), and handle the rest of the exercise with A3-Ts (team charters) and the project plans for each of the improvement tactics referenced in your A3-X (X-matrix). In effect, you can bypass Rounds C and D of the catchball process. As you gain experience, you can slowly expand the circle of involvement.

Throughout the catchball process, the teams that your hoshin team charters negotiate the terms of their organizational contacts. The hoshin team's job is to state *what* these teams must do by *proposing a set of targets*. The chartered teams then respond by stating *how* they intend to hit those targets. The result of a well-managed catchball process is that information is more accurate, thereby reducing costs of managing and enforcing team charters as the teams execute the strategy. Furthermore, catchball gets people invested in strategic intent, which motivates them to achieve the set of targets that you want, rather than merely stating the targets and then punishing teams if they fall short. Therefore, how the hoshin team handles negotiations with its teams, and how the teams follow up with accurate information and deliverable commitments, is very important.

As the catchball process demonstrates, hoshin kanri is revolutionary not only because it supports decentralized decision making by frontline employees, it also relocates organizational power from traditional functional heads to managers leading cross-functional and interorganizational teams. In the beginning, functional managers may try to cling to their authority and continue to optimize their own careers at the expense of the system. But gradually—if you don't give up—systems thinking will take root and grow the company beyond this old managerial behavior.

CATCHBALL ROUND A: EXPERIMENT 4, TACTICAL PROJECTS AND TEAMS

As shown on the hoshin kanri road map (Figure 1-1), the hoshin team plays catchball in Round A and once again in Round E. In Chapter 4, your hoshin team completed the third experiment of the hoshin system by identifying tactics and the processes to deal with them, and by assigning team leaders (managers) and members from the hoshin team for each tactic that appears on the A3-X. So, when the hoshin team meets in round A, it automatically plays catchball with the tactical team leaders. Now in Round A of catchball, hoshin team leaders further develop and deploy the third experiment of the hoshin system—the annual hoshin—by chartering tactical teams and projects to make improvements in Experiment 4 of the hoshin system; the tactics to improve competitive capabilities (intangible assets), e.g., brand equity, technology, business processes, relationships, and human assets.

Catchball Tip: In the Cybernautx case study, catchball is played to confirm 3 of the 6 experiments of the hoshin system: the annual hoshin, tactics, and operations. You can also play catchball to confirm long-term strategy and midterm strategy. For example, catchball can be played with the company's stakeholders—customers, suppliers, shareholders, managers, and employees—to confirm a new mission or vision. You can confirm the midterm strategy in a game of catchball with the company's board of directors. In conducting catchball meetings at the top of the organization chart, simply follow the same steps outlined below. The only difference is that you toss the "ball" of policy "up" instead of "down."

In catchball Round A, the hoshin team will go through the six steps listed below. More or less, the tactical team in Round B and the operational team in Round C will go through these same steps.

1. Prepare for the meeting.
2. Introduce the plan.
3. Discuss the plan.
4. Charter teams with A3-Ts.
5. Study the plan.
6. Complete and confirm the plan.

Hoshin, Tactical, and Operational Team Exercises for Chapter 5: As in Chapter 4, the teams will use the headings above as action items, with further instructions indicated in the text below. The exercises revolve around each team leader deploying the hoshin plan to team leaders at the next level of the organization, who then develop A3-Ts and create project plans for their own teams—and so on until the annual hoshin has been deployed to all managers included in the hoshin process.

Each team has as its *leader* a member of a team at the next level up in the organization, and as its *members* the leaders of teams at the next level down. That is, each team in the hoshin system is a team of team leaders. This structure is called an "overlapping" team structure. It ensures both a smooth deployment during catchball and a responsive reporting system (see Figure 5-1).

Round A, Step 1: Prepare for the Meeting

Every team needs to do several important activities before launching a catchball session. These include:

- Hiring an expert to facilitate the meeting
- Designating a scribe to record the proceedings
- Preparing the meeting room
- Establishing rules for the meeting
- Printing copies of the A3-Xs and A3-Ts
- Making arrangements for food and drink

First, seriously consider hiring an expert to facilitate the meeting. It's extremely difficult to maintain neutrality—a key requirement of good facilitation—in a meeting that will decide the future of your company, division, department, or team. Everyone (except a good facilitator) will naturally take sides. This is particularly true if you intend to invite your suppliers or customers into the hoshin process.

Designate a scribe to record the proceedings of the meeting on the A3-X and supporting documents. Recording agreements and dissenting opinions is not the facilitator's job. Choose someone with good listening, typing, and computer skills; they will be kept busy revising, printing, and distributing new versions of your planning documents.

Prepare the meeting room carefully. The room should accommodate the team comfortably at a large conference table or a classic horseshoe arrangement (see Figure 5-2). We strongly suggest using an LCD projector to share your A3-X with the team. This also permits real-time revisions. Another alternative to consider is printing a blank A3-X in 12 sections, approximately 2 feet high and 3 feet wide. Then assemble them as a giant chart on the wall and use sticky notes to document the various details of your proposal. That way you can involve team members directly in revisions. It also keeps people active throughout the day and promotes lively discussion. A rolling electronic white board that can print is also useful for capturing related points with the team. This saves lots of time. Also, provide plenty of flip charts for short breakout sessions. Try to have a large-format (11″ × 17″) printer in the room and plenty of paper of various sizes. From time to time, people will need to study the latest revision of the your A3s by holding them in their hands. If you are meeting off-site, arrange for breakout rooms where teams may work on project plans. If you are meeting on-site, teams may use their own offices as breakout rooms.

Establish rules for the meeting. You can either provide a handout or discuss these rules at the beginning of the meeting. The most important rules revolve around every team member being responsible for listening actively to what the team leader and fellow team members have to say about the future of the company. This means maintaining eye contact and confirming or disagreeing with what is being said. No checking email is allowed while the meeting is in session, and no taking notes on the computer (paper and pencil are fine), because it breaks contact with the group. It's the scribe's responsibility to take notes and distribute them later.

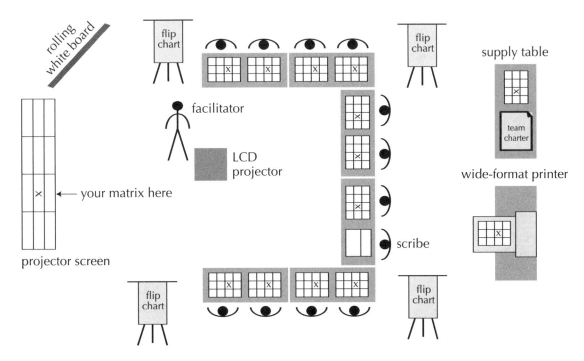

Figure 5-2. Room Set-up for Team Meetings

Print copies of the A3-X and A3-T and instructions from the CD companion in this workbook (CD Forms 1-2 and 1-3). The planning documents are formatted to print double-sided, with the form on the front and instructions on the back. On a supply table, stack extra copies of blank A3-Xs and A3-Ts (X-matrices and team charters), and other forms that you intend to use. Have plenty of pencils—pen and ink are not recommended—and provide a working pencil sharpener.

Arrange for food and drink. Strategic thinking requires fuel. Don't forget healthy snacks. Carbohydrates are good if you're running a marathon, not for seated activities like strategic planning. Protein bars and plenty of fluids will keep people alert in their seats. As people enter the room, collect all cell phones, pagers, and other electronic communication devices and switch them off before the meeting begins.

Round A, Step 2: Introduce the Plan

In Step 2, the hoshin team introduces the hoshin plan to the tactical team leaders and possibly some team members. First, the team presents the midterm plan and then hands out the midterm A3-X, which should be projected on a screen. In this presentation, the hoshin team briefly tells the tactical team leaders what the team should accomplish. If people on these teams have never seen an A3-X, walk them around the matrix, indicating clearly which portion of the matrix you're talking about. Describe how the strategies, tactics, process improvement measures, and results interlock. Carefully discuss the roles and responsibilities section. Point out on the A3-X who the team leaders and team members are for each tactical project. Make it clear that each tactic on the A3-X refers to an improvement project on the process quadrant of the A3-X, and that each team leader is responsible for creating a team charter so that the leader's tactical team can manage the improvement project.

Round A, Step 3: Discuss the Plan

The hoshin team should discuss the plan for about an hour, answer questions about the A3-X, and clarify any points. If the tactical team leaders have reservations or improvement suggestions, list these on the white board or on one of the flip charts. Below is what the Cybernautx hoshin team confronted when it finished reviewing the multiyear profitability analysis in one of its catchball sessions with the hoshin team.

Improvement Suggestions Resulting from a Catchball Session

When the Cybernautx hoshin team reviewed the multiyear profitability analysis prepared during the environmental check, everyone got a wake-up call. Overnight one key assumption of that analysis had changed dramatically. Cybernautx had originally assumed that it would be able to reduce material costs by 5 percent per year over the next four years. But its markets had since changed as the result of rapid political, social, and economic developments. It was now expected that there would be increases of 10 percent per year in material costs over the same three years! The team quickly revised the multiyear profitability analysis to reflect this new and bleak reality (see Table 5-1).

The shocking result of this analysis was that the company would *lose* money for the foreseeable future! Moreover, with global competition for resources, things would only get worse. "Ladies and gentlemen," said the manager, "even if material prices moderate in years 2, 3, and 4, we still need to put our lean program on fast forward."

The team agreed that they would need to involve their most important supplier, Nonesuch Manufacturing, in their hoshin process. Nonesuch's engineering and manufacturing departments could help them contain the cost increase. Moreover, it would be in the interest of both companies to work together.

Round A, Step 4: Tactical Team Leaders Charter Teams

Each tactical team oversees the implementation of improvements on the process quadrant of the A3-X, which means each tactical team leader must draft charters for their own teams. Using the Plan, Do, Check, Act (PDCA) improvement methodologies, the tactical team leader needs to formulate tactical plans in the team charter, establishing specific targets for project. He or she needs to:

- Choose the team members responsible for managing the implementation of policies and objectives
- Choose additional team members based upon the importance of their roles in the implementation process
- Identify salient details for the team charter

The team leader should also think cross-functionally when forming their team. That is, the nature of the project, not formal lines of reporting, should determine team membership. Ask questions like which departments or individuals will provide inputs and which departments or individuals will be affected by the outputs of the project? *Normally, the number of members in each tactical team should not exceed nine.* A smaller number is better. No team should have more than twelve members. Like most teams, you need a core membership of two to three individuals, including the team leader. Or course, membership can extend beyond those present in the room. These team members will become directly involved in

Table 5-1. Cybernautx Profitability Analysis

	This year	Next year	Year 2	Year 3	Year 4
Market size (units)	100,000	100,000	100,000	100,000	100,000
Average sales price	$5,000	$5,000	$5,000	$5,000	$5,000
Market share	10.0%	10.0%	10.0%	10.0%	10.0%
Unit sales	10,000	10,000	10,000	10,000	10,000
Dollar sales	$50,000,000	$50,000,000	$50,000,000	$50,000,000	$50,000,000
Development costs	$1,400,000	$1,400,000	$1,400,000	$1,400,000	$1,400,000
Material costs	$40,000,000	$44,000,000	$48,400,000	$53,240,000	$58,564,000
Conversion costs	$8,000,000	$7,600,000	$7,220,000	$6,859,000	$6,516,050
Value stream profit	$600,000	–$3,000,000	–$7,020,000	–$11,499,000	–$16,480,050
Annual return on sales	1.2%	–6.0%	–14.0%	–23.0%	–33.0%

Cumulative sales	$250,000,000
Cumulative development costs	7,000,000
Cumulative material costs	244,204,000
Cumulative coversion costs	36,195,050
Cumultative VSP	–$37,399,050
Average percent return on sales	–15.0%

the hoshin process in the next round of catchball with the operational teams. Additional action teams will be formed later for implementation (Chapter 6, Experiments 6 and 7). At that time, everyone in the company will be included on one or more teams.

Because the hoshin process moves from the general to the specific, from strategy to tactics and then to daily operations, the tactical team leaders should strive to incorporate salient details on their team charters that may not be listed on an A3-X. If you can't do it at first, don't worry. Your tactical team members will fill these in later. Operational team leaders will use the same documentation and process for operational teams. Figure 5-3 shows that Cybernautx drafted three and Nonesuch drafted two tactical A3-Ts.

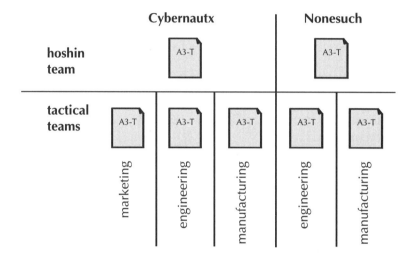

Figure 5-3. A3-Ts (team charters)

Cybernautx and Nonesuch Draft Five Tactical A3-Ts

Note: We will focus on only three tactical teams, for Cybernautx's marketing and engineering department, and Nonesuch's manufacturing department. In Catchball Rounds B and C, we will continue with the operational teams for these departments.

Round A, Step 5: Tactical Team Leaders Study the Hoshin Plan and Prepare the A3-X

Once the tactical team leaders are clear about the projects the hoshin team wants them to undertake, the hoshin team should ask them to think about how they intend to manage their projects and to prepare an A3-X, following the process in Chapter 3 and 4. Before the tactical team leaders leave the hoshin team, conduct a short training on how to use the A3-X. You can follow the detailed instructions in Round A, Step 6, below, as well as use the double-sided A3-Xs that include additional instructions (CD Form 1-2).

The purpose of the training is to ensure that the tactical team leaders have enough information to complete their project plans. If they do not, allow them extra time—up to a week or more—for them to conduct research. This research can involve the deployment of the draft policy and playing the next round of catchball (Round B) with the full tactical teams. In that case, each tactical team focuses on completing its project plan using the process below.

Otherwise, the tactical team leader and core team members on the hoshin team can complete the project plan in a breakout session during Round A of catchball.

Round A, Step 6: Tactical Team Leader Completes the Project Plan

The process for completing the tactical team projects on the A3-X mirrors the process that the hoshin team used for the annual hoshin in Chapter 4. Briefly, there are seven action items for the tactical team leader:

1. Transpose breakthrough strategies.
2. Identify opportunities for the next 6 to 18 months.
3. Document opportunities with A3-Ts.
4. Prioritize, analyze, choose, and record high-impact opportunities.
5. Determine contributions to results.
6. Establish targets for measures of process improvement.
7. Study interdependencies.
8. Assign teams.

Action Item 1: Transpose Breakthrough Strategies

The strategy section of every A3-X at every level of deployment recapitulates the strategy section of the midterm strategy and the annual hoshin. If certain hoshin strategies aren't relevant to the tactical team's project, the tactical team leader may omit them from the A3-X. In addition, if the tactical team leader identifies a strategic theme of critical importance to its endeavor, it may add a new theme to its matrix. Don't delete or add more than one theme at any given level of deployment.

Action Item 2: Identify Opportunities for the Next 6 to 18 Months

Refer to A3-Ts and project plans contained in the hoshin team idea bank and the value stream maps. And don't forget the market/technology matrix. As the hoshin team did in creating the annual hoshin, the tactical team leader can use the market/technology matrix to chart existing, related, and new internal markets, and to explore possibilities for new products and new production processes based on existing, related, and new resources and capabilities.

The Cybernautx hoshin manager asked all tactical teams to prepare intermediate state value stream maps to indicate where they think their functions are now and where they ought to be in twelve months' time. Below is what Cybernautx's tactical marketing team, engineering team, and Nonesuch's manufacturing team prepared.

Marketing Tactical Team—Design for Six Sigma (DFSS) Order Entry Process Lead Time: Interim State

The marketing tactical team's mapping of the marketing process yielded the concept of a co-located cross-functional team of sales, marketing, engineering, and financial personnel responsible for confirming customer requirements, performing engineering feasibility studies, estimating costs, and writing and submitting proposals. The marketing tactical team leader believed that with hard work and good luck he could reduce lead time by 25 percent, from 16 to 12 days (see Figure 5-4) (compare Figure 2-5).

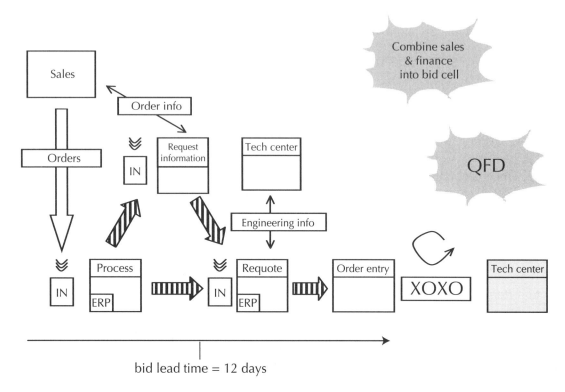

bid lead time = 12 days

Figure 5-4. Cybernautx Marketing Tactical Team—DFSS Order Entry Process Map: Interim State

Engineering Tactical Team—DFSS Engineering Map: Interim State

Process mapping of the engineering process by the engineering tactical team showed that the engineering process is still a "point-based" serial process. That is, engineers work on only "one best idea" at a time in a sequential process that normally ends with throwing a finished but flawed design "over the wall" to manufacturing (see Figure 5-5). In the future state, engineering will use a concurrent, set-based process that begins with the voice of the customer. This idea appears as a "kaizen burst" on the value stream map. Set-based engineering focuses on multiple alternatives instead of "one best" solution and gradually narrows the field in a dialogue between marketing, engineering, and manufacturing. The engineering tactical team leader stated that, based upon his reading and discussions with engineers in other industries, he could possibly reduce engineering lead time by 25 percent from 32 to 24 days in the next product introduction, if he had the resources to train his people. (Compare Figure 2-6.)

Nonesuch Lean Manufacturing Tactical Team Map: Interim State

The reader will recall that Nonesuch Casting, Cybernautx's principal supplier, has been asked to join the Cybernautx hoshin team, to address critical issues of new product introduction and supply chain development. Nonesuch has a lot riding on Cybernautx's success and was eager to participate. When asked his opinion of Cybernautx's emerging strategy, Nonesuch's manufacturing tactical leader stated that the focus should be on reducing the 32-day lead time within the factory. The Nonesuch lean manufacturing

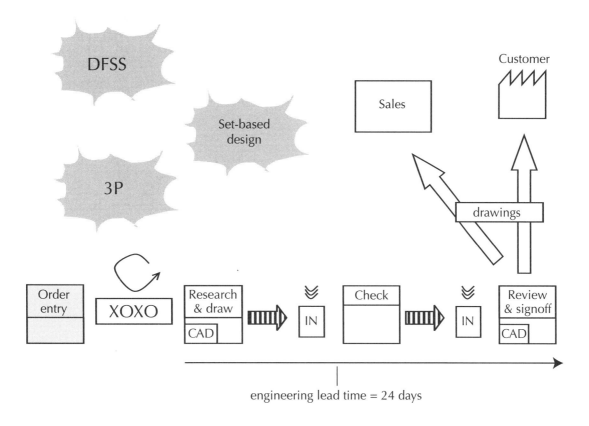

Figure 5-5. Cybernautx Engineering Tactical Team—DFSS Engineering Map: Interim State

tactical team's mapping showed that despite investments in equipment improvement the current state of Nonesuch's manufacturing operations is still traditional mass production, with sequential batch processing, high inventories of raw materials and work-in-process (WIP), low inventories of the right stuff, and high inventories of the wrong stuff (including some obsolete items, too). The vision of the Cybernautx campus includes a perfectly lean manufacturing plant, organized almost completely in traditional U-shaped cells (see Figure 2-8). Nonesuch believes that it can go half the distance this year and may even be able to cut lead time within the factory by 25 percent from 32 to 24 days and reduce inventories of purchased parts in the warehouse by 25 percent as well (see Figure 5-7). The key to this strategy would be to reduce changeover times drastically on Nonesuch's injection molding equipment.

Action Item 3: Document opportunities with A3-Ts

Your tactical team members should now document the breakthroughs they have identified with A3-T team charter proposals (see Tables 1-4 and 1-5 and CD Form 1-3) and update existing A3-Ts with any changes that they have made. There should be a separate A3-T for each breakthrough identified. *Note*: As deployment moves from the hoshin team down through the ranks of the management hierarchy, A3-Ts will become progressively more concrete because members on tactical, operational, and action teams are respectively closer to the particularities of the processes that they manage. This is one of the great benefits of the catchball process.

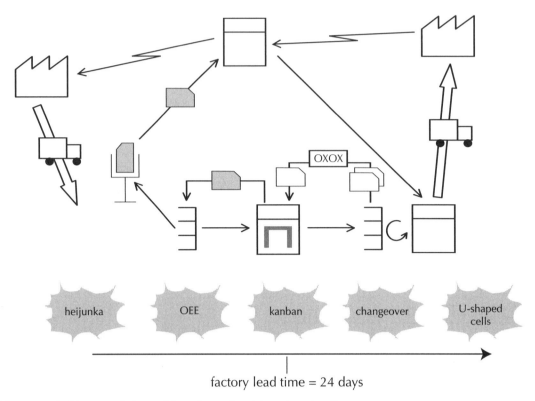

heijunka   OEE   kanban   changeover   U-shaped cells

factory lead time = 24 days

Figure 5-6. Nonesuch Lean Manufacturing Map: Interim State

Action Item 4: Prioritize Opportunities

If the most important opportunities don't jump off your value stream or process maps, use a prioritization matrix to narrow down the field of available solutions to 3 to 5 opportunities. Remember: less is more. (You can print off a prioritization matrix from the CD companion, Form 3-1.)

Action Item 5: Establish Contribution Targets for Results

The results section of each tactical A3-X indicates the amount and structure of the tactical team's contribution to the overall result that appears on the A3-X for the annual hoshin. The format recapitulates the value stream profit and loss (P&L) for a tactical project.

Action Item 6: Establish Targets for Process Improvement

The process quadrant of a tactical A3-X recapitulates the process section of the annual hoshin, but only to the extent that the specific measures listed on the hoshin A3-X pertains to the tactical project. Tactical teams should reinterpret each target that they transpose from the hoshin to their own A3-Xs. High-level measures such as overall equipment effectiveness (OEE) and first time through quality (FTT) may be stratifiable and thus can be easily broken down into their components. However, team members should feel free to add additional measures if necessary to ensure the success of the project. Strive to keep the number of measures low. If the number of measures begins to approach 20, the team should carefully review what they're doing. Often, too many measures on the matrix are an indication of micromanagement. It's better to deploy targets at the next level, where teams can control the process in real time.

Action Item 7: Study Interdependencies and Determine Correlations

Tactical team leaders should analyze their correlation matrices to confirm that relationships transposed from the hoshin A3-X hold at the tactical team level, and to determine correlations in new relationships that result from tactics and process improvement measures that are specific to the tactical project. Be sure to check all four correlation matrices: strategies/tactics, tactics/process, process/results, and results/strategies.

Many teams will feel a strong temptation to strike interdependencies from the agenda to save time. Do the work anyway; or postpone it to Round B of catchball, so that all tactical team members may be involved. Use the Excel comment function to incorporate common understanding and dissenting views directly into the A3-X. Remember President Eisenhower's wartime admonition: *Planning is everything; the plan is nothing.* The conversations behind the A3-X are what count because they build understanding and consensus. It's the memory of what was said and *felt* that creates alignment, not the final piece of paper.

Action Item 8: Assign Teams

At this point, the team leader is ready to assemble the members of the tactical team. Once again, you should choose team members based upon their ability to contribute to the project. To avoid the functional silos of mass production organizations, hoshin teams that originate within specific functions, such as the Cybernautx marketing, engineering, and manufacturing tactical teams, should take care—as Cybernautx has done—to include members from other functions and organizations. When practical, include members drawn from the customer and supplier bases.

Discuss Tactical Project Plans

Having prepared and completed the plan, tactical team leaders formally present their draft A3-Xs to the other members of the hoshin team. Permit about 20 minutes for the presentation and discussion of each tactical matrix. Then discuss the resources required for the successful implementation of the proposed tactical projects. Such resources might include new equipment, extra personnel, consultants, training, travel, release time to work on special projects, and organizational changes.

Revise the Hoshin and Tactical Project Plans

In preparation for deployment to the tactical improvement teams, the hoshin team needs to revise its documents to reflect its provisional understanding of what needs to be done. Permit 30 minutes of discussion about the interrelationships between tactical projects and the hoshin and another 10 to 15 minutes for the scribe to update the hoshin document.

Below are the catchball Round A results of Cybernautx's tactical project plans established by the tactical leaders for Cybernautx's marketing and engineering, and Nonesuch manufacturing (see Figures 5-7, 5-8, and Figure 5-9.) Figure 5-10 is the second draft of the annual hoshin.

Catchball Round A—Hoshin Team Requests Tactical Teams to Address the Four Value Stream Profit Components

Based upon the new assumptions about the pace of improvement, the Cybernautx hoshin team reasoned that the tactical plans should address each of the four major components of value stream profit: dollar sales, development costs, material costs, and conversion costs (see Table 5-1). The revenue plan pivoted on the hope that their customers

---

would agree to a price increase of $500 per unit. The success of the price increase would be the responsibility of the marketing tactical team. With a few layoffs, and with Nonesuch's engineering tactical team involved, the team should be able to achieve the planned reduction of 5 percent in development costs by reducing total people cost. Of this amount, marketing would contribute one third and engineering would contribute two thirds. The large rise in the cost of materials presented a real challenge. Cybernautx's tactical engineering team and Nonesuch's team would each be asked to contribute a 12.5 percent reduction of the materials cost increase. The net effect would be a 7.5 percent rather than a 10 percent increase in the cost of materials for the coming year. By reducing manufacturing lead time by 37.5 percent, engineering and the Cybernautx lean manufacturing team would contribute an estimated 7.5 percent reduction in manufacturing conversion costs (based on the earlier planning assumption of a 5:1 lead time to cost reduction ratio). Of this cost reduction, engineering would contribute 30 percent and manufacturing would contribute 70 percent. This would improve the company's value stream profit to a respectable $3,270,000 next year—assuming of course that *all* hoshin objectives could be achieved. It would be a real stretch.

CATCHBALL ROUND B: HOSHIN EXPERIMENT 5, OPERATIONAL TEAMS AND PROJECTS

Round B of catchball is a *tactical team activity*—the hoshin team is not involved. In Round B, tactical team leaders develop and deploy the fourth experiment of the hoshin system—tactics—by chartering teams and projects to make improvements in the fifth experiment of the hoshin system: current operations. Tactical team leaders may have some awareness of resource requirements when drafting the proposed tactical plans, but they won't necessarily have specific details from deeper within the organization.

It's in this catchball round, after the tactical team leaders communicate the A3-Ts (team charters) and A3-Xs (X-matrices), that tactical team members will research and provide detailed information. This is also the time for tactical teams to suggest to the hoshin team their own ideas for improving company policy and reaching overall objectives. In catchball Round B, the tactical team will follow the same six steps the hoshin team followed (listed on page 82 in this chapter), although, for the purposes of this workbook, we will follow these steps in less detail. *Note*: In the next three rounds, it is the responsibility of the team leaders to deploy the hoshin.

Introduce and Discuss the Tactical Project Plan with Team Members

Having prepared for the meeting, the tactical team leader summarizes the annual hoshin and presents the tactical team charter and tactical A3-X drafted during the first round of catchball to the tactical team members. Take care to explain both how the A3-X works and its contents. Tactical team members need to understand what you want them to do, so let them discuss the A3-X and ask for clarification. They should also give the team leader feedback on the feasibility of the targets, and discuss the core objectives and suggested strategies. List suggestions for process improvements on flip charts.

Operational Team Leaders Charter Operational Teams

Just as there are tactical team leaders on the hoshin team, there are operational team leaders on the tactical team. The process of drafting operational A3-Ts (team charters) is the same as that for the tactical teams. (See Round A, Step 6, page 87 of this chapter.) Operational team

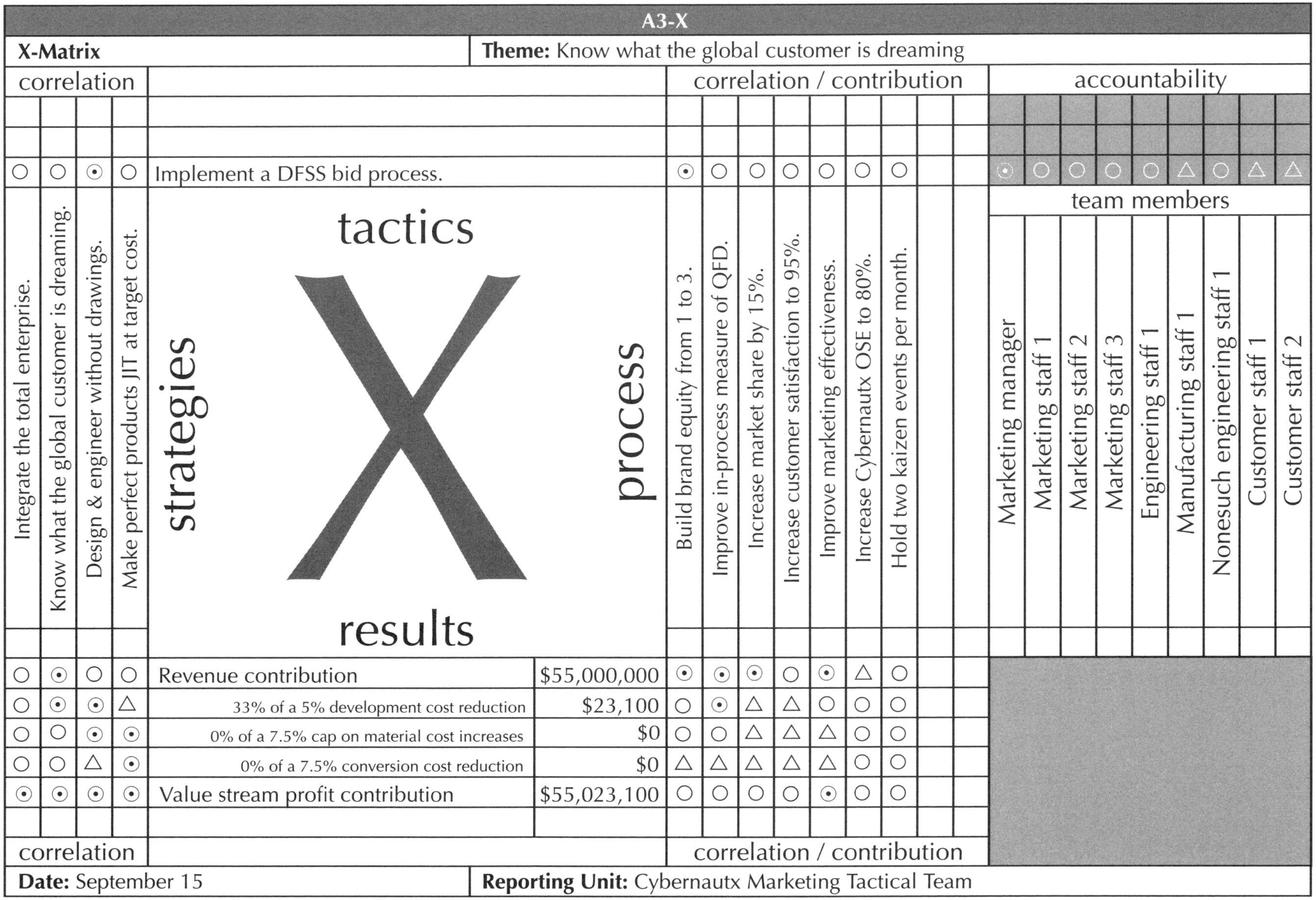

X-Matrix — A3-X

Theme: Know what the global customer is dreaming

accountability — team members

- Customer staff 2
- Customer staff 1
- Nonesuch engineering staff 1
- Manufacturing staff 1
- Engineering staff 1
- Marketing staff 3
- Marketing staff 2
- Marketing staff 1
- Marketing manager

correlation / contribution (process)

- Hold two kaizen events per month.
- Increase Cybernautx OSE to 80%.
- Improve marketing effectiveness.
- Increase customer satisfaction to 95%.
- Increase market share by 15%.
- Improve in-process measure of QFD.
- Build brand equity from 1 to 3.

tactics

- Implement a DFSS bid process.

strategies

- Make perfect products JIT at target cost.
- Design & engineer without drawings.
- Know what the global customer is dreaming.
- Integrate the total enterprise.

results

Results	Value
Revenue contribution	$55,000,000
33% of a 5% development cost reduction	$23,100
0% of a 7.5% cap on material cost increases	$0
0% of a 7.5% conversion cost reduction	$0
Value stream profit contribution	$55,023,100

correlation

correlation / contribution

Date: September 15   **Reporting Unit:** Cybernautx Marketing Tactical Team

Figure 5-7. Catchball Round A Marketing Tactical Team Plan, First Draft

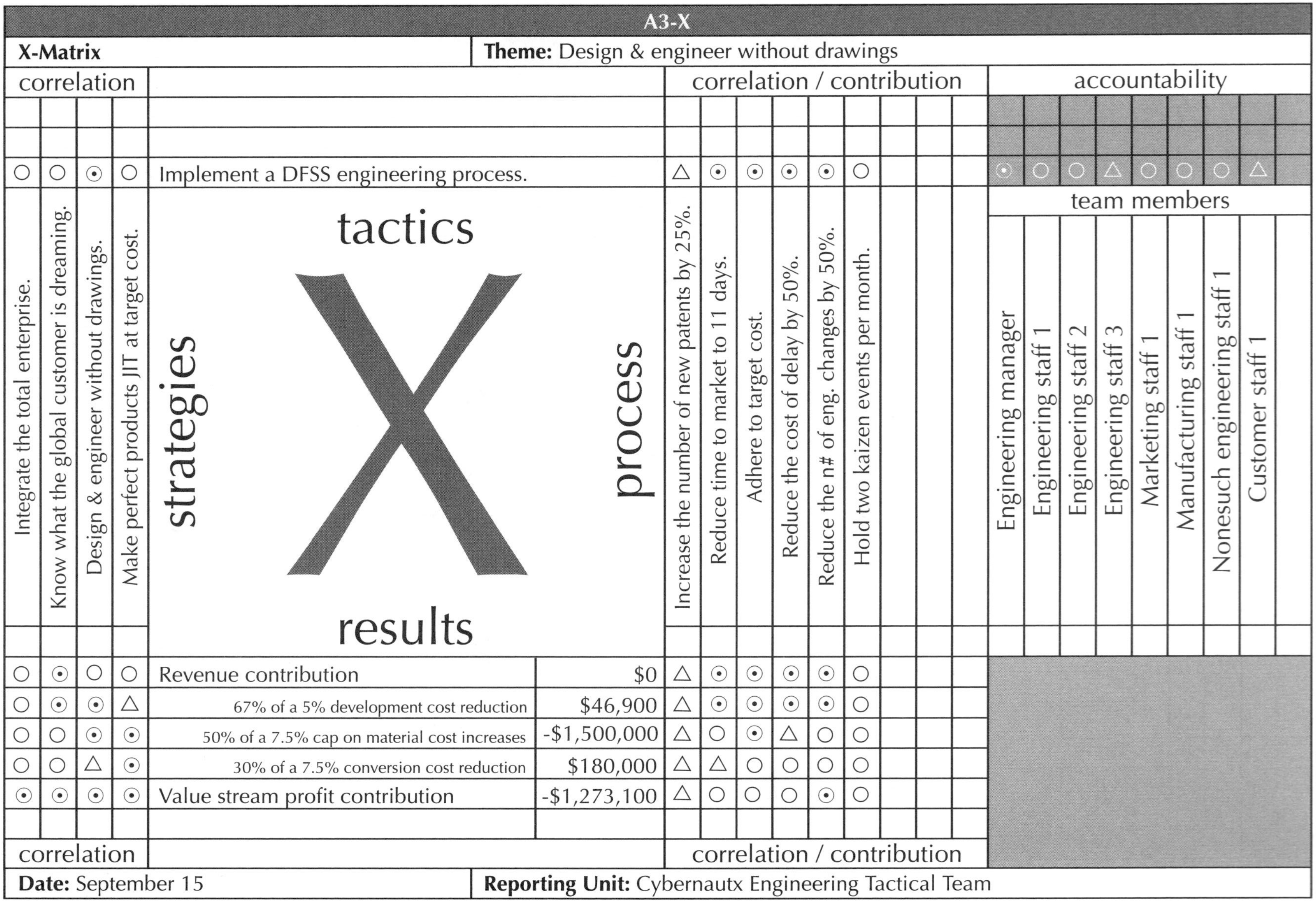

X-Matrix   A3-X

Theme: Design & engineer without drawings

accountability — team members:
- Engineering manager
- Engineering staff 1
- Engineering staff 2
- Engineering staff 3
- Marketing staff 1
- Manufacturing staff 1
- Nonesuch engineering staff 1
- Customer staff 1

correlation / contribution

tactics
- Implement a DFSS engineering process.

process
- Increase the number of new patents by 25%.
- Reduce time to market to 11 days.
- Adhere to target cost.
- Reduce the cost of delay by 50%.
- Reduce the # of eng. changes by 50%.
- Hold two kaizen events per month.

results

Revenue contribution	$0
67% of a 5% development cost reduction	$46,900
50% of a 7.5% cap on material cost increases	-$1,500,000
30% of a 7.5% conversion cost reduction	$180,000
Value stream profit contribution	-$1,273,100

strategies
- Make perfect products JIT at target cost.
- Design & engineer without drawings.
- Know what the global customer is dreaming.
- Integrate the total enterprise.

correlation

Date: September 15   **Reporting Unit:** Cybernautx Engineering Tactical Team

Figure 5-8. Catchball Round A Engineering Tactical Team Plan, First Draft

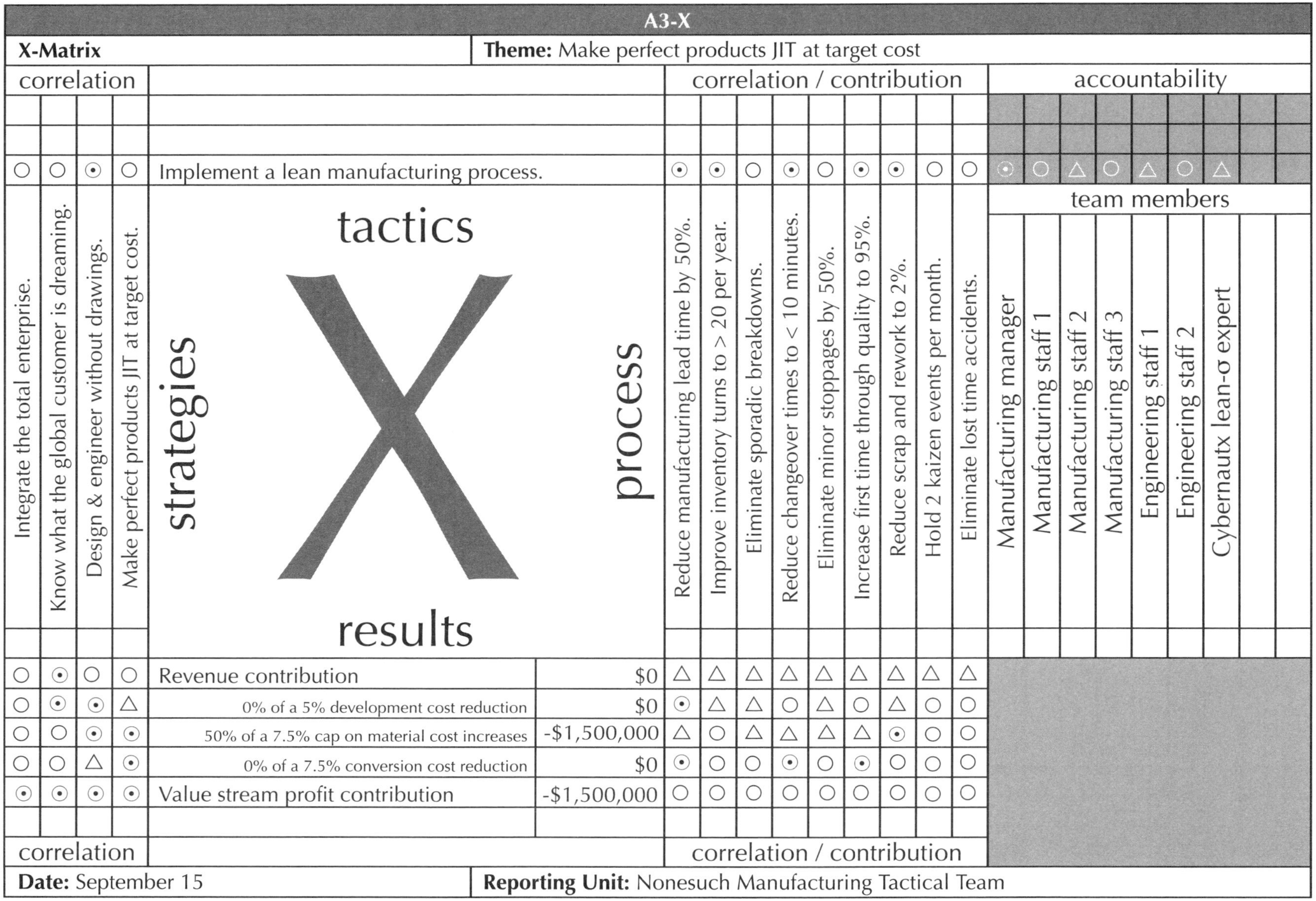

X-Matrix — A3-X

Theme: Make perfect products JIT at target cost

correlation / contribution

Tactics

- Implement a lean manufacturing process.

Process

- Reduce manufacturing lead time by 50%.
- Improve inventory turns to > 20 per year.
- Eliminate sporadic breakdowns.
- Reduce changeover times to < 10 minutes.
- Eliminate minor stoppages by 50%.
- Increase first time through quality to 95%.
- Reduce scrap and rework to 2%.
- Hold 2 kaizen events per month.
- Eliminate lost time accidents.

Strategies

- Integrate the total enterprise.
- Know what the global customer is dreaming.
- Design & engineer without drawings.
- Make perfect products JIT at target cost.

Results

Revenue contribution	$0
0% of a 5% development cost reduction	$0
50% of a 7.5% cap on material cost increases	-$1,500,000
0% of a 7.5% conversion cost reduction	$0
Value stream profit contribution	-$1,500,000

accountability — team members

- Manufacturing manager
- Manufacturing staff 1
- Manufacturing staff 2
- Manufacturing staff 3
- Engineering staff 1
- Engineering staff 2
- Cybernaut lean-σ expert

Date: September 15 **Reporting Unit:** Nonesuch Manufacturing Tactical Team

Figure 5-9. Catchball Round A Nonesuch Manufacturing Tactical Team Plan, First Draft

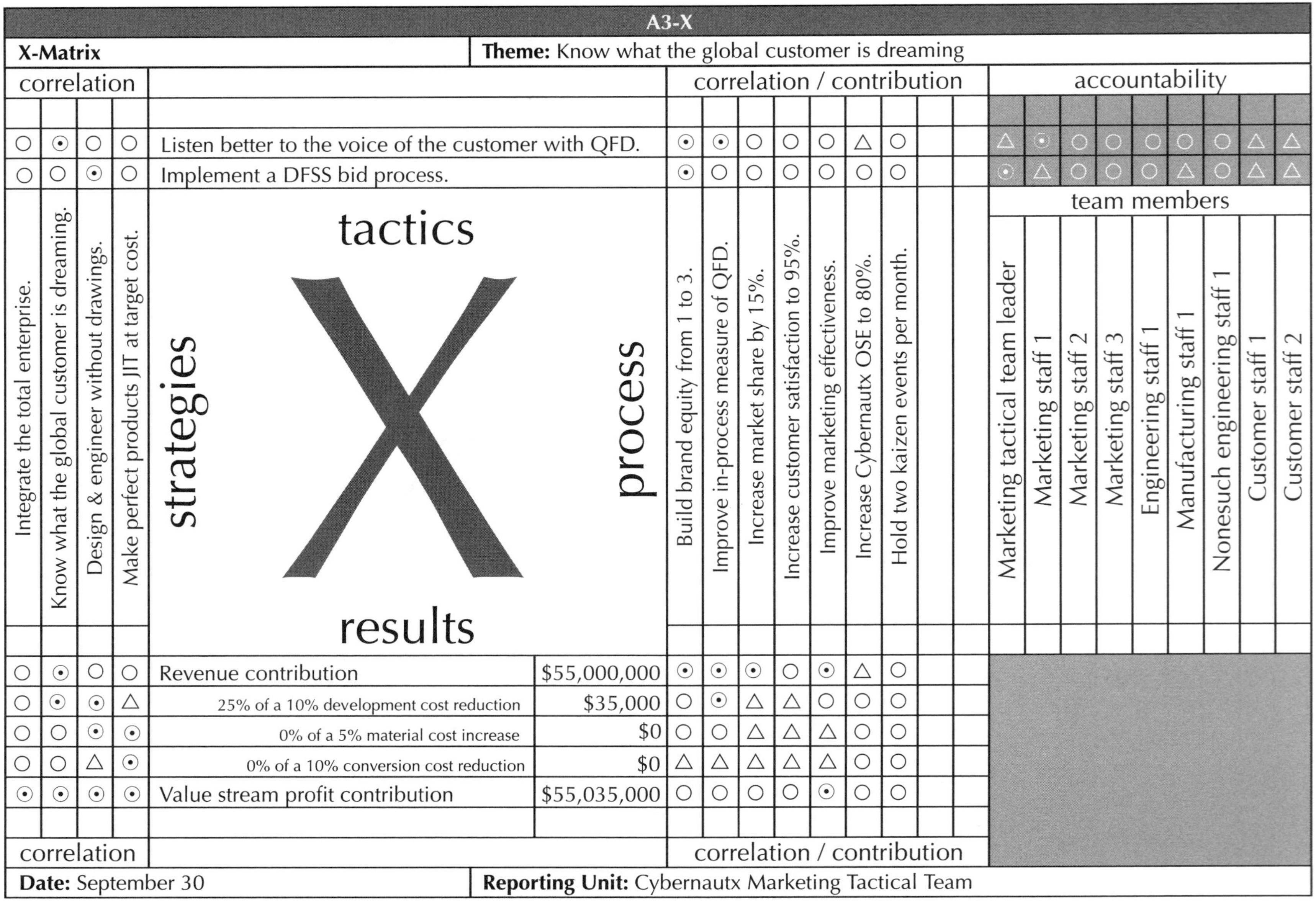

X-Matrix A3-X

Theme: Know what the global customer is dreaming

tactics (correlation / contribution)
- Listen better to the voice of the customer with QFD.
- Implement a DFSS bid process.

process (correlation / contribution)
- Build brand equity from 1 to 3.
- Improve in-process measure of QFD.
- Increase market share by 15%.
- Increase customer satisfaction to 95%.
- Improve marketing effectiveness.
- Increase Cybernautx OSE to 80%.
- Hold two kaizen events per month.

strategies (correlation)
- Make perfect products JIT at target cost.
- Design & engineer without drawings.
- Know what the global customer is dreaming.
- Integrate the total enterprise.

results (correlation / contribution)

Revenue contribution	$55,000,000
25% of a 10% development cost reduction	$35,000
0% of a 5% material cost increase	$0
0% of a 10% conversion cost reduction	$0
Value stream profit contribution	$55,035,000

accountability — team members
- Marketing tactical team leader
- Marketing staff 1
- Marketing staff 2
- Marketing staff 3
- Engineering staff 1
- Manufacturing staff 1
- Nonesuch engineering staff 1
- Customer staff 1
- Customer staff 2

Date: September 30   **Reporting Unit:** Cybernautx Marketing Tactical Team

Figure 5-10. Catchball Round A Cybernautx Annual Hoshin, Second Draft

96

members translate tactical plan targets into operational plans and manageable goals for each tactical deployment objective listed on the A3-X. Recall that once you analyze all of your improvement ideas, you'll have a project plan that covers each breakthrough on your prioritized list. Then you will use this project plan to create an A3-T. (Refer to Chapters 3 and 4 for how to create improvement ideas.) Like the tactical team charter and project plan, the operational team charter and project plan contains many of the elements of a cause-and-effect diagram, but on a more detailed level.

Operational team membership includes middle management, supervisors, and in some cases team leaders. Operational teams do not normally include nonmanagers, and even the participation of supervisors and team leaders is optional. In a mature lean organization, the operational teams would include supervisors, team leaders, and project managers who manage the value-adding frontline action team (frontline action teams are discussed in catchball Round C). The Cybernautx and Nonesuch tactical teams ended up with ten operational teams (see Figure 5-11).

Ten Operational Teams for Cybernautx and Nonesuch

Each of the tactical teams shown here would of course create their own A3-Ts and A3-Xs as part of the catchball process. For the sake of simplicity, we will focus on only the three teams whose team charters we have circled the Cybernautx marketing tactical team and engineering tactical teams and the Nonesuch manufacturing tactical team.

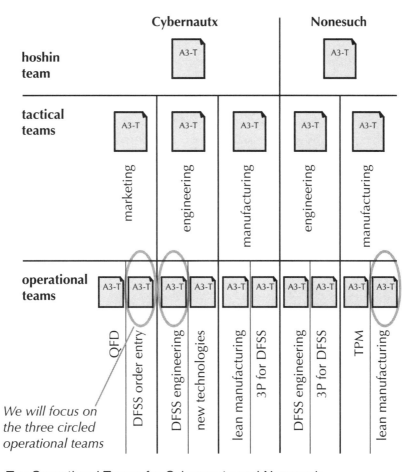

Figure 5-11. Ten Operational Teams for Cybernautx and Nonesuch

Study the Tactical Project Plan

As part of the information gathering, team members who are operational team leaders charter and play Round C catchball with operational team members. It may be necessary to allow a period of time—days or weeks—for the operational team to gather and analyze information to support a commitment to the targets established in your tactical project plans.

Complete the Tactical Project Plan

As required, complete the necessary analysis of root causes, Pareto diagrams, failure mode and effect analyses (FMEAs), and implementation roadmaps. Then the tactical teams fill in their A3-Xs.

- Once again, the strategies section recapitulates the strategies section of the midterm strategy and the annual hoshin. If required, delete or add up to one strategy on each matrix.
- List high priority tactical improvement projects above the "X".
- The results section will indicate the amount and structure of the operational team's contribution to the overall result that appears on the A3-X for the annual hoshin.
- The process section will recapitulate the process section of the annual hoshin, but only to the extent that the specific measures listed on the hoshin A3-X pertain to the operational project. Reinterpret or add additional measures as needed.

In catchball Round B, the two Cybernautx and one Nonesuch tactical teams developed the three matrixes below that are a further development of Figures 5-7, 5-8, and 5-9. Figure 5-10 is the updated annual hoshin.

Catchball Round B—Tactical Marketing Team Proposals

The tactical team leader for the Cybernautx DFSS order entry process focused on the value stream maps prepared earlier during the environmental check and strategic planning (see Chapter 2, page 27). Once assembled, the team was skeptical about the possibility of a price increase, especially in view of their new Asian competitors. But they agreed to do the research with a quality function deployment (QFD) initiative that they included on the tactical marketing team's matrix (see Figure 5-12).

The team quickly ruled out the price increase proposed by the hoshin team. But the team thought that with a strong sales offensive they should be able to increase the company's market share from 10 to 11 percent, which would result in the same increase in revenue, from $50,000,000 this year to $55,000,000 next year. (see Table 5-2).

Catchball Round B—Tactical Engineering Team Proposals

In the first round of catchball, the tactical team leader for the DFSS engineering process focused on current state, future state, and intermediate state maps for reorganizing the engineering department (see page 27). However, the engineering staff on the tactical team grumbled about their 70 percent contribution rate for reductions in development cost. Marketing's bids are always late and they're wrong, too, said the team members—and it was no fault of their own. The tactical team leader (who happened to be the engineering manager) reminded them about the no-blame rule, and so the tactical team had a good discussion about the pros and cons of *set-based engineering* and

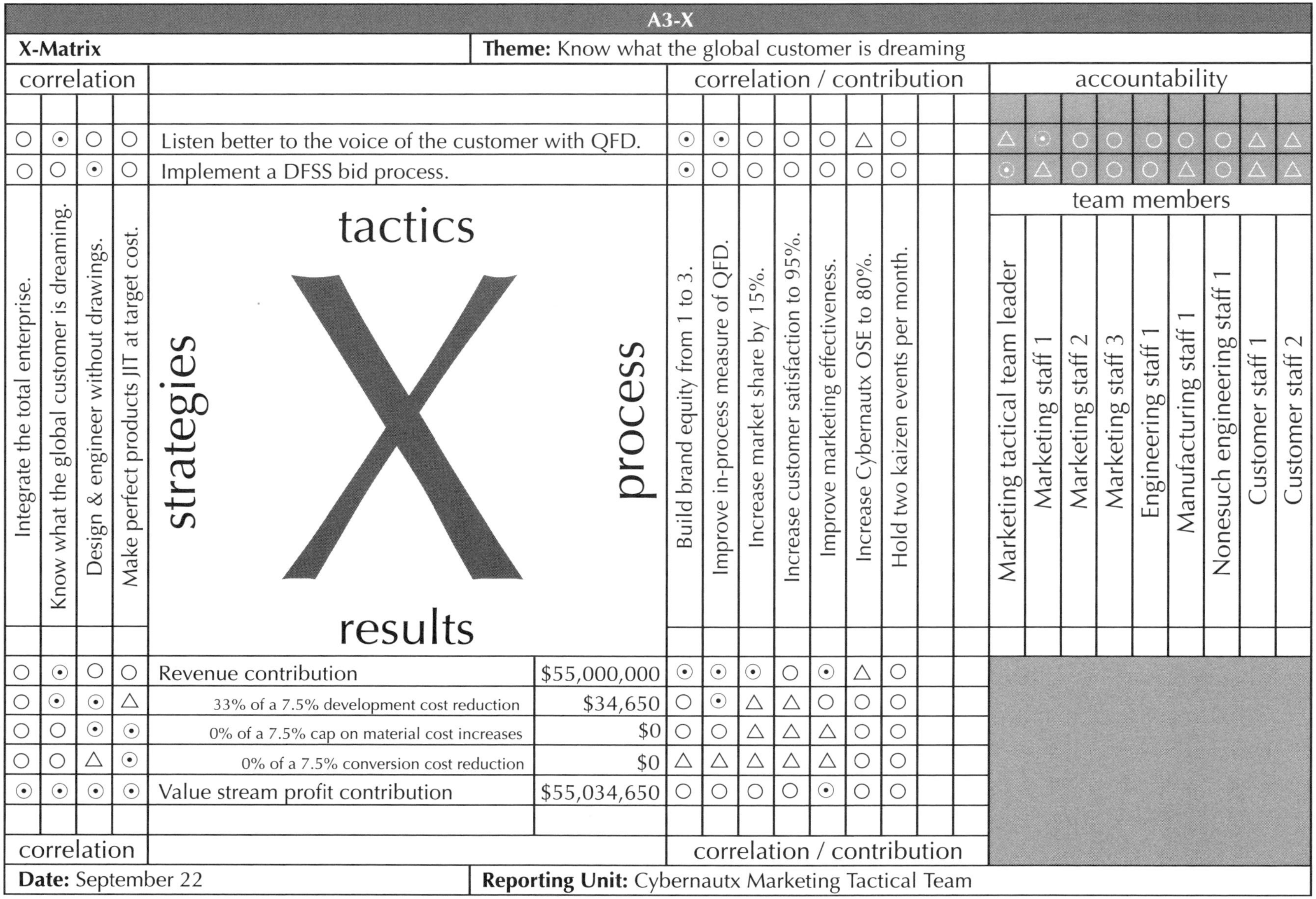

A3-X

X-Matrix

Theme: Know what the global customer is dreaming

Tactics (correlation / contribution):
- Listen better to the voice of the customer with QFD.
- Implement a DFSS bid process.

Process:
- Hold two kaizen events per month.
- Increase Cybernautx OSE to 80%.
- Improve marketing effectiveness.
- Increase customer satisfaction to 95%.
- Increase market share by 15%.
- Improve in-process measure of QFD.
- Build brand equity from 1 to 3.

Strategies (correlation):
- Make perfect products JIT at target cost.
- Design & engineer without drawings.
- Know what the global customer is dreaming.
- Integrate the total enterprise.

Results (correlation / contribution):

Results	Amount
Revenue contribution	$55,000,000
33% of a 7.5% development cost reduction	$34,650
0% of a 7.5% cap on material cost increases	$0
0% of a 7.5% conversion cost reduction	$0
Value stream profit contribution	$55,034,650

Accountability — team members:
- Marketing tactical team leader
- Marketing staff 1
- Marketing staff 2
- Marketing staff 3
- Engineering staff 1
- Manufacturing staff 1
- Nonesuch engineering staff 1
- Customer staff 1
- Customer staff 2

Date: September 22

Reporting Unit: Cybernautx Marketing Tactical Team

Figure 5-12. Catchball Round B Marketing Tactical Team Plan, Second Draft

Table 5-2. Cybernautx's More Aggressive Revised Budget Plan

	This year	Next year	Year 2	Year 3	Year 4
Market size (units)	100,000	100,000	100,000	100,000	100,000
Average sales price	$5,000	$5,000	$5,000	$5,000	$5,000
Market share	10.0%	10.0%	10.0%	10.0%	10.0%
Unit sales	10,000	10,000	10,000	10,000	10,000
Dollar sales	$50,000,000	$50,000,000	$50,000,000	$50,000,000	$50,000,000
Development costs	$1,400,000	$1,400,000	$1,400,000	$1,400,000	$1,400,000
Material costs	$40,000,000	$44,000,000	$48,400,000	$53,240,000	$58,564,000
Conversion costs	$8,000,000	$7,600,000	$7,220,000	$6,859,000	$6,516,050
Value stream profit	$600,000	–$3,000,000	–$7,020,000	–$11,499,000	–$16,480,050
Annual return on sales	1.2%	–6.0%	–14.0%	–23.0%	–33.0%

Cumulative sales	$250,000,000
Cumulative development costs	7,000,000
Cumulative material costs	244,204,000
Cumulative coversion costs	36,195,050
Cumultative VSP	–$37,399,050
Average percent return on sales	–15.0%

concluded that they had no choice but to implement it as quickly as possible. (In set-based engineering, you identify multiple solutions to design problems at the front end of the development process instead of selecting just one.) This would certainly be the only way to meet their targeted contributions to the reduction of material and conversion costs. The groundwork had been laid already. They could start the new process with the next product introduction. The team believed that a lead-time reduction of 37.5 percent was feasible, which should yield a cost reduction of about 7.5 percent in development cost, which the team noted on their A3-X.

The tactical team also noted that the market/technology matrix (see Figure 2-3) indicated important new trends in technology for which the team did not feel that the company was prepared. So they decided to add a tactical objective of researching these trends in depth by conducting *TRI-Z* training, reading journal articles, and attending conferences to network with experts and trusted colleagues in the engineering community. The goal of the activity was to bring new technologies to market to increase the number of new patents by 25 percent per year, as stipulated during catchball Round A (see Figure 5-13).

Catchball Round B—Nonesuch Lean Manufacturing Tactical Team Proposals

The Nonesuch lean manufacturing tactical team's Round B of catchball produced agreement that the team should press ahead with the implementation of lean manufacturing based upon its intermediate state map (on page 88). But the team noted how much easier it would be to succeed if Cybernautx could begin to address problems

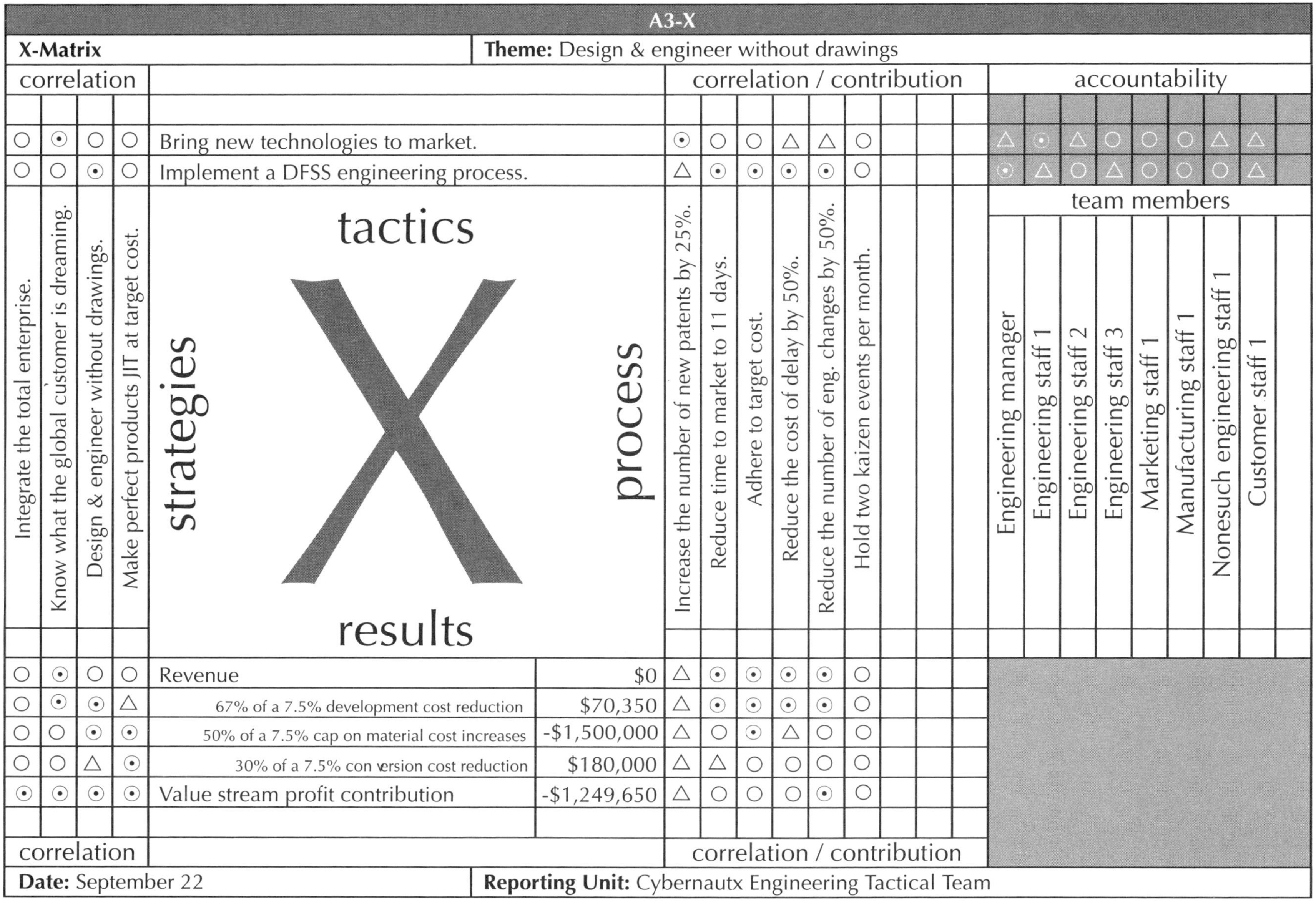

X-Matrix **A3-X** **Theme:** Design & engineer without drawings

accountability — team members

- Engineering manager
- Engineering staff 1
- Engineering staff 2
- Engineering staff 3
- Marketing staff 1
- Manufacturing staff 1
- Nonesuch engineering staff 1
- Customer staff 1

correlation / contribution

tactics:
- Bring new technologies to market.
- Implement a DFSS engineering process.

process:
- Hold two kaizen events per month.
- Reduce the number of eng. changes by 50%.
- Reduce the cost of delay by 50%.
- Adhere to target cost.
- Reduce time to market to 11 days.
- Increase the number of new patents by 25%.

strategies:
- Make perfect products JIT at target cost.
- Design & engineer without drawings.
- Know what the global customer is dreaming.
- Integrate the total enterprise.

results:

Revenue	$0
67% of a 7.5% development cost reduction	$70,350
50% of a 7.5% cap on material cost increases	-$1,500,000
30% of a 7.5% conversion cost reduction	$180,000
Value stream profit contribution	-$1,249,650

correlation / contribution

Date: September 22 **Reporting Unit:** Cybernautx Engineering Tactical Team

Figure 5-13. Catchball Round B Engineering Tactical Team Plan, Second Draft

upstream of manufacturing. The involvement of manufacturing in the new product development process is really a separate project, the team members said. Why not add it to our A3-X? So the tactical team added a new action level project: 3P, or pre-production planning (see Figure 5-14). 3P is an integral part of the set-based engineering process that the Cybernautx program management team has declared it wants to implement. Figure 5-15 is the third draft of the Cybernautx annual hoshin.

X-matrix Tip: When tactical or operations teams add new projects to their A3-Xs, be sure that they link them to strategies (on the left-hand side of the "X") and to measures of process improvement (on the right-hand side of the "X"). Carefully consider whether or not the new project requires new measures of process improvement. If so, add the new measures to the matrix and link them to financial results (beneath the "X").

Operational Team Leaders Present Draft Operational A3-Xs to the Tactical Team

Each operational team leader presents his or her draft matrix to the tactical team leader and the rest of the tactical team. Permit about 20 minutes for the presentation and discussion of project plans for each operational project.

Tactical and Operational Team Leaders Revise the Tactical A3-X

In preparation for deployment to operational improvement teams, the tactical leader and the operational team leaders revise their documents to reflect the hoshin team's provisional understanding of what needs to be done. Permit 30 minutes of discussion about the interrelationships between operational projects and the tactical project and another 10 to 15 minutes for the scribe to update the tactical and operational project plan documents.

CATCHBALL ROUND C: OPERATIONAL TEAM ACTIVITY—ACTION PROJECTS AND TEAMS

In Round C of catchball, operational team leaders deploy the fifth experiment of the hoshin system—current operations—by chartering action teams and action projects with A3-Ts to make improvements in the sixth experiment in the *Do* cycle of the hoshin system: kaikaku, or major, periodic improvements to standardized work. (We will discuss standardized work at length in Chapter 9.) Just as tactical teams consisted of operational team leaders, operational teams consist of action team leaders. Normally, action team leaders are frontline managers such as project team leaders, area leaders, and supervisors.

Action Team Tip: Action teams exist at every level of the organization, not just on the front lines of value-adding operations. If your team isn't involved in the creation and deployment of an A3-X, then your team is an action team. That is, "action team" means nothing more than "next step implementation; no more deployment." This means that there can be action teams attached directly to the hoshin team and the tactical teams, as well as to the operational teams. So you will have a hoshin action team, tactical action team, operational action team, and frontline action team (also called a value-adding action team). Each action team should have its own A3-T, defining the scope and expected outcomes of improvement activity.

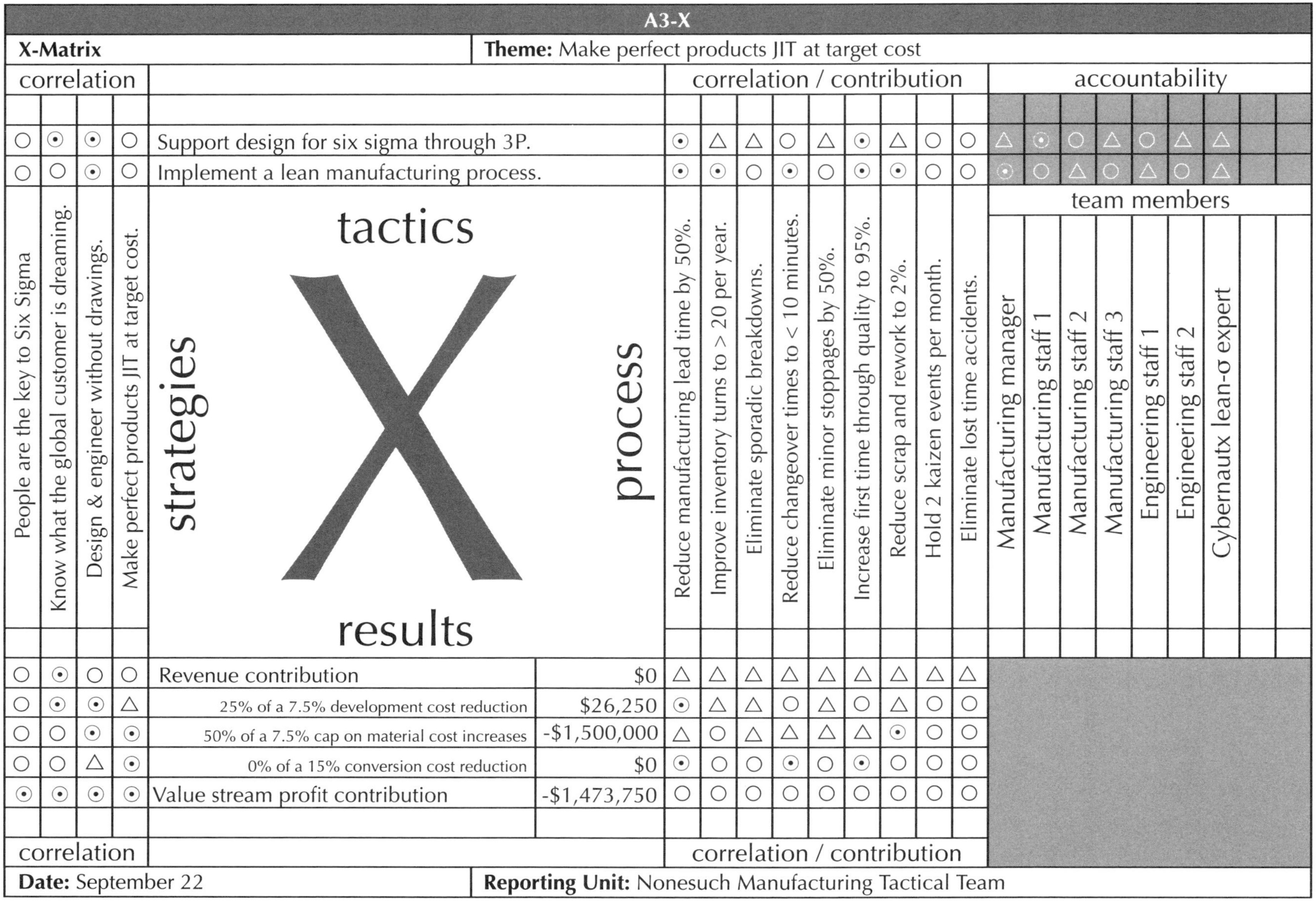

A3-X

X-Matrix

Theme: Make perfect products JIT at target cost

correlation / contribution — accountability — team members

Tactics
- Support design for six sigma through 3P.
- Implement a lean manufacturing process.

Process
- Reduce manufacturing lead time by 50%.
- Improve inventory turns to > 20 per year.
- Eliminate sporadic breakdowns.
- Reduce changeover times to < 10 minutes.
- Eliminate minor stoppages by 50%.
- Increase first time through quality to 95%.
- Reduce scrap and rework to 2%.
- Hold 2 kaizen events per month.
- Eliminate lost time accidents.

Strategies
- Make perfect products JIT at target cost.
- Design & engineer without drawings.
- Know what the global customer is dreaming.
- People are the key to Six Sigma

Results

Revenue contribution	$0
25% of a 7.5% development cost reduction	$26,250
50% of a 7.5% cap on material cost increases	-$1,500,000
0% of a 15% conversion cost reduction	$0
Value stream profit contribution	-$1,473,750

team members (accountability)
- Manufacturing manager
- Manufacturing staff 1
- Manufacturing staff 2
- Manufacturing staff 3
- Engineering staff 1
- Engineering staff 2
- Cybernaut σ lean-σ expert

correlation / contribution

Date: September 22   **Reporting Unit:** Nonesuch Manufacturing Tactical Team

Figure 5-14. Catchball Round B Nonesuch Manufacturing Tactical Team Plan, Second Draft

103

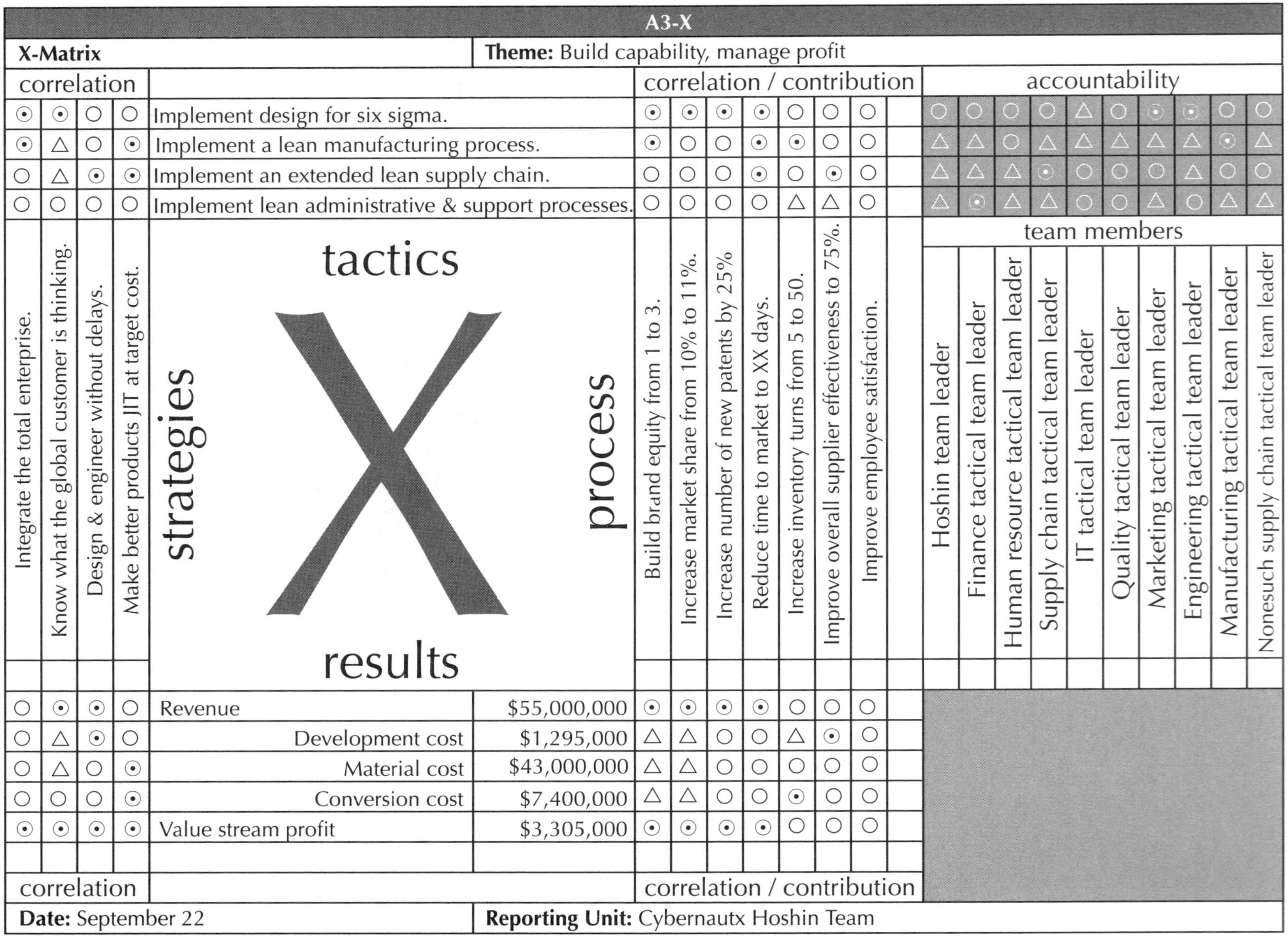

A3-X

X-Matrix | **Theme:** Build capability, manage profit

accountability — team members:
- Hoshin team leader
- Finance tactical team leader
- Human resource tactical team leader
- Supply chain tactical team leader
- IT tactical team leader
- Quality tactical team leader
- Marketing tactical team leader
- Engineering tactical team leader
- Manufacturing tactical team leader
- Nonesuch supply chain tactical team leader

tactics (correlation):
- Implement design for six sigma.
- Implement a lean manufacturing process.
- Implement an extended lean supply chain.
- Implement lean administrative & support processes.

process (correlation / contribution):
- Improve employee satisfaction.
- Improve overall supplier effectiveness to 75%.
- Increase inventory turns from 5 to 50.
- Reduce time to market to XX days.
- Increase number of new patents by 25%
- Increase market share from 10% to 11%.
- Build brand equity from 1 to 3.

strategies (correlation):
- Make better products JIT at target cost.
- Design & engineer without delays.
- Know what the global customer is thinking.
- Integrate the total enterprise.

results (correlation / contribution):

Revenue	$55,000,000
Development cost	$1,295,000
Material cost	$43,000,000
Conversion cost	$7,400,000
Value stream profit	$3,305,000

Date: September 22   **Reporting Unit:** Cybernautx Hoshin Team

Figure 5-15. Catchball Round B Cybernautx Annual Hoshin, Third Draft

104

An action team attached to the hoshin team would be a tactical team, of course, but its project would *not* be *deployed* to the operational level. For example, a tactical action team might be a "tiger" team of experts focused on a new product concept of strategic importance. An action team attached directly to a tactical team would be an operational team, but again it would be a project that is not deployed to the level of value-adding operations. For example, an operational level action team consisting of a team of departmental experts might focus on the implementation of a new information technology. Finally, your frontline action teams are those created through a deployment carried out by an operational team.

Like the hoshin and tactical team, the operational team follows the same six steps in Round A catchball (page 87). In their review, operational teams consider the coordination of improvement activities in their areas, such as corrective action, process improvements, product development, internal communications, customer or supplier relations, and performance measurement. Later, operational teams will suggest to tactical team leader their own ideas for improving company policy and reaching overall objectives.

We will use the Cybernautx operational marketing and engineering team's decision, along with what the Nonesuch lean manufacturing operational team did to show the process for their proposal relating to lean manufacturing activities. Your operational team should consider using some of these tools when discussing, researching, and drafting its own proposal.

Catchball Round C—Cybernautx Engineering Tactical Team Proposal

In its operational team meeting, the engineering tactical team raised the possibility of moving the engineering offices into space freed by manufacturing during last year's lean manufacturing activities. The team reasoned that, in implementing design for six sigma, it was a certainty that all the furniture would be relocated anyway, to promote better communication by team members. Once the furniture was off the floor, why not set it down in the new location? This would promote better communication with the plant, especially during the difficult launch process. The team leader requested team members to research the possibility and to coordinate with manufacturing. The team prepared the value stream map in Figure 5-16.

The team estimated that not only could it meet its conversion cost reduction targets, it could increase the rate of new product introduction. Would this have an additional impact on market share acquisition? Would this help to avoid layoffs? The team estimated that the impact might be an additional 1 or 2 percent in market share per year, but this assumption would have to be confirmed by the marketing team in Round E of catchball.

The team also recognized that the relocation would be pointless without proper training. So it drew up a generic training plan in the form of a bar chart geared to the phases of the new product introduction process (see Figure 5-17). Workshop participants are also listed on the chart.

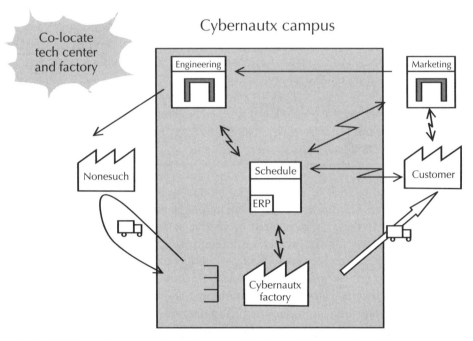

Figure 5-16. DFSS Engineering Team Proposal to Move Engineering Offices

Workshop	Concept selection	Detailed design	Design validation	Production validation	Launch
QFD	Marketing & engineering	Marketing & engineering	Marketing, engineering, & key suppliers	Marketing, engineering, & manufacturing	
Concurrent engineering	Engineering & key suppliers	Engineering & key suppliers	Engineering & key suppliers	Engineering & key suppliers	
3P	Marketing, engineering, & manufacturing	Engineering, manufacturing, & key suppliers	Engineering, manufacturing, & key suppliers	Engineering, manufacturing, & key suppliers	Engineering, manufacturing, & key suppliers

Time →

Figure 5-17. Cybernautx DFSS Training Schedule

Planning Tip: Bar charts (also called Gantt charts) are widely used to graphically display tasks or resources scheduled over time. Use bar charts for short-term projects, or when there are few relationships between tasks, when the number of tasks is small, when you can estimate performance times easily, and for reporting the status of projects. Bar charts are simple to construct and update. They show relationships between task and time, and they are highly visual. Unlike the A3-X, bar charts don't show relationships between tasks, targets, or people.

106

Catchball Round C—Nonesuch's Operational Lean Manufacturing Team Proposal

Nonesuch's operational lean manufacturing team decided to look more closely at the assumptions underlying the estimates of lead-time and cost reduction demanded by Cybernautx. In particular, the team focused on the constraint in their process: injection molding. The OEE on the constraint was currently only 41 percent. The problem was clearly changeovers on the injection molding machines. Changeovers were currently running 4 hours. If they could reduce changeovers to less than 10 minutes—the world class benchmark—OEE could be raised to 82 percent. At this rate, enough capacity would be created to continue current production with only one shift.

Perhaps even more importantly, Nonesuch could perform enough changeovers in a day that it could produce in small batches, ship directly to the Cybernautx plant, and eliminate the need for the warehouse! The team felt confident in committing itself to ameliorating the material cost increase from the current target of 7.5 percent to –5 percent. The team quickly drew up an implementation schedule for the year in the form of a milestone chart (see Figure 5-18).

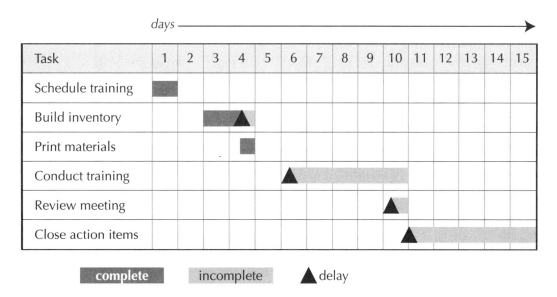

Figure 5-18. Nonesuch Milestone Chart for Conducting a Kaizen Workshop

Hoshin Planning Tip: Milestone charts are bar charts enhanced by information about project start and end dates, review meetings, testing, and other important information. It's common to see a combination of task bars and project milestones. If you're familiar with scheduling software such as Microsoft Project, you are already familiar with this type of milestone chart.

Discuss and Revise Operational and Action Project Plans

Once again, budget enough time for the presentation, discussion, and revision of action and operational team project plans. This is the end of the top-down process, and represents the last opportunity for middle managers to influence the strategic planning process.

This raises the question: How far should the process go? Theoretically, you could extend the process right down to the shop floor until everyone in the company takes a hand in strategic planning. *However, nonmanagers are not normally part of the catchball process.* Even the inclusion of supervisors on operational teams is optional. The circle of involvement in the hoshin process expands slowly in proportion to the maturity of standardized work and continuous improvement on the front line. At the famous NUMMI plant, for example, Toyota included supervisors in the process only ten years after the implementation of the Toyota Production System. So don't be in a hurry.

CATCHBALL ROUND D: OPERATIONAL AND ACTION TEAM ACTIVITY— FINALIZING ACTION AND OPERATIONAL PROJECT PLANS

Up to now, the catchball process has been top-down. Information about the annual hoshin has flowed from the top, down through each level of the management hierarchy. In Round D of catchball, the process has reversed direction and flows from the bottom up. Operational team leaders have already heard the input of their team members. At this point, tactical teams review completed operational A3-Xs and A3-Ts. After discussing the operational plans, each tactical team recommends changes and revises its tactical A3-X in preparation for the final round of catchball with the hoshin team.

Below are the adjustments the three tactical teams made to the operational team's inputs for preparation for Round E, the fifth round of catchball with the hoshin team. Note that the A3-Xs reflect the changes the operational team made in Round C and approved and adjusted by the tactical team.

Catchball Round D—Tactical Team Adjustments to Operational Marketing Team Inputs

An unexpected development occurred in the Cybernautx marketing team meeting, where the DFSS order entry process operational team made its case to create an integrated order entry cell. The marketing tactical team summarized changes in its plans in a revised A3-X (See Figure 5-19). The revisions reflect the team's consensus that it could both deliver a revenue increase and contribute more aggressively to development cost reduction. Marketing has committed itself to contributing a cost reduction of $35,000 in development cost, 25 percent of the total expected reduction.

Catchball Round D—Tactical Team Adjustments to Operational Engineering Team Inputs

In the Cybernautx engineering team meeting, the DFSS engineering process team successfully made its case to move engineering to a new home at the manufacturing plant. Like the tactical marketing team, the engineering tactical team summarized changes in its plans in a revised A3-X (see Figure 5-20). The team's revisions reflect the consensus that it could contribute more aggressively in all cost reduction categories: development cost, material cost, and conversion cost.

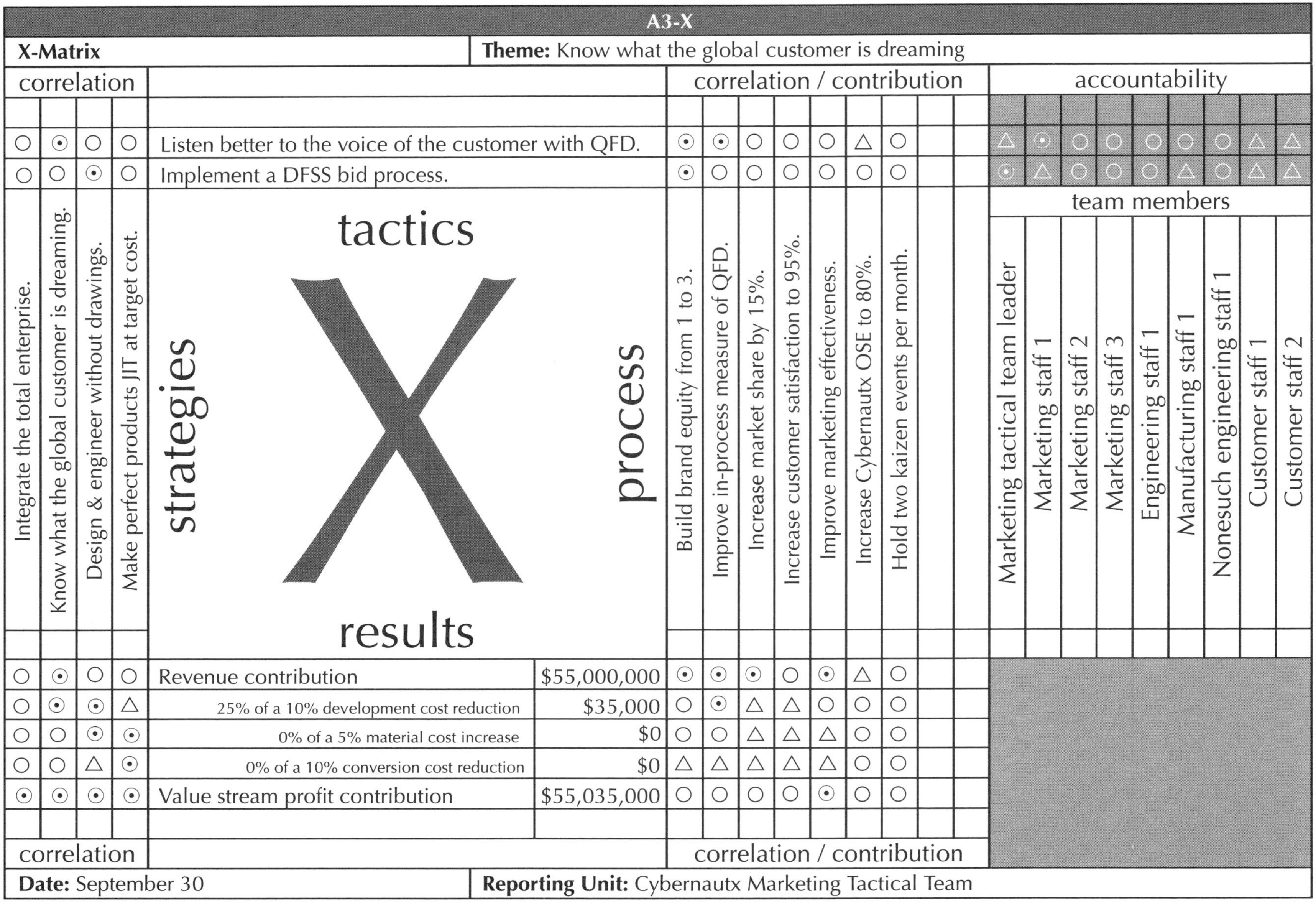

X-Matrix

Theme: Know what the global customer is dreaming

accountability — team members

correlation / contribution

tactics
- Listen better to the voice of the customer with QFD.
- Implement a DFSS bid process.

process
- Build brand equity from 1 to 3.
- Improve in-process measure of QFD.
- Increase market share by 15%.
- Increase customer satisfaction to 95%.
- Improve marketing effectiveness.
- Increase Cybernautx OSE to 80%.
- Hold two kaizen events per month.

strategies
- Make perfect products JIT at target cost.
- Design & engineer without drawings.
- Know what the global customer is dreaming.
- Integrate the total enterprise.

results

Revenue contribution	$55,000,000
25% of a 10% development cost reduction	$35,000
0% of a 5% material cost increase	$0
0% of a 10% conversion cost reduction	$0
Value stream profit contribution	$55,035,000

team members:
- Marketing tactical team leader
- Marketing staff 1
- Marketing staff 2
- Marketing staff 3
- Engineering staff 1
- Manufacturing staff 1
- Nonesuch engineering staff 1
- Customer staff 1
- Customer staff 2

Date: September 30   **Reporting Unit:** Cybernautx Marketing Tactical Team

Figure 5-19. Catchball Round D Marketing Tactical Team Plan, Third Draft

X-Matrix A3-X

Theme: Design & engineer without drawings

tactics
- Bring new technologies to market.
- Implement a DFSS engineering process.

process
- Increase the number of new patents by 25%.
- Reduce time to market to 11 days.
- Adhere to target cost.
- Reduce the cost of delay by 50%.
- Reduce the number of eng. changes by 50%.
- Hold two kaizen events per month.

strategies
- Make perfect products JIT at target cost.
- Design & engineer without drawings.
- Know what the global customer is dreaming.
- Integrate the total enterprise.

results

Revenue	$0
50% of a 10% development cost reduction	$70,000
50% of a 5% material cost increase	-$1,000,000
30% of a 10% conversion cost reduction	$240,000
Value stream profit contribution	-$690,000

accountability — team members
- Engineering manager
- Engineering staff 1
- Engineering staff 2
- Engineering staff 3
- Marketing staff 1
- Manufacturing staff 1
- Nonesuch engineering staff 1
- Customer staff 1

correlation / contribution

Date: September 30   **Reporting Unit:** Cybernautx Engineering Tactical Team

Figure 5-20. Catchball Round D Engineering Tactical Team Plan, Third Draft

110

Catchball Round D—Tactical Team Adjustments to Nonesuch Manufacturing Team Inputs

At Nonesuch, in the manufacturing tactical team meeting, the team presented its X-matrix to the plant manager (see Figure 5-21). The team's plan detailed the rollout of cellular manufacturing across the factory floor, the huge improvement in OEE, the increased frequency of production runs, direct shipments, and the elimination of the warehouse.

CATCHBALL ROUND E: FINALIZING THE HOSHIN AND TACTICAL PLANS

Round E, the fifth and final round of catchball, concludes the *Plan* cycle of PDCA, as stated on the hoshin kanri roadmap (Figure 1-1). Here, the hoshin team reviews the tactical and operational plans prepared by the tactical teams and their respective operational teams. This is the time to fix estimates of the financial impacts of policies and objectives and create a final draft of the annual hoshin A3-X. But be ready for surprises as you prepare to engage your action teams in the sixth experiment in the *Do* cycle of PDCA.

Cybernautx Hoshin Team Finalizes the Three Tactical Plans

In the final round of catchball, the engineering, marketing and Nonesuch manufacturing tactical team leaders presented their plans to the Cybernautx hoshin team to reorganize their units into lean cells. The marketing tactical team presented its plan to create an integrated order entry cell. The engineering tactical team presented its plan to move engineering into the available space at the plant. Nonesuch was declared a hero when it announced its proposal to eliminate the warehouse of purchased parts.

Just before lunch, Cybernautx's manufacturing manager noted that there was probably plenty of space to house the company's entire support staff, so why not relocate everyone at the same time? The Cybernautx hoshin team leader asked the hoshin team to run the numbers, while he ordered take-out. How much space was needed for the sales and marketing cell? How much space was needed for the engineering cell? How much space was available? Both marketing and engineering had already requested permanent participation by each other's departments. Would combining the two cells eliminate the need for additional personnel? Would more space be needed, or less? Would new furniture be required?

That afternoon the hoshin team reconstructed the company's intermediate state value stream map and reestimated the expected reductions in marketing order entry, engineering, and manufacturing launch lead times (see Figure 5-22). The team astounded itself by estimating that the entire process, from concept to color-coded work instructions would be reduced from 80 days (see Figure 2-4) to only 20 days—a reduction of 75 percent! And Cybernautx would be able to take on more business because of its breakthroughs in product development and improvement in throughput on the shop floor. This of course made Nonesuch's value stream leader very happy.

The Cybernautx manufacturing manager was not convinced that the work instructions could be executed without problems. But even if engineering didn't bother to make the product manufacturable, it would be a big improvement over the current situation. "It usually takes months to find out we can't put it together," said Nonesuch's manufacturing team leader.

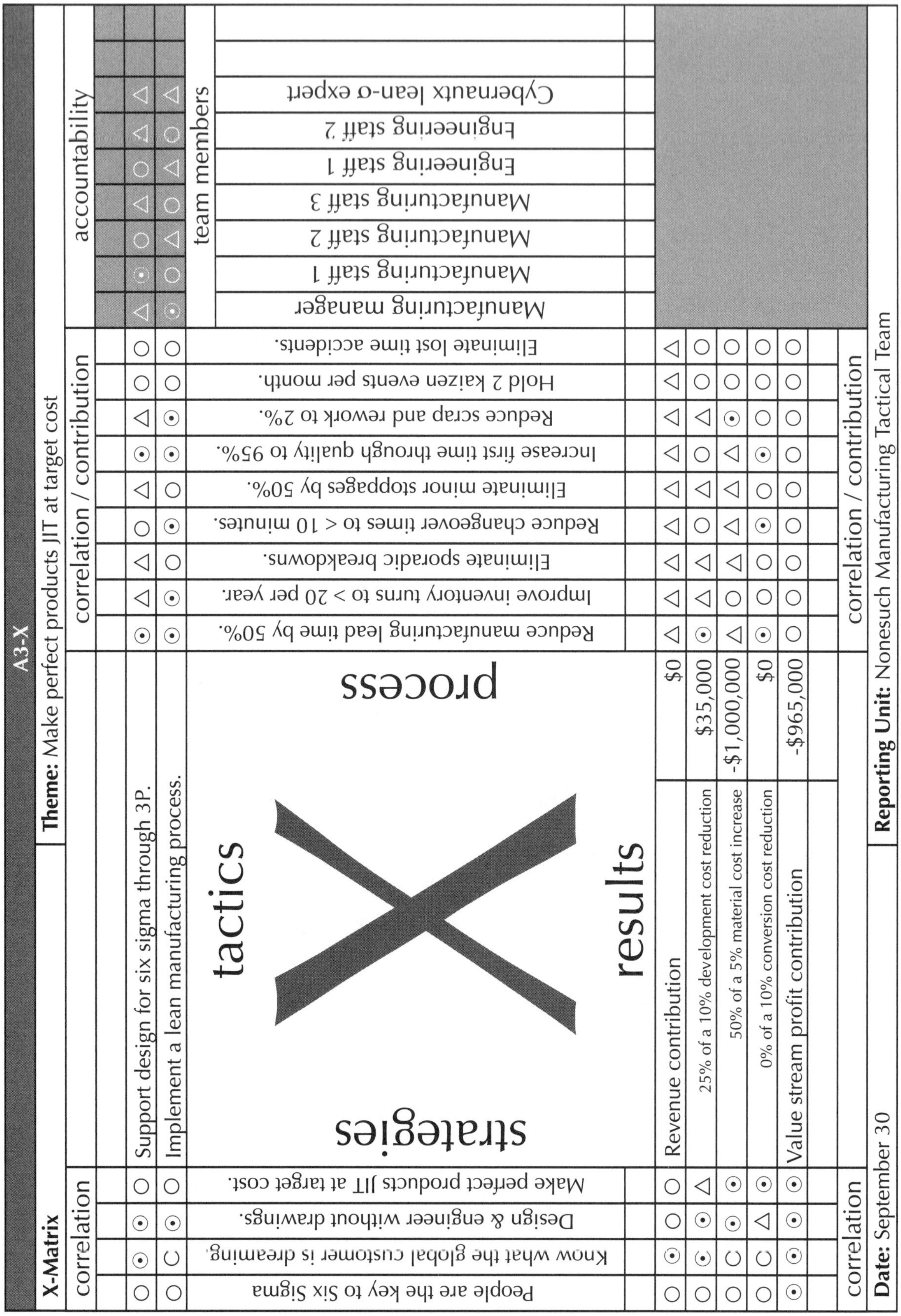

X-Matrix

A3-X

Theme: Make perfect products JIT at target cost

accountability

team members

- Cybernaut lean-σ expert
- Engineering staff 2
- Engineering staff 1
- Manufacturing staff 3
- Manufacturing staff 2
- Manufacturing staff 1
- Manufacturing manager

correlation / contribution

- Eliminate lost time accidents.
- Hold 2 kaizen events per month.
- Reduce scrap and rework to 2%.
- Increase first time through quality to 95%.
- Eliminate minor stoppages by 50%.
- Reduce changeover times to < 10 minutes.
- Eliminate sporadic breakdowns.
- Improve inventory turns to > 20 per year.
- Reduce manufacturing lead time by 50%.

process

tactics

- Support design for six sigma through 3P.
- Implement a lean manufacturing process.

results

- Revenue contribution — $0
- 25% of a 10% development cost reduction — $35,000
- 50% of a 5% material cost increase — -$1,000,000
- 0% of a 10% conversion cost reduction — $0
- Value stream profit contribution — -$965,000

strategies

- Make perfect products JIT at target cost.
- Design & engineer without drawings.
- Know what the global customer is dreaming.
- People are the key to Six Sigma

X-Matrix / correlation

correlation / contribution

Date: September 30

Reporting Unit: Nonesuch Manufacturing Tactical Team

Figure 5-21. Catchball Round D Nonesuch Manufacturing Tactical Team Plan, Third Draft

"When is Nonesuch going to set up shop on our new campus?" the team joked.

Table 5-3 and Figure 5-23 show Cybernautx's revised budget plan and A3-X for next year, reflecting the more aggressive approach suggested by the data gathering and analysis of the sales & marketing, engineering, and manufacturing departments. Figures 24, 25, and 26 show the revised A3-Xs for the Cybernautx marketing, Cybernautx engineering, and Nonesuch manufacturing tactical teams, respectively.

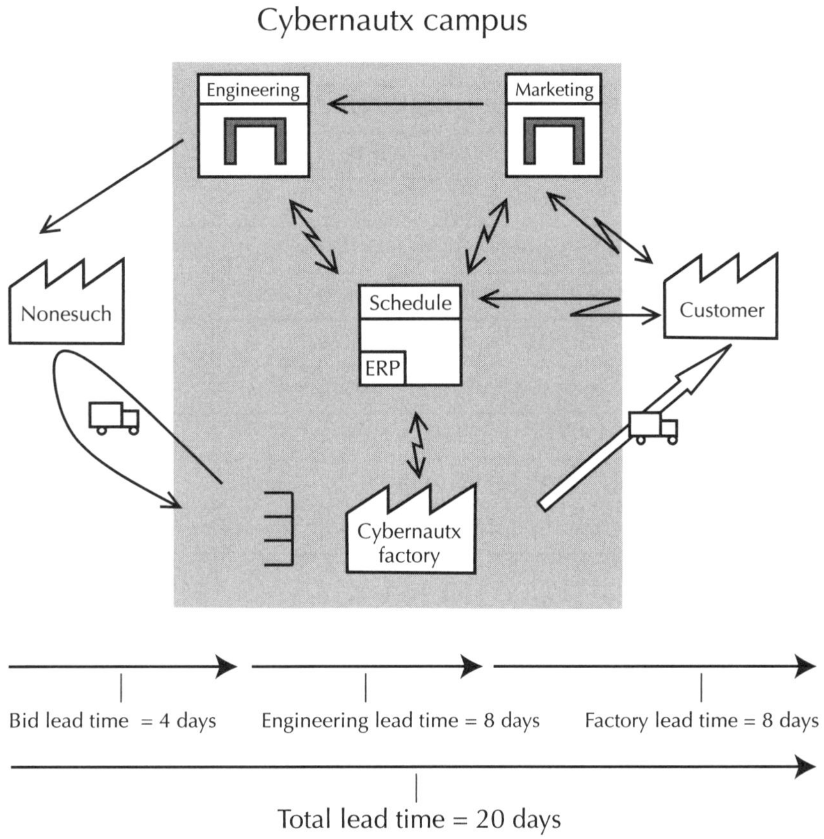
Cybernautx campus
Engineering
Marketing
Nonesuch
Schedule
ERP
Customer
Cybernautx factory
Bid lead time = 4 days
Engineering lead time = 8 days
Factory lead time = 8 days
Total lead time = 20 days

Figure 5-22. Revised Lean Value Stream Map

Table 5-3. Multiyear Value Stream Profit Plan, Final Revision

	This year	Next year	Year 2	Year 3	Year 4
Dollar sales	$50,000,000	$60,000,000	$70,000,000	$80,000,000	$90,000,000
Development costs	$1,400,000	$1,190,000	$1,011,500	$859,755	$730,809
Material costs	$40,000,000	$44,100,000	$49,980,000	$57,120,000	$64,260,000
Conversion costs	$8,000,000	$6,800,000	$5,780,000	$4,913,000	$4,176,050
Value stream profit	$600,000	$7,910,000	$13,228,500	$17,107,225	$20,833,141
Annual return on sales	1.2%	13.2%	18.9%	21.4%	23.1%

Cumulative sales	$350,000,000
Cumulative development costs	5,192,084
Cumulative material costs	255,460,000
Cumulative coversion costs	29,669,050
Cumultative VSP	$59,678,866
Average percent return on sales	17.1%

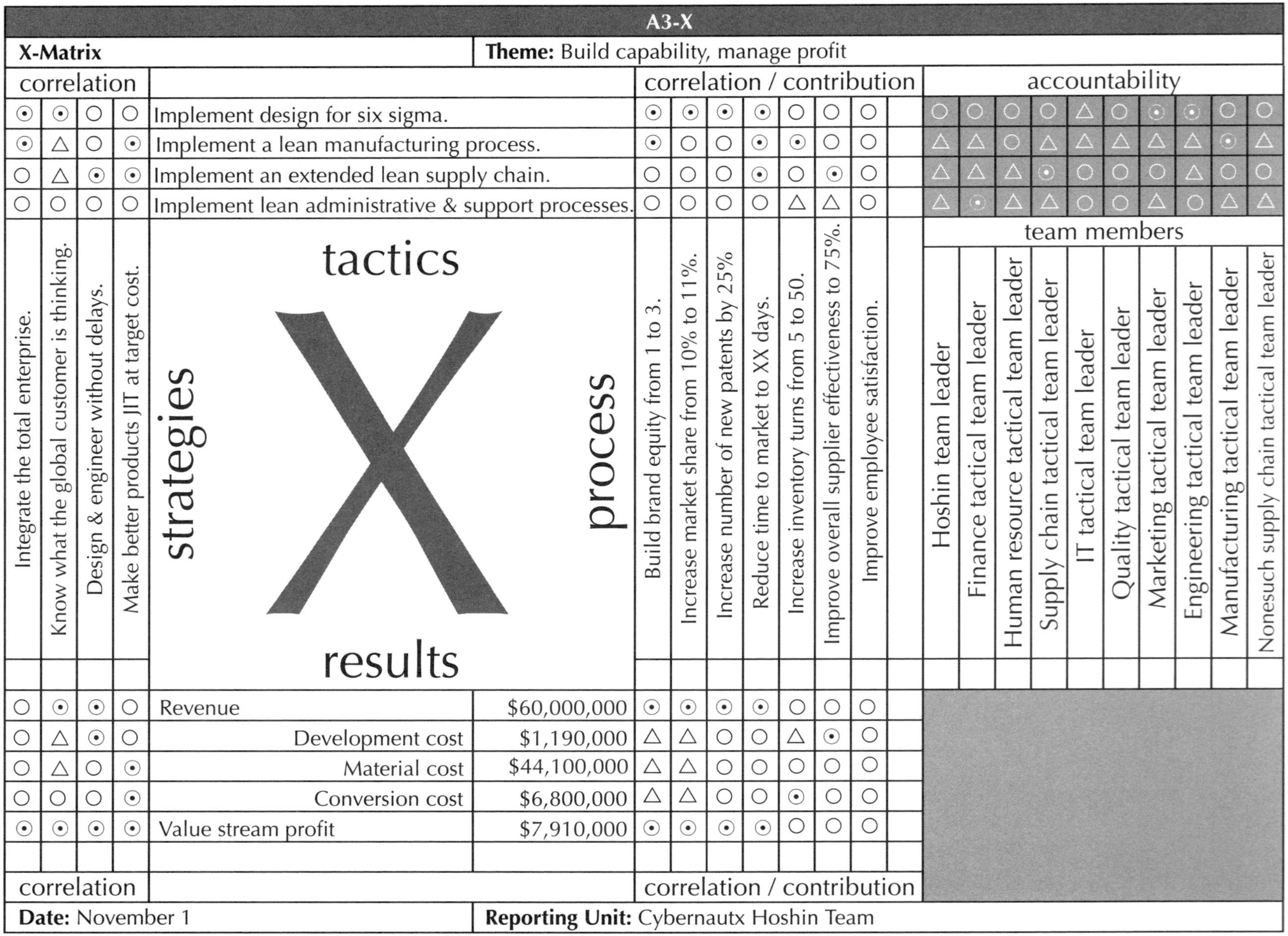

X-Matrix — **A3-X**

Theme: Build capability, manage profit

Tactics
- Implement design for six sigma.
- Implement a lean manufacturing process.
- Implement an extended lean supply chain.
- Implement lean administrative & support processes.

Process (correlation / contribution)
- Build brand equity from 1 to 3.
- Increase market share from 10% to 11%.
- Increase number of new patents by 25%
- Reduce time to market to XX days.
- Increase inventory turns from 5 to 50.
- Improve overall supplier effectiveness to 75%.
- Improve employee satisfaction.

Strategies (correlation)
- Make better products JIT at target cost.
- Design & engineer without delays.
- Know what the global customer is thinking.
- Integrate the total enterprise.

Results

Results	
Revenue	$60,000,000
Development cost	$1,190,000
Material cost	$44,100,000
Conversion cost	$6,800,000
Value stream profit	$7,910,000

Accountability — team members
- Hoshin team leader
- Finance tactical team leader
- Human resource tactical team leader
- Supply chain tactical team leader
- IT tactical team leader
- Quality tactical team leader
- Marketing tactical team leader
- Engineering tactical team leader
- Manufacturing tactical team leader
- Nonesuch supply chain tactical team leader

Date: November 1 **Reporting Unit:** Cybernautx Hoshin Team

Figure 5-23. Catchball Round E Cybernautx Annual Hoshin, Final Draft

114

X-Matrix

Theme: Know what the global customer is dreaming

accountability — team members:
- Marketing tactical team leader
- Marketing staff 1
- Marketing staff 2
- Marketing staff 3
- Engineering staff 1
- Manufacturing staff 1
- Nonesuch engineering staff 1
- Customer staff 1
- Customer staff 2

correlation / contribution (process):
- Build brand equity from 1 to 3.
- Improve in-process measure of QFD.
- Increase market share by 15%.
- Increase customer satisfaction to 95%.
- Improve marketing effectiveness.
- Increase Cybernautx OSE to 80%.
- Hold two kaizen events per month.

tactics:
- Listen better to the voice of the customer with QFD.
- Implement a DFSS bid process.

strategies:
- Make perfect products JIT at target cost.
- Design & engineer without drawings.
- Know what the global customer is dreaming.
- Integrate the total enterprise.

results:

Revenue contribution	$60,000,000
25% of a 15% development cost reduction	$52,500
0% of a 5% cap on material cost increases	$0
0% of a 15% conversion cost reduction	$0
Value stream profit contribution	$60,052,500

Date: November 1 **Reporting Unit:** Cybernautx Marketing Tactical Team

Figure 5-24. Catchball Round E Marketing Tactical Team Plan, Final Draft

X-Matrix — A3-X

Theme: Design & engineer without drawings

Tactics:
- Bring new technologies to market.
- Implement a DFSS engineering process.

process

Process (improvement priorities):
- Increase the number of new patents by 25%.
- Reduce time to market to 11 days.
- Adhere to target cost.
- Reduce the cost of delay by 50%.
- Reduce the number of eng. changes by 50%.
- Hold two kaizen events per month.

tactics

results

Results:

Revenue	$0
50% of a 15% development cost reduction	$105,000
50% of a 5% cap on material cost increases	-$1,000,000
30% of a 15% conversion cost reduction	$360,000
Value stream profit contribution	-$535,000

strategies

Strategies:
- Make perfect products JIT at target cost.
- Design & engineer without drawings.
- Know what the global customer is dreaming.
- Integrate the total enterprise.

correlation / contribution

accountability — team members:
- Engineering manager
- Engineering staff 1
- Engineering staff 2
- Engineering staff 3
- Marketing staff 1
- Manufacturing staff 1
- Nonesuch engineering staff 1
- Customer staff 1

Reporting Unit: Cybernautx Engineering Tactical Team

Date: November 1

Figure 5-25. Catchball Round E Engineering Tactical Team Plan, Final Draft

X-Matrix   **A3-X**

Theme: Make perfect products JIT at target cost

accountability — team members:
- Manufacturing manager
- Manufacturing staff 1
- Manufacturing staff 2
- Manufacturing staff 3
- Engineering staff 1
- Engineering staff 2
- Cybernaut lean-σ expert

correlation / contribution

Tactics:
- Support design for six sigma through 3P.
- Implement a lean manufacturing process.

Process:
- Reduce manufacturing lead time by 50%.
- Improve inventory turns to > 20 per year.
- Eliminate sporadic breakdowns.
- Reduce changeover times to < 10 minutes.
- Eliminate minor stoppages by 50%.
- Increase first time through quality to 95%.
- Reduce scrap and rework to 2%.
- Hold 2 kaizen events per month.
- Eliminate lost time accidents.

Strategies:
- Make perfect products JIT at target cost.
- Design & engineer without drawings.
- Know what the global customer is dreaming.
- People are the key to Six Sigma

Results:

Revenue contribution	$0
25% of a 15% development cost reduction	$52,500
50% of a 5% cap on material cost increases	-$1,000,000
0% of a 15% conversion cost reduction	$0
Value stream profit contribution	-$947,500

correlation / contribution

Date: November 1   **Reporting Unit:** Nonesuch Manufacturing Tactical Team

Figure 5-26. Catchball Round E Nonesuch Manufacturing Tactical Team Plan, Final Draft

117

CHAPTER SIX

DO: Engage the Workforce to Execute the Strategy

Now it's time for team leaders to learn how to do what they have planned in a way that empowers local decision makers to improve quality, reduce lead time, and control cost using the scientific methods of lean and six sigma. As Table 2-1 shows, your action teams will conduct Experiment 6, which entails making both critical adjustments in daily work with focused breakthrough improvements called kaikaku by every single manager and employee using the Plan, Do, Check, Act (PDCA) cycle. Like its close cousin kaizen, kaikaku requires that you have standardized work and is part and parcel of a hoshin operating system. (We will discuss Kaizen, Experiment 7 of the hoshin system, in Chapter 9.)

As stated in the *Do* phase in your hoshin kanri roadmap (Table 1-1), the action teams need to conduct this experiment under controlled conditions that only standardized work provides. At a minimum, a company needs to implement and promote adherence to hoshin's kaikaku objectives through intensive training in productivity and quality methods. These kaikaku projects usually last one week to three months. Without this training, as well as instilling kaizen's ongoing problem solving in the course of daily work, a company will find itself repeatedly solving the same problems. This is why we treat these two experiments as an extension of the deployment process and why there is an emphasis on different training regimens.

For a mature lean enterprise, executing the sixth and seventh experiments of the hoshin process—making adjustments to standardized daily work—is primarily a matter of ensuring adherence to project targets and milestones. This requires the development of a specific schedule for meeting hoshin targets in each project or work center. Next, implementation must be integrated with the goals and targets of daily work. However, most organizations are not mature lean enterprises, but rather are in the process of strategic change from mass thinking to lean thinking. This makes experiments six and seven all the more critical for executing hoshin objectives because enormous work is involved in changing an organizational culture stuck in the last century to one that is continuously eliminating the 7 deadly wastes, installing standardization, mentoring and training your workers, and developing leadership.

ENGAGE THE ACTION TEAMS

Hoshin kanri defines a system of nested experiments, each defined by a team charter. Every team leader—whether a project manager or frontline supervisor—is one part scientist and one part project manager, responsible on the one hand for ensuring adherence to the PDCA process of reliable methods, and on the other hand for delivering targeted results according to a project schedule. The intent of hoshin kanri is to encompass *all* improvement activity within your company and align it with your strategic intent. You have now chartered the hoshin team, tactical teams, and operational teams that include all your managers. The targets of the strategic, tactical, or operational projects of a top executive, division head, department head, section leader, area manager, or supervisor relate to a variety of broad, or relatively broad, objectives. Now that you have finalized the hoshin, the circle of involvement will expand to action teams, which include every employee in your company, as represented in our Cybernautx case study (Figure 6-1).

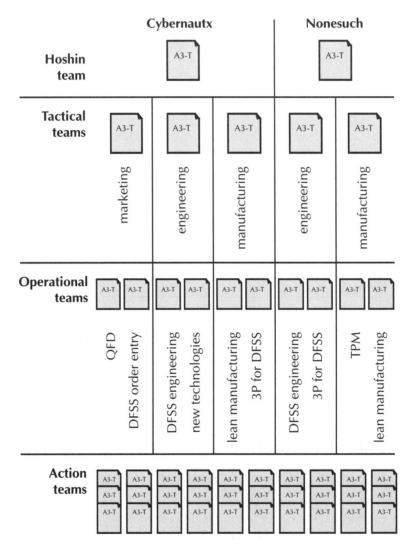

Figure 6-1. Cybernautx and Nonesuch Circle of Involvement Expands to Action Teams

Exercise Good organization is essential for a successful catchball process. Figure 6-1 is essentially a tree diagram designed to verify the scope of the deployment process and keep track of the many teams involved. Draw the planning diagram on a large white board first, then transfer the information to a tabloid-size planning sheet. (See CD Form 6-1.) You may wish to post the planning sheet on your hoshin management board. *The instructions given below are written for a deployment process with four levels of detail, like the process in the workbook.* If there will be more than four levels or fewer than four levels of deployment, you may still use these instructions; but please read the special instructions after step 6 below before you begin.

1. At the top of column 1, briefly list the deliverables of the planning process for which the hoshin team will be responsible: hoshin team charter, hoshin project plan, midterm strategy, annual hoshin, and so forth. Next, record the name of your hoshin team on the left-hand side of a white board or large sheet of paper. This is the first level of detail.

2. At the top of column 2, briefly list the deliverables of the planning process for which the tactical teams are responsible. Next, identify the tactical teams whose team leaders will be members of the hoshin team. Indicate the tactical team names as branch headings in column 2 for the second level of detail.

3. At the top of column 3, list operational team deliverables. Next, for each tactical team in your diagram, identify the operational teams whose team leaders will be members of that tactical team. Indicate the operational team names as branch headings linked to that tactical team in column 3 for the third level of detail. Repeat this branching process for each tactical team.

4. At the top of column 4, list action team deliverables. Next, for each operational team in your diagram, identify the action teams whose team leaders will be members of that operational team. Indicate the operational team names as branch headings linked to that tactical team in column 4 for the fourth level of detail. Repeat this branching process for each operational team.

5. Verify the diagram by retracing the branches to the lowest level. Verify the diagram by retracing the diagram backwards, from the action team level through operational teams and tactical teams all the way back to the hoshin team.

6. When the number of teams involved is large, it's a good idea to assign each team a number or alphanumeric code. For example, the hoshin team series might be designated as H.0. The tactical team series might be designated as H.1, H.2, H.3, …. The operational team series might be designated as H.1.1, H.1.2, H.1.3, … H.2.1, H.2.2, and so forth. And the action team series might be H1.1.1, H1.1.2, H.1.1.3, …, H.2.1.1, H.2.1.2, etc.

Special instruction for companies with more than four levels of deployment: For each additional level of deployment, repeat the branching process that appears in steps 2, 3, and 4 above. CD Form 6-1 includes two additional columns for this purpose. Note that the hoshin team leader will need to assign a name to each additional level.

Special instruction for companies with fewer than four levels of deployment: For companies just beginning the deployment process, it's not unusual to have only two or three levels of deployment. In this case, simply delete step 3, or steps 3 and 4.

Special instruction for interorganizational planning: If you plan to use hoshin in planning strategy jointly with another company, you may simply include your planning partner's teams as tactical, operational, or action teams on your own diagram. You may also note your partner's hoshin team on your diagram, as in Figure 6-1. For this purpose, you may need to print more than one copy of CD Form 6-1.

The success of lean enterprise is the result of a thousand things done well. Nowhere is this more evident than at the action team level of the hoshin process. In addition to adhering to standardized work, action teams focus on thousands of specific improvements to those standards, such as improvement in particular technologies and product features, or to the improvement of specific processes and physical areas. Through action team activity, strategic intent is connected to the daily work of everyone in the organization. As we'll see in Chapter 9, the culture of standardized work and kaizen creates a community of knowledgeable first-responders who don't wait for management's okay to act when problems arise. Meanwhile, management does not hesitate to help when called. Hoshin kanri exploits the lean organization's attitude of improvement by connecting it systematically to strategic improvements in competitive capability, the kaikaku or "breakthrough" objectives of the annual hoshin. This is the real secret to rapid organizational learning, dramatic improvement, and sustainable results in lean enterprises like Toyota.

Everybody Gets Involved

Most business organizations in the United States and Europe are not mature lean organizations. They're still in the process of becoming lean, and the objectives of the annual hoshin are related to implementing basic lean and six sigma technologies effectively. As a practical matter, how many people should you involve in executing a strategic change initiative focused on lean manufacturing, six sigma, or lean sigma? What should their responsibilities be? How should you train them for their new roles? Table 6-1 below assumes that you will integrate your hoshin objectives into the daily work of every executive, manager, staff member, and hourly associate.

Some six sigma consultants recommend a higher ratio of change agents to employees, but hoshin kanri process assumes that everyone is responsible in a lean and six sigma organization. As a result, you need fewer specialized change agents because every manager is, by definition, a change agent. In other words, every manager is a leader, because leading is all about making sustainable change for the better.

It has probably occurred to the reader that you can use hoshin kanri to manage lean manufacturing or six sigma programs effectively, but there is ultimately no need for the lean or six sigma bureaucracies that often crop up in large companies. Furthermore, the existence of a lean or six sigma program office fosters the view that you can delegate lean and six sigma. *You cannot.* Using hoshin to delegate strategic change dooms it to failure because hoshin is not merely a tool of project or program management. Hoshin kanri is nothing less than the business operating system of the 21st century. In a mature lean enterprise, you use the project plans and budgets of the hoshin process to manage *everything that moves*, not just high profile projects. And that includes the daily activities of finance and accounting, the CEO, and the board of directors.

Hoshin Team Exercise: Print out your completed CD-Form 6-1 and compare it to the circular organization chart that you built in Chapter 1 to help you choose the hoshin team members. Recall that you also built the circular organization chart to highlight the need for all managers at all levels in the organization to support value-adding operations on the front lines of functional activity in manufacturing, engineering, marketing, etc. Have you included all senior and middle managers in the hoshin exercise? Have they delegated or resisted strategic change? Do you have plans to involve them in improvement process? Or are they waiting to see results? If they're not formally involved, many of the roles in Table 6-1 will be left unfilled, and improvement efforts on the front line will lack the necessary support. Review Table 6-1, taking note of who might fill these roles as you expand the circle of involvement to action teams and in the future to additional tactical and operational team members higher on the organization chart.

Table 6-1. Roles and Responsibilities in Execution

Role	Responsibility	Recommended Preparation	Planned Preparation	Recommended Staffing	Planned Staffing
Executives	Executives drive the lean initiative. They develop lean business systems and establish corporate strategies and tactics to implement these systems companywide.	Company leaders are educated and mentored in lean principles and management methodologies by a qualified external consultant. Executives must participate in at least one shopfloor kaizen.		All executive level managers	
Corporate lean coordinator	The corporate lean coordinator reports directly to the company CEO and is responsible for the day-to-day management of the lean initiative. He is the leader of the corporate lean-s team.	The lean coordinator can be an established sensei. Otherwise he/she should be trained and certified in all relevant lean and six sigma methodologies and tools by a qualified external consultant.		One for every strategic business unit (SBU) or value stream	
Corporate lean team	The lean team trains, educates, and mentors site champions. Lean team members should be upwardly mobile individuals. Lean team participation becomes a prerequisite for promotion to executive management.	The lean team should be trained and certified by external sensei or the corporate lean coordinator at the equivalent of a six sigma master black belt level or higher in all relevant lean and six sigma methodologies and tools by the corporate lean coordinator or by a qualified external consultant.		One to two lean masters for every strategic business unit (SBU) or value stream	

Table 6-1. Roles and Responsibilities in Execution, *continued*

Role	Responsibility	Recommended Preparation	Planned Preparation	Recommended Staffing	Planned Staffing
Site champions	Site champions work with middle managers to implement process-improvement plans and disseminate the lean and six sigma methods to middle mangers, hourly associates, and staff members through regular kaizen events.	Site champions should be trained and certified at the equivalent of a six sigma black belt level or higher in a subset of lean methodologies and tools relevant to a specific site implementation.		One or more per site or business function (recommended ratio = 1:200 associates)	
Project Managers & Supervisors	These middle managers own specific business processes. They ensure that standardized work is implemented and adhered to, and that continuous process improvements eliminate waste and reduce variability.	When applying new methods, these individuals should be trained and certified by site champions in the equivalent of a six sigma green belt level or higher in regular kaizen events in a subset of lean methodologies and tools relevant to the improvement of a specific business process		All middle managers	
Staff and hourly associates	Staff and hourly associates own specific business operations and tasks. They ensure that standardized work is performed, and that when defects, errors, or equipment abnormalities are discovered, they are immediately corrected or managers summoned to contain the problem and help solve it.	When applying new methods, these individuals should be trained and certified by project leaders or supervisors in the equivalent of a six sigma green belt level in a subset of lean methodologies and tools relevant to the improvement of a specific business process.		All staff and hourly associates participate in implementation, if only through the continuous improvement of standardized work.	

FINALIZE PROJECT PLANS

All projects in the annual hoshin and all teams throughout the organization follow traditional rules of good project management. In this chapter, we will briefly review some of the basics of project planning and then discuss special considerations involved in implementing lean and six sigma methods for the first time. Finalizing the plan is perhaps the most critical step at the front end of a project. The hoshin team has already completed much of the work as part of the hoshin planning and deployment process, and team leaders will already have shared drafts—in the form of A3-Ts—of tactical, operational, and action project plans in Rounds A, B, and C of the catchball process. But in many cases the A3-Ts may require additional work before implementation can begin, such as developing:

- Implementation roadmaps
- Detailed budgets
- Detailed schedules
- Schedule reviews

The entire team should work out these details after the project has been approved through the catchball process. The level of detail in your plan depends on the size and nature of your project. The project plan for a small project may require nothing more than a schedule and a budget. The plan for a large and complex project may need a detailed definition of the technical approach and a staffing plan.

Implementation Roadmaps

Tactical, operational, and action teams should break each project down into manageable elements so that they can:

- Control the work
- Assign responsibility and accountability
- Establish cost estimates
- Monitor schedules, cost, and performance

If you've followed the approach laid out in this workbook, your hoshin, tactical, and operational teams have already created implementation roadmaps of the major phases of their breakthrough strategies. Some of this information may already be imbedded in the A3-T for your specific project. At this point, you may need a more detailed implementation roadmap than the roadmaps you developed when you analyzed and prioritized breakthrough strategies (see Figure 3-4). Your detailed roadmaps might resemble the roadmap that the Design for Six Sigma (DFSS) engineering tactical team developed for Cybernautx (see Figure 6-2).

If you're a more advanced lean enterprise, you may have created tree diagrams to describe different levels of work involved. How much more detail is required? In most cases, three to four levels of detail are sufficient. Too many levels means that either the project is very large and should probably be divided into subprojects; or you're trying to micromanage the project, which defeats the purpose of hoshin kanri: localized decision making in real time.

Add Detail to the Budget

A lean enterprise budget translates hoshin project plans into dollars. A project budget sets a financial performance goal for the project. It will measure progress by comparing actual revenues and costs to budgeted revenues and costs. The budgeting process brings you face-to-face with the competing demands for quality, schedule, and cost that the project managers must manage. When developing their budgets, the teams will often wrestle with trade-offs between their estimated resource requirements and the quality and profit goals of the project.

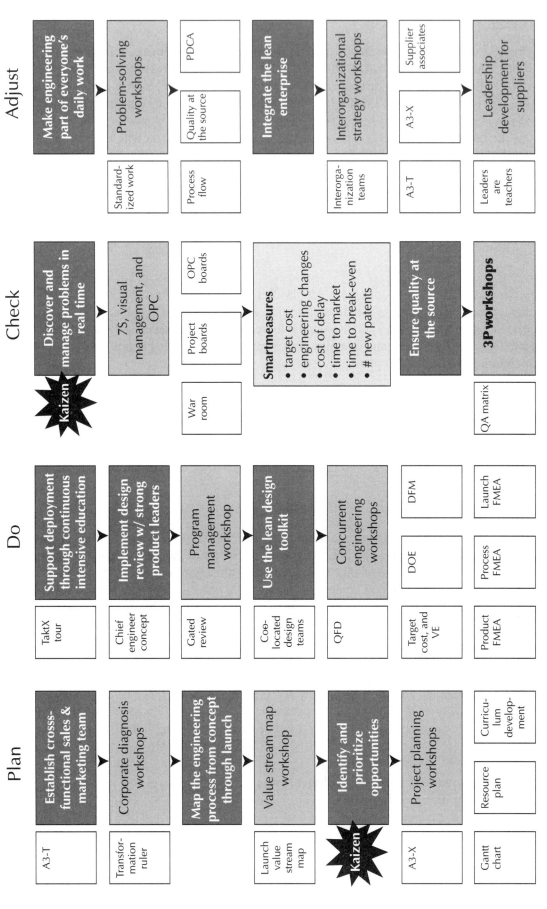

Figure 6-2. Cybernautx Implementation Roadmap for DFSS Concurrent Engineering

Consider using the value stream profit and loss statement as a method of open book management, the practice of sharing financial information with employees and engaging them directly in profit management. This works better, of course, if you couple profit management with gain-sharing in some form, be it profit sharing, pay-for-knowledge, or a balanced paycheck that rewards individuals based upon multiple criteria, including individual, team, and company performance.

Make a Detailed Schedule

After the teams complete their implementation roadmaps, they can develop accurate implementation schedules. After scheduling all tasks detailed on the roadmap, assign team or staff members to every task. The team leader must also estimate the time that each activity will take and determine if any activities have priority over any others. This is the next step in the ongoing process of resource allocation. In the previous chapter, you saw how you could use bar charts and milestone charts in scheduling. (See Figures 5-17 and 5-18.)

> **Action Team Exercise:** Action team leaders at all levels of the organization—hoshin, tactical, operational—should finalize project plans by developing implementation roadmaps detailing the budgets and schedules. Break each project down into manageable and controllable elements by assigning responsibility and accountability, and establishing cost estimates. If necessary, provide basic training in project management to middle managers who are not familiar with project management tools. Also, be prepared to provide project management software for complex projects that may require it. In Chapter 7, we'll see how teams use these tools to monitor schedules, cost, and performance as they keep their projects on track.

DEVELOP LEADERS WHO CAN TEACH

For companies in the process of implementing lean manufacturing or six sigma, execution is primarily a matter of training, educating, and mentoring, carried out through the kaizen workshops or "workouts" that are identified as tactics and action items in your company's A3-Xs (X-matrices). It may seem odd to find a discussion on training in a workbook on hoshin kanri. But training is a form of communication, perhaps the most powerful form of communication there is, especially when it comes to communicating with an entire workforce. In this sense, training is a natural extension of hoshin kanri's deployment process. What makes hoshin training different from most other forms of training is that it takes place on the job, where each employee applies the PDCA to his or her task. Of course, the workshops in which people learn the new, scientific methods of self-control to accomplish these tasks also transform your operations. With hoshin kanri, such transformation becomes a permanent feature of how you do business; that is, through continuous training you are continuously improving and becoming an organization that learns.

Fortunately, much is known about effective training, thanks to the United States government. In World War I and again in World War II, the United States faced an enormous training problem, because it was necessary to increase industrial production at a time when experienced workers—mostly male—were shipped overseas to fight. In World War I, the government turned to vocational instructor Charles Allen, who developed a four-step method for training supervisors in the country's busy shipyards (See Table 6-2).

In World War II, the problem was bigger than ever. The government responded with *Training Within Industry* or TWI and the three job programs, Job Instruction, Job Methods,

Table 6-2. Charles Allen's Four Rules of Training

Preparation	Connect the learning experience with the learner's own experience.
Presentation	Present new information in small doses to prepare for Step 3.
Application	Apply new ideas and show that the participant can do it.
Testing	Repeat the application of new ideas without help from the instructor.

and Job Relations, each having their own four-step method. TWI instructed plants on how to multiply the impact of Allen's four-step method by training and certifying trainers to cascade organizational learning. Table 6-3 shows the three job programs and how they relate to Allen's four steps, kaizen, PDCA, and the scientific method.

By the end of the TWI program, 1,750,650 people from 16,511 plants and unions had been trained and certified. The impact on wartime productivity is legendary. After the war, many countries adopted TWI, including of course Japan. Toyota continues to utilize some parts of the original TWI materials today.

If you expect your employees to absorb the new, scientific methods of working, you should follow Charles Allen's four steps. Allen's method requires the physical presence of the instructor; so don't get too excited about web-based training, which relies almost entirely on the student to absorb and apply information without the benefit of a coach. If you expect to train your workforce quickly *and* effectively, you must train leaders that act as on-the-job instructors and coaches. Table 6-4 shows five reliable models of certification that can do the job.

The first model is what we may call a one-on-one apprenticeship. Toyota utilized this model at both NUMMI, a brownfield site, and Toyota Georgetown, a greenfield site. The second model is the method of the kaizen blitz, which focuses on the rapid transformation of brownfield sites or facilities. The founders of the famous Japanese consulting firm, Shingijutsu pioneered this model for Toyota's suppliers. The third model is a traditional train-the-trainer approach, based on TWI methodology. The fourth model focuses on the intensive education and mentoring of a select group of high potential managers, who become certified leaders of lean transformation. The fifth model is the six sigma model, a sort of do-it-yourself approach to certification.

These models have different costs and benefits, as illustrated by Table 6-4. The programs are compared in terms of the scope of lean subject matter, the depth (or number of repetitions) of training in each subject, the external and internal costs of implementation, and the relative effectiveness of each program. We will briefly discuss these models.

The Toyota Model: One-on-one Apprenticeship

Toyota's apprenticeship of course tops the chart in all categories, including cost and effectiveness. In transferring the Toyota Production System to the United States, Toyota employed a resource-intensive, but devastatingly effective method. Sixty Japanese managers, all experts in Toyota's management systems and production methods, were paired one-on-one with sixty American managers—*for two years*. The American managers were in effect educated on the job in their new roles and responsibilities. This apprenticeship was mirrored on the shop floor. At Toyota, intensive training and mentoring are a permanent feature of how business is done and is one of the major facets of being a lean learning organization. Both Honda and Nissan used similar, if less intensive, programs in their American startups, too.

Table 6-3. How Allen's 4 Rules Relate to TWI, Kaizen, Scientific Method, and PDCA

		TWI Four Step Method for Each Job Program					
Steps	Allen's Four Rules of Training	Job Instruction	Job Methods	Job Relations	Kaizen	Scientific Method	PDCA
1	Preparation	Prepare the worker	Break down the job	Get the facts	Observe and time current process	*Observation*: Define the problem and its parameters	Plan
2	Presentation	Present the operation	Question every detail	Weigh and decide	Analyze current process	*Hypothesize*: Suggest a possible explanation or solution	Plan
3	Application	Try-out performance	Develop the new method	Take action	Implement and test new process	*Testing*: Collect information (data) and test hypothesis	Do
4	Testing	Follow up	Apply the new method	Check results	Document new standard	*Results*: Interpret the results of the test to determine if hypothesis is correct	Check
						Conclusion: State a conclusion that others can independently evaluate. (Start process over.)	Act

Source: Parts of this table were amended from *Training Within Industry, Three Essential Skills of Supervisors*, Patrick Graupp and Bob Wrona, Productivity Press Inc., 2006. Columns were added for PDCA and Allen's Four Rules.

Table 6-4. Five Reliable Certification Models

Program Model	Participation	Scope of training	Depth of training	Cost	Effectiveness
Apprenticeship	Total Population	Total	Highest	Highest	Highest
Kaizen blitz	Selective	Operations focus	High	Medium	Medium
Train-the-trainer (TWI methodology)	Trainers	Subject matter focus	High	Low	Medium
Journeyman's tour	Total population	Total	High	High	High
Six sigma	Project leaders	Operations focus	Medium	Medium/ low	Medium

The Kaizen Blitz

The consulting firm Shingijutsu founded in 1987 by Taiichi Ohno's protege, Yoshiki Iwata, pioneered the kaizen blitz. Lean promotor Norman Bodek dubbed it "five days and one night," because each workshop lasted from Monday through Friday, and typically on Wednesday night everyone participating in the event would be up half the night moving, rewiring, and replumbing equipment into the classic U-shaped cells of lean manufacturing. Shingijutsu concentrated on repeating the same kaizen blitz, as it came to be called, in different areas of a plant until the entire facility had been cellularized and knit together with kanban. The more kaizen workshops the client signed up for, the faster and more complete the implementation. The kaizen blitz is a standard component of all remaining certification programs described below. Although the content of the kaizen blitz was lean manufacturing, the structure of the training was clearly consistent with Charles Allen's four steps, as codified by Training Within Industry (see Table 6-5).

Table 6-5. Structure of a Kaizen Blitz

	Allen's Four Rules		PDCA	
Monday	Prepare/present	plan	Principles and concepts	
Tuesday	Apply	plan	Data collection	
		plan	Goals and objectives	
		do	Shop floor improvements	
Wednesday	Apply	do	Shop floor improvements	
		do	equipment relocations	
Thursday	Test	check	Validation of improvements	
Friday		act	Presentation to management	

Train-the-Trainer

Other lean consulting companies, notably Productivity Inc. and the Kaizen Institute, have developed lean training programs based on a combination of the kaizen blitz and Training Within Industry's train-the-trainer approach. These programs tend to offer a wide variety of training modules, each focused on a particular method, such as cell design, quick changeover, problem solving, etc. Table 6-6 shows that to become certified in a particular module, a candidate completes the classic course of train-the-trainer instruction. The main benefit of train-the-trainer programs is their high quality, standardized training materials. The main drawback of train-the-trainer programs is that they lack inherent mechanisms for learning to choose the appropriate tool and to integrate multiple tools. While train-the-trainer programs have been effective in developing individual skills, such programs have not been nearly as effective as Toyota's apprenticeship or the kaizen blitz in transforming entire facilities and organizations.

Table 6-6. How to Become a Trainer

Four Steps to Become a Trainer	Participation Level
1. Participate as a team member	The candidate participates simply as a team member.
2. Participate as a team leader	Candidates learn how to organize and lead a small kaizen team to make focused improvements on a tight schedule.
3. Cofacilitate the workshop	Candidates assist the trainer in preparing for and conducting the workshop. In addition, they deliver sections of material chosen by the trainer facilitating the event.
4. Facilitate the workshop solo	Finally, candidate delivers the entire class by herself, under the observation of the certifying trainer.

Leadership tip: Internal change agents in lean enterprises, such as lean coordinators and master black belts, need to be good trainers, of course; but more than that, they need to become well developed internal consultants to their own organizations. Good consultants play three roles well:

- **Star player:** A problem-solving virtuoso who knows how to use PDCA tools to gather and analyze information, prescribe corrective action, and execute it effectively using the tools of project management.
- **Master teacher:** A crackerjack instructor who knows how to convey important information effectively to others. Teachers of lean methods specialize in using the Socratic method, which is based on asking students leading questions, forcing students to solve problems by themselves.
- **Head coach:** A coach and mentor who knows how to help others by working with them, giving them feedback on their performance, and demonstrating a better way to do the job.

It is not enough to play only one role well. Good consultants master all three. The mark of a *really* good consultant, a sensei, as they are known in the lean consulting business, is knowing when to play these roles and how to combine them.

Journeyman's Tour

Yet another approach to implementing lean emerged within the world of Japanese transplants, initially under the guidance of consultant Clyde Haugan, at that time a consultant for Misaki Imai's Kaizen Institute. Haugan combined the benefits of Toyota's apprenticeship program, the kaizen blitz of five days and one night, and a train-the-trainer program. Like the Toyota apprenticeship, little differentiation was made between lean champions and managers.

All managers who expected to be promoted within the client organization had to sign up for the program. Also, the client was also expected to adopt a Toyota-style management system, based on hoshin kanri. As a target, each facility in the client's system was expected to host at least two kaizen workshops per month. To this Haugan added a well-structured train-the-trainer program of 13 one-week kaizen workshop modules for an elite group of managers. To become certified in the program, each candidate had to complete a classic course of train-the-trainer instruction for all 13 modules. In all, each certified lean expert completed *52 weeks* of instruction and mentoring. In order to maximize their exposure to the number of modules and workshops, candidates in the program traveled with Haugan and other certified experts *on tour* from client site to client site, thus shortening the total lead time of certification.

The Six Sigma Style Approach

Another important approach to implementation emerged from the Japanese Union of Scientists and Engineers (JUSE). To promote the spread of total quality management methods, JUSE developed a six-week program for executives and TQM experts that Motorola would later brand as "six sigma." At the core of the program is four weeks of intensive training in quality methods. In between each of the training weeks, the trainee carries out a "six sigma" project, to apply what she has learned. After the successful completion of four weeks of training and three successful projects, the trainee is certified as a "black belt." Some six sigma programs also require passing a written exam. The six sigma certification structure is independent of its content. Table 6-7 shows an application of the method to the training and certification of black belts in lean manufacturing.

Table 6-7. Six Sigma Style Certification Program for Lean Manufacturing

		Week 1 Plan	Onsite execution	Week 2 Do	Onsite execution	Week 3 Do	Onsite execution	Week 4 Check Act
M	AM	Hoshin kanri		Reports		Reports		Reports
	PM			Quick changeover		Mistake proofing		QS 9000
T	AM	JIT		Standardization and operator process control		Lean administration		Total plant layout
	PM							
W	AM	Value stream mapping		100 PPM quality		Program management		Kanban
	PM							
Th	AM	Kaizen event management		7S and visual management		Preproduction pioneering		Total site implementation planning
	PM							
F	AM	Assignment		Assignment		Assignment		Graduation

Unlike the Toyota apprenticeship, the kaizen blitz, and journeyman's tour, the candidates in six sigma style programs do not normally receive intensive, onsite mentoring over a significant period of time. Mentoring by a sensei is always recommended but is normally optional; some mentoring is carried out by email or telephone, rather than in gemba (the actual place). The main appeal of the six sigma style approach is its low cost relative to other certification programs. Coupled with the right kind of coaching, however, the approach can be quite effective.

APPLY RELIABLE PDCA METHODS IN TRAINING YOUR EMPLOYEES

Whether we're talking about lean manufacturing or six sigma, we're talking about methods and tools that work. All these methods and tools have one thing in common: They're all based on the scientific method. The scientific method is the systematic, firsthand observation of facts as a means of understanding what happens—and therefore how to affect or *control* what happens—in the world. Scientific knowledge is based upon the testing of hypotheses and theories of how observed events are related to one another. In the world of business, scientific investigation follows the pattern of PDCA. As we have shown earlier (see Table I-1), PDCA is a pocket edition of the scientific method, as is six sigma's DMAIC (Define, Measure, Analyze, Improve, Control) process and CEDAC (Cause and Effect Diagram with the Addition of Cards). They are all fundamentally the same.

Scientific thinking and organizational learning are the whole point to hoshin kanri, and to lean manufacturing and six sigma as well. Unfortunately, lean (just-in-time) and six sigma are often imposed on the workforce without their involvement. Such efforts always fail because you are imposing methods on the workers in a mechanical way, without PDCA thinking. The business and work environments are so dynamic that, without PDCA's built-in ability to adapt, even best-in-class methodologies become limitations that obscure new data and delay or even prevent corrective action. PDCA thinking of course requires a real delegation of authority that many managers are unwilling to make.

Hundreds of PDCA methods and tools are available to choose from, some of which are in the Recommended Reading list. Methods such as just-in-time and six sigma deal with all phases of the PDCA process. Tools such as visual control and poka yoke may deal with one process phase or another. Visual control and poka yoke, for example, deal with the *check* and *act* phases of PDCA. Don't rely solely on textbook methods. The best companies invent new methods to solve unique problems. In the implementation phase of the hoshin cycle, your teams should review improvement approaches recorded in the area manager's or supervisor's idea banks to avoid reinventing the wheel. Associates unfamiliar with any selected improvement approach need training, of course. If you've followed one of the reliable certification methods listed earlier in this section, you'll be well prepared to do the job, no matter how large or small your workforce may be.

Hoshin Team Exercise: Table 6-8 is a Leadership Certification Matrix that shows the progress of Cybernautx's teams and key individuals in developing facility with the methods and tools of lean enterprise. Use Table 6-4 to choose one of the five reliable certification models that best fits your company and needs. Remember, your goal is to develop leaders who can teach the methods of lean enterprise to your entire workforce. Print the Leadership Certification Matrix (CD-Form 6-2) and follow the steps below to track the progress of your company's teams and individuals. (Note: Consider using a plotter to print the matrix on poster size paper.)

---

1. ***Analyze breakthroughs for training requirements.*** Analyze breakthrough opportunities on your company's X-matrices for methodologies that are new to the company and in which training will be required to support implementation. Then list these methods across the top of your Leadership Certification Matrix. (*Note*: Because there are so many lean methods and tools, this list can quickly grow out of control. Consider using the categories of the Transformation Ruler (see Chapter 8) or a productivity prize system such as the Shingo Prize as a way of organizing your list into manageable categories.)

2. ***List leaders to be certified.*** List the leaders to be certified down the left-hand side of the matrix. Because leaders should be teachers, every one of your executives and managers should be on the matrix. (*Note*: While it's a good idea to identify a core group of individuals who will lead the education process, they must not be viewed as the team that "does lean". In a lean enterprise, every leader must become a teacher. The "lean team," if you have one, exists only as a resource to enable all managers to grow new, lean capabilities.)

3. ***Post the matrix in the workplace.*** It's a common practice to post "cross-training" boards in the work areas of hourly associates.

4. ***Record levels of certification.*** As your leaders-in-training complete their certification for a particular methodology, color in the quadrants of the certification "wheel" beneath the related method or technique as indicated in Table 6-9. (*Note*: The basic certification wheel recapitulates the phases of Charles Allen's training cycle (see Table 6-2) and levels of mastery of a particular methodology. The outer circle represents a particularly high level of mastery that will often identify a candidate for advancement within the organization, and participation in the next round of training and certification.)

5. ***Repeat the process.*** As indicated in Table 6-10, there are five certification cycles, one for each of the four teams in the hoshin system, and a final cycle at the highest level of the organization. The cycles are differentiated primarily by the extent to which they incorporate training in hoshin kanri and advanced tools and techniques. After completing certification for a particular set of methodologies, leaders may graduate to the next cycle of certification. Place another empty certification "wheel" under the appropriate methods to indicate that the individual has begun the certification process again at a higher level.

Table 6-8. Cybernautx's Hoshin System Cross-training Matrix for all Managers

Methods and tools → / Leaders ↓	Foundations of lean thinking	Process and value stream mapping	The president's diagnosis	Hoshin kanri: midterm strategy	Profit management & lean accounting	Building the annual hoshin	Managing the catchball process	Leadership development	Lean transactional management	Project management	Hoshin review system	Visual management	Managing suggestion systems
To be certified													
Hoshin team leader	⊕⊕⊕⊕●	⊕⊕⊕⊕●	⊕⊕⊕⊕●	⊕⊕⊕⊕●	⊕⊕⊕⊕●	⊕⊕⊕⊕●	⊕⊕⊕⊕●	⊕⊕⊕⊕●	⊕⊕⊕⊕●	⊕⊕⊕⊕●	⊕⊕⊕⊕●	⊕⊕⊕⊕●	⊕⊕⊕⊕●
Corporate lean champion	⊕⊕⊕●	⊕⊕⊕●	⊕⊕⊕●	⊕⊕⊕●	⊕⊕⊕●	⊕⊕⊕●	⊕⊕⊕●	⊕⊕⊕●	⊕⊕⊕●	⊕⊕⊕●	⊕⊕⊕●	⊕⊕⊕●	⊕⊕⊕●
Six sigma master black belt	⊕⊕⊕⊕●	⊕⊕⊕⊕●	⊕⊕⊕⊕●	⊕⊕⊕⊕●	⊕⊕⊕⊕●	⊕⊕⊕⊕●	⊕⊕⊕⊕●	⊕⊕⊕⊕●	⊕⊕⊕⊕●	⊕⊕⊕⊕●	⊕⊕⊕⊕●	⊕⊕⊕⊕●	⊕⊕⊕⊕●
Tactical team leaders	⊕⊕●	⊕⊕●	⊕⊕●	⊕●	⊕●	⊕●	⊕⊕●	⊕●	⊕●	⊕●	⊕⊕●	⊕●	⊕●
Functional lean champions	⊕⊕●	⊕●	⊕⊕●	⊕⊕●	⊕⊕●	⊕⊕●	⊕⊕●	⊕⊕●	⊕⊕●	⊕⊕●	⊕⊕●	⊕⊕●	⊕⊕●
Six sigma black belts	⊕⊕●	⊕●	⊕⊕●	⊕⊕●	⊕⊕●	⊕⊕●	⊕⊕●	⊕⊕●	⊕⊕●	⊕⊕●	⊕⊕●	⊕⊕●	⊕⊕●
Operational team leaders	⊕⊕●	⊕●	⊕●	⊕●	⊕●	⊕●	⊕●	⊕●	⊕●	⊕●	⊕●	⊕●	⊕●
Action team leaders	⊕●	●	●	●	●	●	●	●	●	●	●	●	●

Table 6-9. Leadership Certification Matrix Legend

Action team member	◔ In PDCA training for the first time. Cannot replicate method with supervision.	◑ Knows how to apply PCDA and follow a project plan with supervisions.	◕ Knows how to use a structured PDCA method without supervision.	● Can train on reliable methods and help groups understand PDCA.	● PDCA is commonly used to improve standardized daily work.
Action team leader/ Operations team member	●◔ In training as a lean supervisor or team leader for the first time.	●◑ Can lead a workshop team with supervision.	●◕ Able to follow standards created during a workshop and lead a team without supervision.	●● Able to improve standards after a workshop.	●● Is able to select and execute appropriate tools for continuous improvement.
Operations team leader/ Tactical team leader	●●◔ In training as a trainer for the first time.	●●◑ Can lead and coach a workshop team with supervision.	●●◕ Can facilitate a workshop with supervision.	●●● Can facilitate a lean workshop without supervision.	●●● Able to adapt a workshop to specific cases and coach others.
Tactical team leader/ Hoshin team member	●●●◔ In lean project leader training for the first time.	●●●◑ Can lead projects involving lean tools with supervision.	●●●◕ Can lead projects involving lean tools without supervision.	●●●● Can select focus of improvement, plan, and coordinate resources to execute major projects with supervision.	●●●● Can select focus of improvement with supervision, but plan, and coordinate resources to execute major projects without supervision.
Hoshin team leader	●●●●◔ In advanced subject matter training for the first time.	●●●●◑ Can facilitate advanced subject matter training with supervision in multiple areas.	●●●●◕ Can facilitate advanced subject matter workshops and coach black belts and black belt candidates in multiple subject matter areas without supervision.	●●●●● Can adapt & integrate advanced subject matter workshops and coach and mentor black belts and black belt candidates in multiple subject matter areas to address specific cases.	●●●●● Able to build a complete curriculum of workshops and coach other lean coordinators (master black belt).

Table 6-10. Certification Cycles

●	At the action team level, the methodologies involved are the classic methods of lean operations, such as problem solving, just-in-time (JIT), quick changeover, and poka yoke, which directly affect daily work on the manufacturing shop floor as well as in administrative areas. There is no need for formal training in hoshin kanri.
●●	At the operations team level, team members should ideally complete the action team certification cycle, moving on to a curriculum that includes training in project selection, team chartering, the X-matrix, catchball, coaching teams, and project management. Remember that operational team members are by definition action team leaders.
●●●	At the tactical team level, the curriculum incorporates the president's diagnosis, mentoring of coaches, and training in methods, tools, and techniques that are specific to the business functions that tactical team leaders may manage. Remember that tactical team members are operational team leaders.
●●●●	At the hoshin team level, the curriculum focuses on the methods of the environmental scan, lean finance, the president's diagnosis, and how to conduct quarterly review meetings focused on process improvement. Once again, hoshin team members ideally should complete the first three courses of certification before advancing. Remember that hoshin team members are by definition tactical team leaders.
●●●●●	Ideally, the hoshin team leader will strive to become a true sensei, a person who knows the content of lean enterprise in detail, and who is a master at developing leaders at all levels of the organization. At this level, the curriculum is largely self-determined, or determined in close cooperation with a recognized sensei, who can direct the hoshin team leader to advanced or emerging methodologies, tools, and techniques.

CHAPTER SEVEN

CHECK: Create a Lean-Thinking Environment

Now that your teams have initiated the seven experiments, you need to check on the implementation of the strategies and tactics on each team's A3-X (X-matrix). You've already used the hoshin process to charter teams with each team chartered to perform an experiment. Furthermore, you've structured each experiment as a project with specific deliverables: improvements in the resources and capabilities you need to beat your competitors. The catchball process you went through in Chapter 5 created alignment among team members and management. In Chapter 6, you finalized your action project plans and now know what certification models you will use to develop leaders. You also know what scientific method (PDCA, CEDAC®, DMAIC) you will use to engage the action teams and entire workforce. The teams have begun to execute and now you must use the *Check* phase to validate the progress of the experiments in real time to make sure they are having the intended effect. But to be able to accomplish this, your company needs a few important features of lean thinking to empower its workforce.

CREATE A NO-BLAME ENVIRONMENT

In a lean enterprise, everyone's job is to know what's really going on—in real time, not after the fact. In that case, your company must eliminate the mass-production thinking of managers and employees assigning blame when things go wrong. Instead, you need to train your people to recognize and eliminate problems. Problems are treasures of hidden waste and variability that you want workers to find and eliminate through continuous process improvement. If your workers do not perceive problems, there can be no improvement. In a lean enterprise, people are rarely the problem but in fact are your most valuable problem solvers. Therefore, as a project manager, you should maintain open communications and be in constant contact with your project team members below and with management above.

As the imprisonment of Galileo centuries ago demonstrated, scientific investigation is difficult when authorities are threatened by the truth; those in the know won't tell them for fear of reprisals. Work hard to ensure that your teams feel safe communicating problems to you. This avoids the "shoot the messenger" mentality and increases trust. It's also the only way to solve systemic problems at the root cause level. One technique you can use to build trust is to have your teams use the 5-why method for root cause analysis. It keeps the team focused on solving problems rather than disintegrating into the blame game. Blame is, after all, just another form of waste. To understand the cultural state of your company, you need to approach it at a systems thinking level, as Cybernautx did below.

Cybernautx Current Status of Its Lean Cultural Development

Figure 7-1 shows a radar chart that the Cybernautx hoshin team constructed to analyze the current status of its lean cultural development. The team's discussions revealed that while team members felt that the company had begun to overcome its functional orientation, in their opinion the company was still no more than a "3" out of "10" with respect to true, "systems thinking". The recent adoption of hoshin kanri led the team to conclude that the company might actually focus on the process instead of demanding results. So the team rated the company a "4" in this dimension of lean culture. Meanwhile, team members agreed that "we have a long way to go," especially on the shop floor, where supervisors often failed to listen to hourly associates. Problems were definitely not considered to be treasures, and as a result, problems persisted—indefinitely. So the team rated the company a "2" in this dimension. Finally, the team rated the company a "1" in the dimension of "no judgment/no blame," because each team member could remember a recent instance when he or she had "shot the messenger" bearing news of bad results.

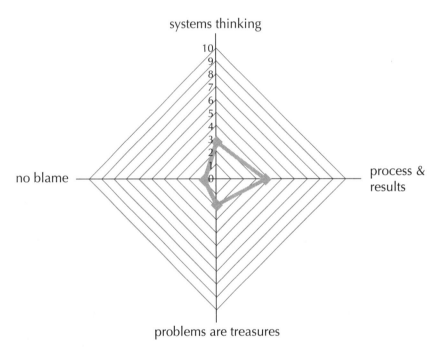

Figure 7-1. Cybernautx Radar Chart of Lean Cultural Development

Hoshin Team Exercise: A no-blame environment is the product of systems thinking and encourages the sharing of vital information about problems—and the opportunities they represent. Quality guru W. Edwards Deming found that only 6 percent of failures were the result of worker error. The remaining 94 percent were the result of not adhering to an established system of management and work. Are you still blaming the workers? Using a simple radar chart, ask your team to rate your organization in how it performs or delivers in the four dimensions below. The team should rate your organization in each dimension on a scale of zero to ten in which zero is bad and ten is good.

1. **Systems thinking.** A system is a network of interconnected events. A small change in any part of the network can cause a disproportionately large change in any other part of the network. Mass production organizations are full of functional thinkers who attempt to optimize their local concerns, frequently at the expense of the organization's strategic intent. Lean organizations see themselves as systems and pay attention to small details. Lean thinkers are "systems thinkers" who invite input from all levels of the management hierarchy. This is one of the important rationales for hoshin kanri.

2. **Process not results.** Results-oriented managers achieve hollow victories for their organizations by demanding "performance," frequently without reference to the intangible causes of success. Lean thinkers focus on the process to sustain results over time.

3. **Problems are treasures.** Mass productions thinkers often see problems as criminal activities attributable to bad employees, who must be punished as a warning to others. Lean thinkers invite and even provoke problems as opportunities to learn more about the unknown complexities of organizational systems.

4. **No judgment, no blame.** Results-oriented managers drive information about organizational systems into hiding by shooting the messenger, whenever one finds the courage to appear. Lean thinkers *reward* the messenger for news of hidden problems in the system.

Most management teams will normally rate their organizations between 3 and 6 in most of the four dimensions. Teams composed of hourly associates will frequently rate their organizations between 0 and 3.

MANAGE VISUALLY

Another lean technique is to set up feedback and corrective action in real time to make your lean company responsive to its customers. The most immediate way that you can verify adherence to your vision is to *go see* (going to *gemba*). Visual management presents information in a way that people can readily receive or retrieve and assimilate it "at a glance." This is absolutely vital in fast-paced environments where multitasking is the order of the day. It's an essential characteristic of Toyota's lean production system and its phenomenal throughput and profitability.

Figure 7-2 shows a comparison of two plants that have installed andon, a powerful type of visual control, installed at each operator's station. When problems occur that cannot be corrected within takt time (the time allocated for performing standardized work), the operator triggers the andon. The supervisor is summoned by flashing lights and sound to help solve the problem. In extreme cases, the entire production line might be stopped, to prevent bad parts from moving to the next process. A recent study has shown that at Toyota, the andon was triggered over 2,500 times in a single shift. At GM, where they have recently implemented lean production, the andon was triggered only 10 times a day (or roughly 5 times per shift). Toyota doesn't have more problems than GM. It's *solving* more problems, because it has installed visual controls and responds to even minor issues in real time. One can easily understand how Toyota's numerous products continue to top the quality charts—and make more money for Toyota's shareholders.

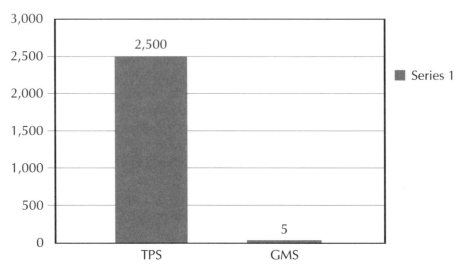

andon triggered (times / shift)
3,000
2,500
2,000
1,500
1,000
500
0
2,500
5
Series 1
TPS
GMS

Source: Christine Tierney, "Big Three play catch-up to Toyota plant prowess," *The Detroit News*, Sunday, February 22, 2004.

Figure 7-2. Comparison of Two Plants Using Andon

The visual management pyramid in Figure 7-3 demonstrates how the techniques of workplace organization, visual control, and poka yoke (mistake-proofing) are combined to create an environment in which your workers can spot problems and correct them in real time—rather than waiting for them to become six sigma projects or hoshin strategies and tactics.

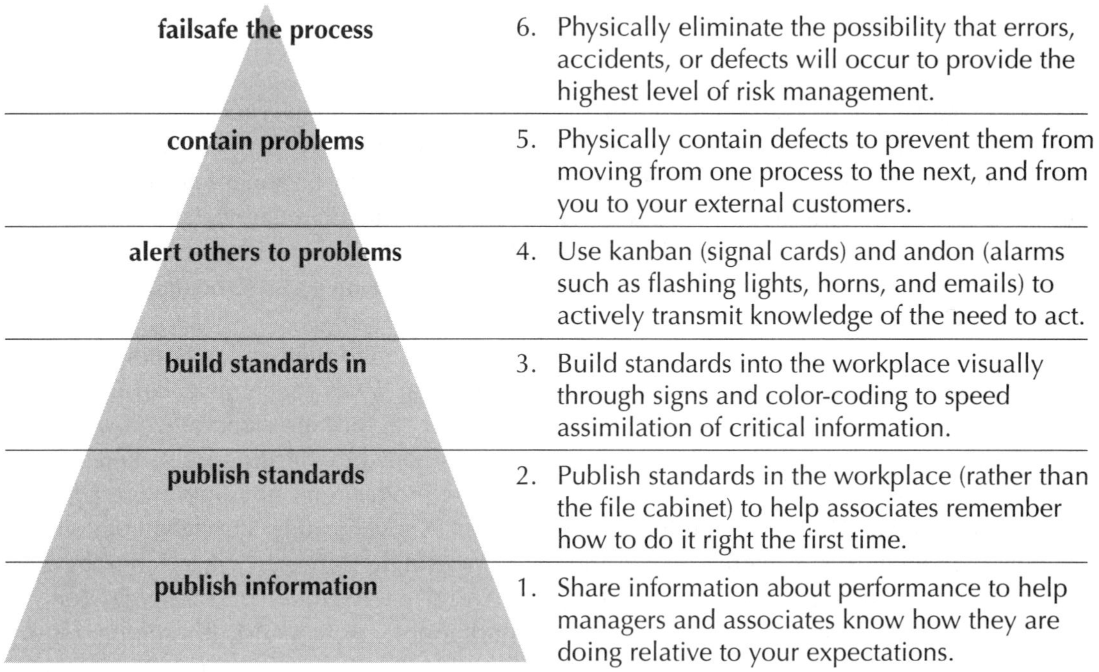

failsafe the process
6. Physically eliminate the possibility that errors, accidents, or defects will occur to provide the highest level of risk management.
contain problems
5. Physically contain defects to prevent them from moving from one process to the next, and from you to your external customers.
alert others to problems
4. Use kanban (signal cards) and andon (alarms such as flashing lights, horns, and emails) to actively transmit knowledge of the need to act.
build standards in
3. Build standards into the workplace visually through signs and color-coding to speed assimilation of critical information.
publish standards
2. Publish standards in the workplace (rather than the file cabinet) to help associates remember how to do it right the first time.
publish information
1. Share information about performance to help managers and associates know how they are doing relative to your expectations.

Figure 7-3. Visual Management Pyramid

HOSHIN MANAGEMENT BOARDS

Visual management applies to the executive function as well as to operators and project team leaders. The best way to do this is to place a *hoshin* management board where everyone in the company can see it, including your suppliers and your customers! (See Figure 7-4.)

Although there is no substitute for visual management in *gemba*, you can usefully share the same information via a website hosted on your intranet. A hoshin website becomes indispensable, however, whenever you involve your suppliers in planning new products and joint improvement initiatives.

Hoshin Team Exercise: Create a hoshin management board. On one side of a board, post your organization chart and document the flow of the hoshin process (See Figure 7-4) and standard documentation (A3-Xs, A3-Ts, A3-SRs, A3-SSRs, A3-Ps, transformation ruler, etc.). On the other side of the board, post summaries of all your tactical and action team projects. Insist that team leaders keep their project reports up-to-date.

Step 1. Discuss the hoshin team's need to *know* information concerning adherence to the strategic improvement targets of the company. (*Hint:* Treat the company's policies and objectives as standard operating procedures.) Where do the events to which such information refers occur? Within the boardroom? Outside the boardroom? Are team members co-located or not? How does such information reach the members of the team? Is the process simple or complex? Is communication effective? How should information be shared with corporate management team members?

Step 2. Discuss the hoshin team's need to *share* certain information with others who are not formally members of the team. How is this information shared? Is the process simple or complex? Is communication effective? How should information be shared with individuals outside the boardroom?

Step 3. For each lean measurable and financial impact on each A3-X, discuss and then decide how to report the measurable to team members.

Step 4. Discuss who should collect measurable data and who should compile the data, calculate, and report the stratified measurable to team members.

Step 5. Discuss how nonaggregated data from deployment teams should be collected and compiled for the calculation of companywide figures.

Step 6. Discuss the drawbacks of data aggregation. Can the numbers in the boardroom ever correspond truly to gemba? Devise a plan for ensuring that the numbers in the boardroom are correctly interpreted with true reference to gemba.

Step 7. Design and model a hoshin center. Please use the following guidelines:
  • All measurables should be reported graphically.
  • The hoshin management center must support real-time corrective action as well as "management by walking around".
  • The hoshin management center should be completely self-explanatory, so that visiting deployment team members suppliers, and of course customers can easily understand what is being measured, the targets that have been established, and the performance trends experienced by each team.

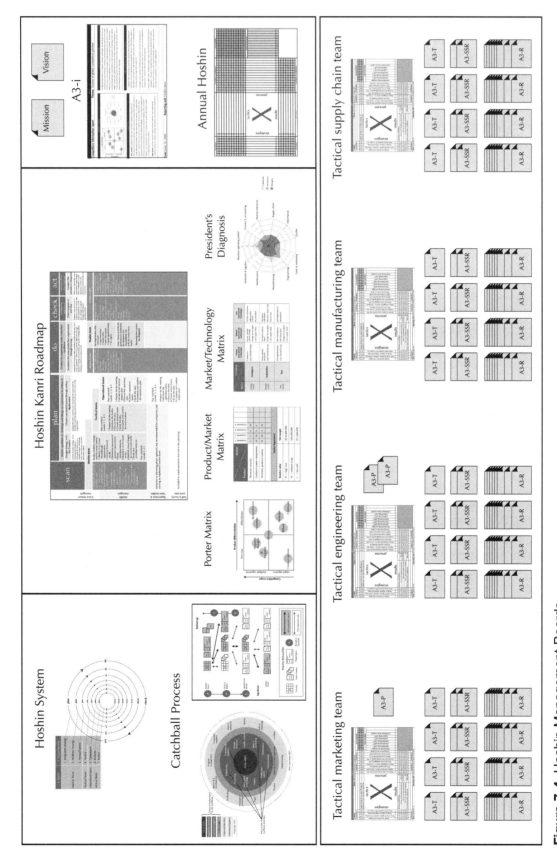

Figure 7-4. Hoshin Management Boards

Step 7. *(continued)*

- Deviations from standard or target values should be clearly reported, together with the status and effect of corrective action.
- The hoshin management center might incorporate a method for alerting team members of the need for real-time corrective action.
- Standard procedures for gathering, recording, calculation, and reporting should be clear.
- All necessary tools and materials for the proper maintenance of the information center should be incorporated into the overall design of the center.

If you have the capability, assign someone to develop a hoshin website where, among other relevant data, you can post the hoshin management board on the website where anyone who is interested can check on what is happening.

USE A3-SRS TO DOCUMENT ACTION TEAM ACTIVITY

Use the A3-SR (see Table 1-4 and CD Form 1-4) status report form to document results of all action team activities systematically and in a standardized format. Each A3-T bundled into your system of X-matrices will give rise to a series of monthly A3-SRs. This checking mechanism ensures that action teams focus on contributing to the process improvement and financial targets recorded on the A3-Xs of chartering tactical and operational teams. Figure 7-5 is an example of an A3-SR completed by the engineering action team chartered to implement design for six sigma in engineering. *Note*: While tactical and operational teams also have A3-Ts (teach charters), and while they may also use the A3-SR to create monthly status reports, higher-level teams will normally have multiple projects (stated on an A3-X) to track. Therefore, tactical and operational teams may find it more useful to report their progress using the A3-SSR (see below).

USE A3-SSRS TO DOCUMENT TACTICAL AND OPERATIONAL TEAM ACTIVITY

The A3-SSR (see Table 1-4 and CD Form 1-5) is a valuable tool for hoshin, tactical, and operational team leaders to summarize the progress of teams listed on their respective A3-Xs. The hoshin team uses the A3-SSR to summarize the progress of all tactical teams on the A3-X defining the annual hoshin. Each tactical team uses the A3-SSR to summarize the progress of operational teams listed on their respective A3-Xs. Operational teams use the A3-SSR to summarize the activities of action teams on their A3-Xs. Figure 7-6 is an example of an A3-SSR completed by the engineering tactical team to summarize the activities of operational teams listed on the A3-X that appears as Figure 5-25 in Chapter 5.

Hoshin, Tactical, Operational Team Exercise: Print out the blank A3-SSR from the CD Companion, CD 1-5. As team leader, write a progress report for your team. A well-written report gives the reader a good idea of the overall progress made over the reporting period. Describe accomplishments during the reporting period, including any deliverables completed or key events that took place. Identify things that did not go as planned as well as things that went well. This is especially important if a situation arises that can affect getting the job done correctly, on time, and within budget. You should circulate the progress reports electronically and post them on your *hoshin* management board and website.

A3-SR

Status report

Theme: DFSS implementation on track

BACKGROUND

For the past five years, our engineering process has involved many steps, rework, and delays that have resulted in an average engineering lead time of 32 days for new products. This has contributed to significant cost overruns of over $1,000,000. To address this problem, the engineering tactical team planned 3 workshops to promote flow in the engineering process and reduce product and parts variety and parts complexity. In addition, the company's many CAD platforms were to be consolidated on a single platform.

TARGET STATEMENT

Decrease engineering process lead time to 24 days by the end of the next fiscal year.

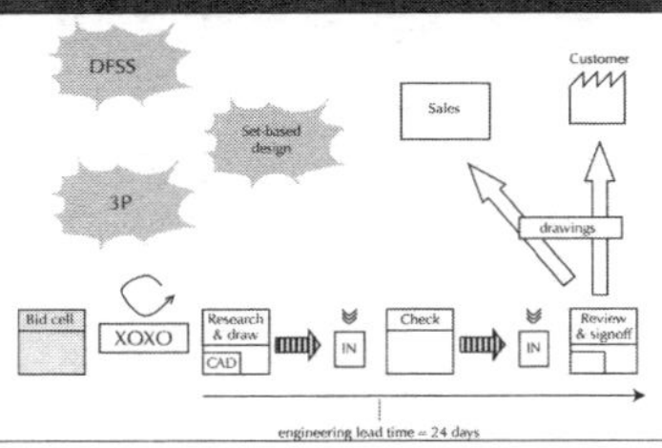

IMPLEMENTATION STATUS

Action	Responsibility	Due	Complete
• Conduct engineering kaizen	• Tom Jackson	Jan 15 /	Jan 15 /
• Conduct product reduction kaizen	• Don Makie	Jan 30	Jan 30
• Purchase CAD software	• Dave Niemann	Feb 03	Feb 03
• Conduct parts reduction kaizen	• Don Makie	Feb 24	Feb 24
• Complete CAD training	• CAD vendor	Mar 15	
• Begin CAD conversion	• Dave Niemann	April 15	

IMPACT

Engineering kaizen	Product complexity	Parts complexity
Engineering lead times have already been cut to the project 24 days for three new products ordered since January 15.	Product complexity has been reduced by 40% as a function of the number of product configurations now offered in the catalog.	Part complexity has been reduced by 55% as a function of the total number of parts that will be used to design and manufacture new products.

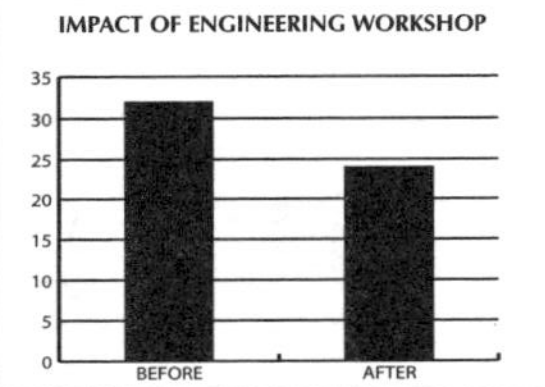

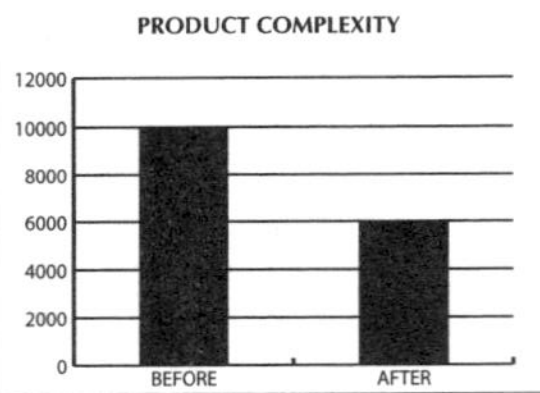

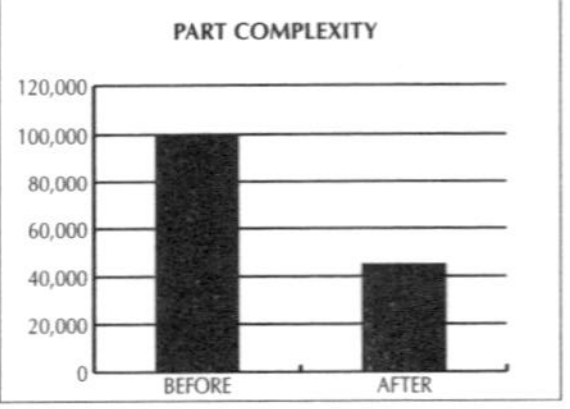

UNRESOLVED ISSUES

1. **Customer reaction to product/part reduction unknown.** Reaction to product/part reduction is not known. The reaction of the field sales staff is "cautiously optimistic."

2. **Slow follow up after kaizen workshop.** Long "treasure chest" lists of to-do items were generated at each of the 3 engineering kaizen workshops. The lean champion for manufacturing has become involved to make sure action items are completed on time.

3. **Possible space constraint.** After moving the engineering team to the Cybernautx plant, there may not be enough space to consolidate the marketing team's order entry cell.

4. **CAD training and design conversion.** While new Pro-E CAD software has been purchased, CAD training of staff has only begun. No problems are anticipated. The engineering staff is eager to be trained and certified and to begin the work of CAD conversion.

Date: April 17   **Reporting unit:** Engineering tactical team

Figure 7-5. Engineering Tactical Team A3-SR Status Report

A3-SSR

Summary Status Report | Theme: Engineering tactical team implementation on track

RESULTS 3-year record (yearly average)

measure	3 years ago	2 years ago	Last year
Time to market	4 months	3 months	2 months
Adherence to target cost	Not measured	Not measured	15%
Cost of delay	Not measured	Not measured	$200,000
Engineering changes per launch	100	80	75
# kaizen events	0	0	1
Poka yoke devices per launch	0	0	3
Project control boards	0	0	0

THIS PERIOD

measure	target	performance	comments
Time to market	11 days	30 days	New process
Adherence to target cost	75%	50%	New process
Cost of delay	$10,000	$25,000	New process
Engineering changes/product	20	15	They listened!
# kaizen events	3	4	Hard work
Poka yoke devices	10	11	Good training

PRESENT CONDITION

The implementation of a design for six sigma (DFSS) concurrent engineering process is on track.

OUTLOOK FOR NEXT PERIOD

1. Design changes will be made to ensure both ease of assembly and manufacture.
2. The preproduction pioneering process will be applied again in laying out the new production process, and again during launch, to ensure that target quality, target cost, and takt time can be met.
3. Engineering and manufacturing personnel will be trained in poka yoke (mistake proofing).

CATEGORY	STEPS TAKEN
1. Design Process	1. Design process value stream mapped with the participation of marketing and production. 2. Standard procedures written and deployed. 3. Engineering team co-located with marketing personnel in Cybernautx production facility.
2. Technical Risk Management	1. All engineering trained in Failure Modes and Effects Analysis (FMEA). 2. FMEA applied to first new product. 3. Risk Probability Numbers (RPNs) established and control plans developed for high risk items.
3. Preproduction Pioneering (3P)	1. Marketing, engineering, and production trained in 3P tools, including the 7 alternatives. 2. 3P tools applied in marketing and design phases of new product development process.

Review period: 3rd quarter | **Reporting Unit:** Engineering tactical team

Figure 7-6. A3-SSR

The Cybernautx engineering tactical team A3-SSR for the third quarter appears as Figure 7-6. Note how the targets tracked in the report correspond to the targets recorded in the team's A3-X at the end of Chapter 5 (Figure 5-25). The team has been busy in three main areas related to their effort to implement Design for Six Sigma (DFSS): (1) the redesign of their product development process, (2) technical risk management, and (3) preproduction pioneering (3P). (In the fourth quarter, the engineering tactical team will revisit these categories in the Act phase of the hoshin process when they participate in the president's diagnosis. See Chapter 8 and CD Form 8-10.)

CONDUCT REGULAR REVIEW MEETINGS

Hoshin kanri manages by exception. For hoshin kanri, this means the way you manage continuous improvement via the strategic goals based on the organizational mission and vision, customer expectations, and competitive benchmarks established during the scan and *Plan* phase. The backbone of any business or quality operating system is for the various teams to hold regular review meetings that focus on measures of process improvement. Table 7-1 broadly shows the time, purpose and responsibilities of all employees involved in hoshin kanri, while Tables 7-2 and 7-3 show the agenda for daily stand-up meetings, and the weekly, monthly, and quarterly review meetings, respectively. (*Note*: These tables are also on the CD companion. See CD Forms 7-1, 7-2, and 7-3.) Depending on which improvement has been deployed, project teams can handle many deviations from the annual hoshin more or less in real time. Only the most important or intractable issues should appear on review meeting agendas.

Daily, standup meetings of all workgroups and project teams, *including the hoshin team*, in addition to periodic review meetings, should be encouraged at the start or end of the workday to promote real-time information gathering and decision making. Daily meetings should last from 5 to 15 minutes. Table 7-2 shows a sample agenda.

On a technically demanding project, it's helpful to have frequent, short, informal project meetings. This ensures that everyone knows what everyone else is currently working on. It's important that everyone be brought up-to-date promptly on overall project activities. It's vitally important that teams communicate any change in commitments, schedules, or deliverables to everyone on the project. Daily meetings are a vehicle for this communication. Periodically, the hoshin team should meet in front of their hoshin management board (see Figure 7-4 above) to review progress. You should expand the quarterly review to two days.

CONDUCT AN ANNUAL REVIEW

We saw how, in the *Check* phase of the strategic improvement cycle, the attitude of PCDA was built into daily work, together with policy. At the end of the strategic improvement cycle, the entire company must return to PDCA again, looking back on results achieved and on problems and surprises encountered. Hoshin teams must pause to review the company's performance figures from the previous year to discover any critical gaps between actual performance and stated goals. Teams in these companies must also review stated or implied assumptions made in business strategy to discover gaps between assumptions on the one hand, and changed reality on the other. The outcome of policy analysis is a list of important problems that are recognized to affect the company's continued progress towards its vision. (*Note*: The list of problems developed in the annual review should lead to the creation of one or more A3-i competitive information reports and A3-Ts.)

Table 7-1. Example of Hoshin Review Meetings Involving the Entire Workforce

Meeting		Time	Purpose	Responsibilities
Action teams	Operators; project team members	*In real time*	Review own performance and conditions of production by means of andon cords and buttons	• Feedback to supervisors, action team members • Andon activation • Problem resolution
		Daily	Review own performance by means of operator process and team project control boards	• Feedback to action team members • Exception reporting • Problem resolution
Operations teams	Supervisors and area team leaders; project team leaders	*Daily*	Review own performance by means of operator process and team project control boards	• Feedback to action team leaders and members • Exception reporting • Problem resolution
		Weekly/daily	Review local performance; interpret priorities; evaluate activities; detect early warning signals	• Feedback to action team leaders and members • Exception reporting • Problem resolution
Tactical teams	Functional department heads, and cross-functional team leaders	*Monthly/weekly/daily*	Review scorecards, evaluate programs; support resource decisions; explain performance outliers	• Feedback to operations team leaders and members • Exception reporting • Problem identification
Hoshin team	Functional department heads, cross-functional team leaders, value stream managers, product managers	*Quarterly/monthly*	Review scorecards; evaluate strategy execution; support resource decisions; identify cross-functional issues; identify theme; select overall goals and targets	• Feedback to tactical teams • Exception reporting • Commitment process
		Annually	Review vision, strategies, tactics, process measures, results	• Define and deploy annual/semiannual vision

Table 7-2. Example of Fifteen-Minute Daily Standup Meeting

Daily Standup Meeting		
Agenda		
Purpose of meeting		To keep the workgroup or team focused on adhering to standard work and meeting requirements and expectations of daily work.
Outcomes of meeting		• An energized workgroup or team • The communication of new information about conditions of quality on-time production or performance • Initiatives to correct nonstandard conditions
8:00 AM	Orders of the day	Supervisor or team leader communicates daily production requirements or other expectations of team performance that day.
8:05 AM	Review of problems	The team reviews problems encountered on the preceding day or shift. Team members communicate awareness of abnormal conditions or other problems not previously documented.
8:10 AM	Related matters	Corrective action is planned for new problems. Other team matters, including vacations, birthdays, etc., may be discussed.
8:15 AM	Adjourn	

Hoshin Meeting Note: The hoshin team conducts the annual and quarterly reviews. (See Table 7-1 and CD Form 7-3). The tactical, operational, and action teams conduct the monthly and weekly reviews. Weekly reviews are optional for the tactical teams. I have been in large facilities, however, where the plant manager, as hoshin team leader, conducted a weekly review to accelerate organizational learning. Daily stand-up meetings are for action teams. In some facilities, operating teams might also have a midday meeting to address important quality issues. The number and frequency of meetings depends upon management's ability and desire to learn.

Hoshin review meetings at all levels should focus on process improvement.

USE A3-PS TO DOCUMENT COURSE CORRECTIONS

The best-laid plans of mice and men often go awry. It goes without saying that you will need to make a few course corrections in implementing your annual hoshin. Your A3-SRs and A3-SSRs will not always describe a steady, unimpeded progress towards your goals. You will run out of resources. You will set stretch targets that are too aggressive. Equipment will break down and people will stress out. The list of probable failures goes on. When failure does occur, use the A3-P (see Figure 1-4 and CD Form 1-6) to get yourself back on track. The A3-P is very similar to the A3-T, because both documents follow the same PDCA format. The "P" simply stands for "problem," or, if you like, the "impromptu" nature of the activity (because it was not part of the plan). Figure 7-7 shows an example of an A3-P that the Cybernautx engineering and tactical marketing teams drew up when they discovered (on the third day of a 5-day kaizen activity!) that there was not quite enough space to co-locate the engineering and marketing teams as was originally planned.

Table 7-3. Example of Agenda for Top Management Review

Weekly/Monthly/Quarterly Review Meeting		
Agenda		
Purpose of meeting		To review progress toward implementing lean in divisional plants and functions.
Outcomes of meeting		Documented analysis and short-term corrective action ideas to adhere or make small adjustments to current implementation plans.
8:00 AM	Introduction	Introduce meeting participants to the meeting process and system of documentation.
8:15 AM	Plan phase review	Review plan phase of implementation roadmap, including the lean organization and training resources; document facts, opinions, and questions for further research.
9:30 AM	Break	
9:45 AM	Brainstorm	Generate and document ideas for corrective action.
10:45 AM	Prioritize	Prioritize ideas for corrective action and assign responsibility for implementing the best ideas.
12:00 Noon	Lunch	
1:00 PM	Pilot phase review	In breakout sessions chaired by lean champions, review pilot phase of implementation roadmap and document facts, opinions, and questions for further research.
2:30 PM	Break	
2:45 PM	Brainstorm	In breakout sessions chaired by lean champions, generate and document ideas for corrective action.
3:30 PM	Prioritize	In breakout sessions chaired by lean champions, prioritize ideas for corrective action and assign responsibility for implementing the best ideas.
4:00 PM	Report	With all meeting attendees present, each lean champion gives a short report on the status of implementation in the plan and pilot phases, and gives an overview of corrective action.
5:00 PM	Adjourn	

Note: The discussion of issues in weekly, monthly, and quarterly review meetings should be supported by your system of A3 reports. Prior to each review meeting, use the A3-SR and A3-SSR to identify relevant exceptions, then document the exceptions with the A3-P.

A3-P

Problem solving report | **Theme:** Failure to move marketing team to Cybernautx plant

PROBLEM STATEMENT

The engineering and marketing tactical teams have been unable to consolidate order entry operations at the Cybernautx manufacturing plant according to the implementation schedule. As a result, the total product gestation lead time is currently 30 days—10 days longer than the original target of 20 days.

TARGET STATEMENT

The engineering and marketing tactical teams still believe that it is possible to move order entry operations and achieve the projected 20 day lead time soon enough to avoid revising market share growth and profit projections.

ANALYSIS

Why? Space available was insufficient to accommodate existing furniture and cubicles from the old office facilities.

Why? 20-year old furniture and cubicles are adapted to functional operations.

Why? Some upstairs office space was devoted to manufacturing MRO supplies.

COUNTERMEASURES

- The engineering and marketing tactical teams have rescheduled the original consolidation kaizen event.
- New Herman Miller furniture will be ordered to replace the old office cubicles. The following features of the new furniture promote close teamwork:
  - Requires 40% less space and has flexible overhead "conduit" to permit easy setup
  - Plenty of vertical space for visual displays and project management tools
  - Permits direct line of sight and impromptu communication
  - "Cone of silence" canopies available for managers
- Manufacturing will conduct an MRO kaizen to eliminate unnecessary supplies and consolidate the rest more efficiently. A 50% space reduction is expected.

IMPLEMENTATION PLAN

Action	Responsibility	Date
Make preliminary design of new layout	G. Peurasaari	Xx/xx/xx
Order new furniture	M. Sinnochi	Xx/xx/xx
Conduct MRO kaizen	M. May	Xx/xx/xx
Conduct order entry kaizen, round 2	R. Cooper	Xx/xx/xx

CHECK AND ACT verification and follow up

Date: June 19 | **Reporting unit:** Engineering and marketing tactical teams

Figure 7-7. Engineering and Marketing Tactical Team A3-P Problem Report

CHAPTER EIGHT

CHECK: The President's Diagnosis

In addition to the more or less traditional methods of review outlined in Chapter 7, hoshin kanri has a review method all its own: *the president's diagnosis*. The method is so called because at the end of every year, the hoshin team, which is normally led by the company's president, personally visits each of his or her company's sites to check on the vitality of the system and recognize achievement. In other words, the president's diagnosis involves your company's top leaders directly in the systematic review of organizational fitness resulting from the development of new competitive capabilities.

In Chapter 2, the hoshin team was introduced to the president's diagnosis as one of the tools it could use to establish the state of its own competitive resources and capabilities, as well as those of competitors and suppliers. In this chapter, all four hoshin teams—tactical, operational, and action teams as well as the hoshin team itself—will learn how to use it annually as a diagnostic system to systematically check the progress of development of your management systems and the state of your competitive resources. Furthermore, the teams will learn how to use the president's diagnosis to assist in coaching and mentoring the entire organization in correctly developing its resources and capabilities—aligned with becoming lean. The president's diagnosis is one of the most powerful ways to build a lean culture, because it encourages the proper growth of important resources and capabilities like brand equity, new technologies and copyrightable new ideas, relationships with your suppliers, and lean manufacturing processes—the soft side of competitive advantage. It's also an excellent tool for promoting long-term strategic change and a good early warning system of potential financial problems. Motorola and GE both have used a form of the diagnosis to promote the development of six sigma capabilities. The president's diagnosis can also be an important element of supply chain integration. For many years, Toyota has diagnosed its suppliers to promote their development of lean manufacturing capabilities.

As in the short-term reviews covered in Chapter 7, the focus of the president's diagnosis is on process first and results second. While the methods in Chapter 7 focused on discovering and addressing assignable causes of short-term process deviations or failures, the president's diagnosis focuses directly on checking the management systems that support organizational development.

ARE WE LEAN YET?

Every man, woman, and child on the planet has at one time or another asked the irritating question, "Are we there yet?" Anyone who initiates a process of strategic change, such as implementing lean or hoshin kanri, had better be ready to answer these five questions:

1. What is the standard by which we measure the development of competitive resources and capabilities initiated by hoshin kanri?
2. What resources or capabilities should we be measuring?
3. What measurement scale should we use?
4. Where are we now?
5. How will we know if we are there yet?

President's Diagnosis Tip: Japan's Deming Prize predates both hoshin kanri and the president's diagnosis and was their origin. There are several excellent and readily available diagnostic systems from which to chose, including the criteria for the Deming Prize and all the quality and productivity prizes to which it gave birth (for example the Baldrige Award, and the Shingo Prize), which may all be downloaded free from the Internet. In addition, there are the proprietary criteria of Iwao Kobayashi (the 20 Keys), Isaaki Imai, and Richard Schoenberger. They are all worth studying. In fact, you may conduct the president's diagnosis on the basis of any of these systems. The best companies develop their own diagnostic systems focused on issues of specific concern to their own industries. See Recommended Reading under the President's Diagnosis for a list of resources.

Many companies use diagnostic criteria designed to highlight a continuum of transformative phases they will pass through as they change from one state into another. To answer the first three questions above, this workbook provides an updated version of the criteria first published in *Corporate Diagnosis*. There, for the first time, a *comprehensive* set of criteria was presented that addressed the developmental requirements of lean management, human resource development, supply chain management, quality, manufacturing, and product development. Previous diagnostic systems had tended to focus on particular business functions such as quality (the Deming Prize and Baldrige Award) or productivity (the Shingo Prize). To a large extent, this is still true today.

In redeveloping the criteria for this workbook, we have reorganized the diagnostic categories (originally called "keys") to strongly emphasize the operational and strategic integration of an entire lean supply chain. Complete criteria are offered here for finance and accounting, information systems, marketing, product development, and supply chain development, as well as for quality and manufacturing, and human resource systems. The criteria for finance and accounting and marketing are entirely new, while the criteria for product development and supply chain management are greatly expanded.

To assist in answering all of the questions above, we have also introduced a new measurement system, called the *transformation ruler*, which adopts the PDCA structure of hoshin kanri and the 5 rules of lean "DNA."

PDCA AND THE 5 RULES OF LEAN DNA

As a method, hoshin kanri imbeds PDCA thinking in all decision making, at every level of your organization. Thus, the major question in assessing development is: *To what extent has scientific PDCA thinking become part of the company's culture?* No matter what type of development an organization is attempting to promote—be it to become lean, achieve six sigma quality, reposition an entire brand, or increase the number of innovative patents, this question is a constant. PDCA thinking is a constant because it's the basis of all organizational learning.

The hoshin team was introduced to the transformation ruler at the end of Chapter 2 (Table 2-4) as part of the discussion around the using the president's diagnosis as a scanning tool. As you will see below, we've expanded the ruler to address five important themes central to the development of a mature lean enterprise. Steven Spear and H. Kent Bowen in the landmark article, "Decoding the DNA of the Toyota Production System," reemphasized the central role of PDCA in the development of lean enterprise. Spear and Bowen articulated 4 rules of lean DNA and outlined the scientific reasoning process that they saw inside Toyota. We have renamed and restated these rules in the context of hoshin kanri as follows:

- **Rule 1:** *Standardize processes and standardize work.* Standardized processes and work practices reduce variability and improve quality in your products in services. More important, they ensure that there will be controlled conditions for experiments with your company's systems and processes at all seven levels of the *hoshin kanri* system (see Figure 1-1).
- **Rule 2:** *Zero ambiguity.* This rule states that requirements of internal and external customers be absolutely clear to everyone in the value stream, including requirements that we change the way we do things to develop new resources and capabilities. This reduces ambiguity and thus improves the signal-to-noise ratio in information systems (computerized and otherwise).
- **Rule 3:** *Flow the process.* This rule states that the flow of material and information be as direct as possible. In other words, the system works best if there is a clear, waste-free flow of material and information with very few paths of variation.
- **Rule 4:** *Speak with data.* This rule states that decisions taken to correct or improve the system should be taken at the lowest possible level, in as close to real time as possible, and based upon the scientific method (PDCA).

In their original article, Spear and Bowen imbedded the statement, "guided by a coach or mentor," in rule 4. This actually rises to the level of a fifth rule.

- **Rule 5:** *Develop leaders who are teachers.* This rule states that leaders must be teachers and coaches of their employees as they learn to apply PDCA methods in real time.

In their article, Spear and Bowen carefully described how each of the 4 (now 5) rules of lean DNA functions by forming a hypothesis and then identifying and responding to problems. Table 8-1 liberally reinterprets, restates, and generalizes Spear and Bowen's original findings from activities on the shop floor to *all* activities in a lean enterprise, in every function, at every level, and throughout the supply chain.

Table 8-1 describes in detail what any diagnosis of a lean enterprise is looking for. This is what we expect to see in a mature lean enterprise. Everyone is a good scientist, operating under controlled conditions in a clean laboratory fee of waste, in which research priorities are clear, and the next step in the process is always obvious. If any of these conditions fail, immediate steps are taken to improve the situation.

THE TRANSFORMATION RULER

How can you operationalize the pure form of lean thinking of the 5 rules and hypotheses? Spear and Bowen describe a perfect universe in which everyone applies PDCA in real time. They don't give us much guidance as to what mass production thinkers should do to become lean. This is where the transformation ruler comes into play (see Table 8-2 and CD Form 8-1).

Table 8-1. The PDCA and Five Rules and Hypotheses of Lean DNA Enterprise

	Rule	Hypothesis	Sign of a problem	Response
RULE 1 **Standardize work** *How people and machines should work*	All human and mechanical work should be highly specified as to content, sequence, timing, work-in-process inventory, and outcome.	The person or machine can do the activity as specified.	The activity is not done as specified.	Determine the true skill level of the person or the true capability of the machine and train or modify as appropriate.
		If the activity is done as specified, the good or service will be defect free.	The outcome is defective.	
RULE 2 **Zero ambiguity** *How people and machines should connect*	Every customer-supplier connection should be direct, and there should be an unambiguous yes-or-no way to send requests and receive responses.	Customers' requests will be for goods and services in a specific mix and volume.	Responses don't keep pace with requests.	Determine the true mix and volume of demand and the true capability of the supplier; retrain, modify activities, or reassign customer-supplier pairs as appropriate.
		The supplier is capable to respond to customers' requests.	The supplier is idle, waiting for requests.	
RULE 3 **Flow the process** *How value streams should be constructed*	The pathway for every product and service must be simple and direct, free from waste and variability.	Suppliers connected to the value stream are required.	A person, machine, organization or other supplier is not actually required.	Determine why the supplier wasn't needed, and redesign the value stream.
		Suppliers not connected to the value stream are not required.	A nonspecified supplier provides an intermediate good or service.	Learn why the nonspecified supplier was actually required, and redesign the value stream.
RULE 4 **Speak with data** *How to improve continuously*	Any improvement must be made in accordance with the scientific method, under the guidance of a sensei, at the lowest possible level in the organization.	A specific change in an activity, machine, connection, or value stream will improve cost, quality, lead-time, batch size, or safety by a specific amount.	The actual result is different from the expected results.	Learn how the activity was actually performed or the connection or value stream was actually operated. Determine the true effects of the change. Redesign the change.
RULE 5 **Develop leaders who can teach**	Leaders must be systems thinkers and teachers thoroughly well-versed in the Socratic methods of instruction as well as their particular areas of technical expertise.	94% of all problems are the result of system failures, not failures of intelligence or character.	All of the signs above regularly recur without being fixed or without preventive measures being put into place.	Use window analysis to identify the nature of systems failure (see Table 9-2). Train, retrain, or apply poka yoke where standards exist. Create or improve standards through employee involvement.

All the rules require that where possible, activities, connections, and value streams have built-in test mechanisms, called poka yoke, to signal problems automatically. It is the continuous response to problems in real time that makes this seemingly rigid system so flexible and adaptable to changing circumstances.

Source: Adapted from Spear and Bowen, "Decoding the DNA of the Toyota Production System," *Harvard Business Review,* September–October, 1999.

Table 8-2. The Transformation Ruler: Lean Development Pattern Defined

Lean DNA	mass		Lean DNA		lean
	1 scan	2 plan	3 do	4 check	5 act
Standardize Work	Standards not documented. No two people could do same job twice in the same way if they wanted to.	Some standards documented. Training sporadic. Adherence to standards very poor.	Everyone trained in how to create and maintain standardized work, but standards still documented by engineers. Adherence to standards poor.	Hourly associates & staff document standards. Good adherence because of understanding and buy-in. Standards reinforced by effective audit system.	Standardization of work content, sequence, timing, and work-in-process inventory obvious "at a glance." Standardization used to drive kaizen activities.
Flow the Process	Non-value-adding waste chokes process flow. Value-added ratio < 5%. Flow not a primary consideration of layout. Process flow looks like a bowl of spaghetti.	Individual strategy of waste elimination and variability reduction seen as thrust of lean enterprise. Value stream mapping begins.	Value stream mapping techniques taught to all. Flow of products and services improves as gross process waste identified and removed.	There is a good flow of products and services as waste in operations is greatly reduced. Product flow is primary consideration in advanced engineering and product development.	Direct flow of products and services w/little process or operations waste. Goods & services flow like water as waste of movement is addressed systematically.
Zero Ambiguity	Customer requirements unclear in daily work. Poor feedback and feed forward hinder supply chain management.	Customer and supplier requirements clear and data being used to evaluate and improve performance.	Visual controls such as kanban introduced in all business functions to clarify customer requirements. Feedback/feed forward improved.	Visual control systems identify defects, errors, and abnormalities and support real-time problem solving.	Visual controls replace written standards. Systems anticipate customer.
Speak with data (PDCA)	No plan-do-check system. Problems go unaddressed for years.	The company firmly grasps concept of PDCA and its central role in lean enterprise. New PDCA system designed.	New plan-do-check system formally introduced. Managers and associates systematically trained in PDCA methods. Old problems addressed but new ones crop up quickly.	A sound plan-do-check system focuses on defects and errors. New problems addressed as they arise.	A refined plan-do-check system focuses on abnormal conditions. Problems anticipated before they occur.
Develop Leaders Who Are Teachers	Leaders are bosses. People expected to do what the boss says. Messengers who carry bad news are frequently "shot."	Leaders see potential in their people, but most training dollars still spent on managers.	Development of leaders who are teachers begins as managers train in lean methodologies, and learn how to teach and coach workforce.	Decision making done at levels close to actual processes.	Managers come running when hourly associates & staff signal for assistance in solving problems.

On the one hand, a mature lean organization would find lean DNA functioning in every function and at every level of a lean enterprise. In addition, a fully developed lean culture has internalized PDCA. The president's diagnosis determines the *gap* between this ideal state and your own current state, prescribes corrective action, and helps everyone implement it. Therefore, the transformation ruler describes what you would expect to find with respect to each of the five rules of lean DNA at each of the five phases of the organization transformation process.

On the other hand, teams throughout a less mature lean company will use the new transformation ruler to assess where they are with respect to ideal lean thinking and practice. In addition to PDCA, we have added a fifth dimension to the ruler, namely, "scan" to determine the company's awareness of the need to change. In Chapter 2, the hoshin team scanned the company's market conditions, but in this case tactical, operational, and action teams will also scan to determine their development in relation to how mass or lean they really are, answering question 4 above, "Where are we?" Once you establish this, you can then move forward in the PDCA cycle to determine, "How will we know if we're there yet?"

While the ruler is useful in theory, it's too abstract to be practical. What does the practice of lean thinking look like in marketing? In engineering? In manufacturing? To address these and other questions, this workbook provides a *new, comprehensive system of diagnostic categories* and supporting criteria—expressed in the form of convenient *progress tables*—to diagnose all elements of an integrated lean enterprise. The whole system is called "The transformation ruler," after the PDCA measurement system on which it is based. It includes criteria for marketing, design engineering, manufacturing, and supply chain integration, and people, bringing it to a total of eleven criteria. The eleven categories are based on eleven distinct business functions frequently found in the management hierarchy. Table 8-3 lists the eleven categories (business functions) down the left-hand column, with a description, measure, and methodology provided for each category.

To assist all four types of hoshin teams in using the transformation ruler, we have developed eleven progress tables, specifying specific criteria for each of the eleven diagnostic categories and their related subcategories. For each category or function in the transformation ruler, a corresponding progress table maps the category and its respective subcategories against the five distinct levels of development: scan, plan, do, check, and act. The subcategories describe specific PDCA methodologies, tools, and techniques that lean enterprises employ to achieve their extraordinary performance. The progress tables describe specific conditions of organizational development that you should expect to see in each subcategory (i.e., with respect to specific lean methods, tools, or techniques) at each level of development. The progress tables will help hoshin, tactical, operational, and action teams use the transformation ruler to identify the company's progress from plan to do to check and to act with respect to all normal business functions as they adopt lean methods, tools, and techniques. The teams will also be able to identify and close strategic gaps in these areas. Figure 8-1 shows the logic of lean enterprise for Cybernautx and Table 8-4 shows an example of its progress table for marketing and sales. The complete transformation ruler, including all eleven progress tables, may be printed from the companion CD (CD Forms 8-1 through 8-14).

Table 8-3. Categories of the Transformation Ruler

	Categories of Diagnosis		
	Description	**Measures**	**Methodologies**
Management	Lean enterprises apply PDCA to strategy, tactics, and operations, as well as daily work. A continual process of realigning a business's organization and productive capacity w/its strategic intent, in particular, through involvement of teams and employees in planning process.	• Value stream profit • EBITDA • Adherence to strategic targets	• Hoshin kanri • Balanced scorecard • Strategy maps • Scenario building • Game theory
Finance & Accounting	Lean enterprises know their real costs to design and produce products and services in as close to real time as possible.	• Target profit • Target cost • Kaizen cost • Time to close	• Profit management • Strategic cost management • Order line profitability analysis
Human Resource Development	Developing human resources key to developing intangible assets of brand, technology, process, and relationships. Continual process of constructing a post-modern organization of vertical and horizontal networks of individuals and teams that leverages learning capability of all employees.	• # kaizen workshops • # lean leaders certified • # employees cross-trained • Employee satisfaction	• Kaizen events • Train the trainer • Black belt programs • Employee surveys • Gainsharing
Supply Chain Management	Continual process of building long term, cooperative relationships w/external stakeholders of organization, including government and local communities, but especially suppliers.	• Supplier on-time delivery • Supplier quality • Supplier cost	• Supplier certification programs • Supplier development programs
Information Management	Good information has a very short shelf life. In a lean enterprise, decisions made as close to process as possible. Thus, lean information systems are designed to provide local decision makers at all levels of organization w/information they need in as close to real time as possible.	• 5S, 6S, 7S levels • Strategic information coverage index • First time through in admin. processes	• 5S, 6S, 7S • Visual management • Poka yoke • ERP • Knowledge management
Quality Assurance	Quality in a lean enterprise means quality at the source. Quality cannot be inspected into a product or a process. Every single person throughout a lean supply chain is responsible to inspect incoming material, and to certify quality of their work. When a problem is discovered, process stops until it is fixed.	• External ppm • Internal ppm • Scrap • Rework	• CEDAC® • Six sigma • Q7 • N7 • O certification

159

Table 8-3. Categories of the Transformation Ruler, *continued*

		Categories of Diagnosis		
	Description	Measures	Methodologies
Marketing & Sales	Decoding voice of customer is first of three essential targets of business competition. Continual process of aligning a business's strategic intent w/actual stated, unstated, and latent requirements of its customers; and discipline to stay focused on that intent from order to delivery.	• Profit and market share growth • Quality levels • Complaints • On-time Delivery	• Quality functional deployment • Customer surveys • Focus groups • Process mapping
Engineering Operations	Translating voice of customer faithfully into a concrete design second target of business w/team-based methods of concurrent engineering and mass customization that ensure product concepts translated swiftly and efficiently into robust designs that can be executed flawlessly.	• Time to market • Time to market acceptance • New product as % of sales	• Concurrent engineering • Value analysis • Life cycle costing • QFD, DFM, FMEA, FMEI, DOE, VRP, VRP
Manufacturing Operations	Faithfully executing good design is third and final target of business competition. Team-based methods of just-in-time production (JIT) that remove non-value-adding wastes (e.g., waiting, inspection, transport, motion, overproduction, defects, inventory) from production process.	• Mfg Lead Time • Value-Adding Ratios • Overall equipment effectiveness (OEE)	• Process mapping & value analysis • Group technology & cell design • Autonomation
Maintenance Operations	In a lean manufacturing environment, downtime a luxury no one can afford.	• OEE • Mean time to failure • Mean time to repair	• Autonomous maintenance • Six sigma
Materials Management	In a lean enterprise, good and services flow like water.	• Inventory turns • Dock to dock	• Value stream maps • Kanban • Heijunka • Water spider • Containerization

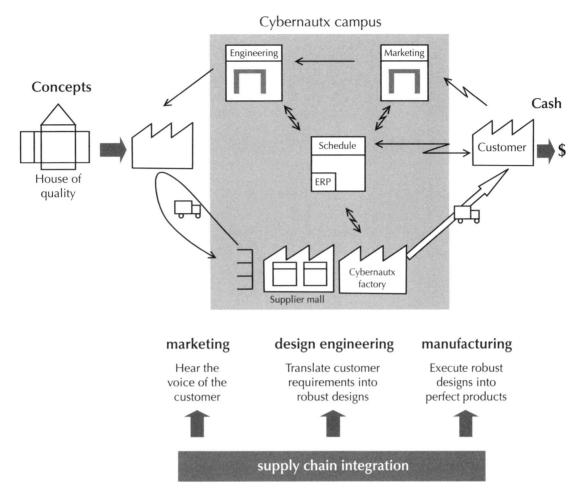

Figure 8-1. The Logic of Lean Enterprise

Hoshin, Tactical, Operational, and Action Team Exercise: Before conducting a diagnosis, have all participating team leaders review Tables 8-1 through 8-4. Teams at all levels should meet to discuss the concepts, review the tables, and become versed in the terminology. If you begin the exercise with a hoshin team meeting, you may use a process similar to the deployment process described in Chapter 4 to transmit the transformation ruler down the management hierarchy. The main goal is to have a clear understanding of the transformation ruler so that team members will be able to fill out their own progress tables. Team leaders should discuss Table 8-4, becoming familiar with the terminology and layout. Recall that there are eleven blank progress tables, one for each category in the transformation ruler. Each progress table specifies the subcategories for each of the eleven criteria in the diagnostic categories. These eleven progress tables are on your companion CD (CD Forms 8-4 to 8-14). Have team leaders print his or her forms and assign them to each team member for further study. In the coming exercises, each team will be using the appropriate table to help them fill out generic diagnostic scorecards and diagnostic forms (Tables 8-5 and 8-6). It may be helpful to have the team review the examples in workbook, including the diagnostic scan in Chapter 2, Figure 2-4.

Table 8-4. Example of a Progress Table for Marketing and Sales

	1	2	3	4	5
	mass				lean
	scan	plan	do	check	act
Voice of the Customer	No one knows what QFD is or why they may need it.	QFD not practiced. Customer sees product only after it's launched. No one knows what customer says let alone what she wants.	Marketing personnel have been trained in QFD, but the voice of the customer is still not clear. The customer sees a prototype.	QFD and value engineering are routinely applied and customers involved in critiquing prototypes. QFD captures the voice of the customer for both marketing and engineering.	Customers are formally part of the new product team from concept to design and execution.
Market Dimensions	There is no good picture of the value stream; surveys are infrequent, markets are not segmented.	Total value stream mapping and regular surveys begin. Market segments are sorted out with a product/market matrix.	Products are repositioned to meet the needs of customers in specific markets.	Your value streams are well understood. Markets segments yield benefits to you and your customers.	Competitors, suppliers, and market trends are well understood. Markets are properly segmented and surveyed once a month.
Marketing and Sales	Customers don't get the right information. Prices are based on cost-plus. You have never stapled yourself to an order.	Product-out orientation. The order-to-delivery process has been mapped and obvious problems are fixed.	Marketing & sales staff trained to understand strengths and weaknesses of companies core value-adding processes.	Market-in orientation. Customers get the info they need. Prices are competitive. The order-to-delivery process has been streamlined.	Service orientation. Customers are savvy. Product pricing is based on perceived value. The order-to-delivery process is like clockwork.
Perfect Service	Customers don't know whom to turn to for service. Employees are not well informed. Customer retention rates are low.	Your service process is mapped. Obvious problems are fixed.	Marketing and sales staff are trained in how to deliver perfect service.	Frontline employees are empowered to please the customer and have the information they need to act.	The entire organization is geared to respond to customer requests. You regularly surprise your customers with great service.

Table 8-4. Example of a Progress Table for Marketing and Sales, *continued*

	1	2	3	4	5
	mass		**Marketing and Sales**		lean
	scan	plan	do	check	act
Knowledge of the Customer	Customer experience is not tracked. Cross-functional communication is contentious.	Only serious customer complaints tracked.	Systematic customer tracking begins, but crossfunctional communication is still a problem.	A cross-functional database is developed to support frontline employees in serving the customer.	Cross-functional database tracks customer experience. Employees can take appropriate and timely action to serve customers.
Brand Equity	The brand has no clear position. Don't know what the customer says let alone what she wants in most market segments.	A brand charter is created, but while the customers' spoken needs are sometimes met, unspoken needs are not known.	The brand charter is now effectively communicated to customer in all important market segments.	The brand is well positioned. Spoken needs are met in all segments. Unspoken needs are met in major market segments.	You know what the customer is dreaming about. Your brand excels at giving customers what they really want. Loyalty soars.
Supplier of Choice	You do not measure your effectiveness as a supplier to your customers.	Your overall supplier effectiveness (OSE) is low. OSE = external quality $\times$ customer cost $\times$ delivery performance.	Immediate steps ensure perfect quality. Value stream maps illuminate opportunities for improvement of cost and delivery.	OSE is strong compared to your competitors, and steadily improving.	Delivery on demand with lean thinking and continuous replenishment. OSE > 98%.

THREE STAGES IN THE PRESIDENT'S DIAGNOSIS

No matter what system of diagnostic criteria you choose, the president's diagnosis has three stages:

1. All tactical, operational, and action teams self-diagnose their level of PDCA development.
2. The hoshin team conducts the president's diagnosis for designated teams.
3. President recognizes achievement for all team leaders (managers).

Stage 1: Tactical, Operational, and Action Teams Self-diagnose Their Level of PDCA Development

Despite its name, the president's diagnosis is actually a companywide system of *self-diagnosis* among all four types of hoshin teams. Teams throughout the company use the same criteria to assess their own progress as well as the progress of the entire company. Teams should diagnose their development at least once a year.

For purposes of Stage 1, we will assume that all teams conduct a diagnosis of their own functions and/or business processes, without involving other teams. As a practical step, teams often diagnose one another leading up to the hoshin team's diagnosis, which is described in Stage 2. Tactical teams diagnose their constituent operational teams; operational teams diagnose their constituent action teams; tactical teams may diagnose other tactical teams; and so forth. Diagnosis may move from the bottom up as well as the top town, in which case action teams may diagnose an operational team, or an operational team may diagnose a tactical team. In all cases where teams diagnose one another, team leaders should review and follow the procedures set out for the hoshin team in Stage 2 below, omitting the previsit report and the companywide score. Whether or not teams diagnose one another, they should always diagnose themselves. This promotes empowerment and also prepares team members for constructive interaction with external teams, including the hoshin team, that perform any external diagnosis.

Diagnostic tip: Some companies use diagnostic categories, criteria, and measures like those found in the transformation ruler as a system of certification to promote self-development and also award recognition and benefits. Action teams seeking certification make a formal application, usually to the operational team of which its own team leader is a member. It's a good idea to require the team seeking certification to provide documentation proving that it has maintained its new status for 3 to 6 months before certifying the unit at the new level.

Tactical, Operational and Action Team Exercises: Each team needs to follow the headings and instructions below to gather performance data, prepare the team, and prepare the diagnostic form. The site visit will entail its team diagnostic team members to *go see*, to make observations, review improvements, ask questions, and see firsthand what the team, or site has accomplished in the categories of lean culture. The team diagnostic team will also coach and mentor, and record observations. To complete these exercises, you will need to print from the companion CD, the transformation ruler and all supporting documents, CD Forms 8-1 through 8-14.

Gather Performance Data

For a tactical, operational, or action team to make its diagnosis, it will need information about its own performance. For example, it should have estimates of engineering and manufacturing lead times, changeover times, overall equipment effectiveness (OEE), first pass quality, supplier quality, and so on. Much of this data will be readily available if the teams have implemented operator process control boards, visual project boards, and if there is a visual hoshin board, as recommended in Chapter 7.

Prepare the Team

The teams should review their respective strategies, tactics, and targets articulated on their A3-Xs and/or A3-Ts. Then, as in the exercise for the hoshin, tactical, and operational team on page 157, review the basics of the diagnostic system, including the eleven criteria and the transformation ruler. Be sure that everyone understands the definition of each category and subcategory and the diagnostic logic of PDCA.

The teams will focus on specific categories and criteria related to the business functions and processes for which they have direct responsibility. For example, a manufacturing tactical team's diagnosis of the production department will utilize the criteria listed on the progress table for the manufacturing operations category. An engineering operational team's diagnosis of an engineering technical center will use the criteria on the progress table for the engineering systems category. In addition to criteria specifically related to the team's own functions and processes, teams should include in their diagnosis all general management criteria for hoshin kanri, including criteria in the following categories:

- Business operating system
- Finance and accounting systems
- Human resource systems
- Information systems
- Quality systems

While not all criteria for specific subcategories listed under these five categories may apply to a given business function, many will. In general, teams closer to the top of the organization should expect to include the most subcategories in their diagnosis. Teams closer to the bottom of the organization, in particular the action teams, may need to omit some subcategories in the criteria related to their business processes as well as in the general criteria. The hoshin team should give guidance on this point before deploying the diagnostic criteria. Tactical teams may wish to edit the criteria before transmitting them to operational teams; operational teams may wish to edit the criteria for the action teams. Because your company's functional structure may not match the structure of the generic sample questions, we encourage you to adapt these questions to your own requirements. In lieu of a detailed deployment of criteria, Table 8-5 (also CD Form 8-2) shows a generic diagnostic scorecard that might be applied to any tactical, operational, or action team. All that a given team has to do is to specify any specialized lean systems and tools that may apply to the functions or process under its control.

Prepare the Diagnostic Form

As part of its diagnosis, each team will make a visit of its own work site. Before the site visit, the team prepares a diagnostic form (Table 8-6; also CD Form 8-3) for each category and subcategory examined during the diagnosis.

At the top of the diagnostic form, team members enter the relevant categories and subcategories examined. They identify the team and its members, followed by a summary of

Table 8-5. Diagnostic Scorecard

		The Transformation Ruler								
			1		2		3		4		5
			mass		plan		do		check		lean
			scan								act
Management Systems		1		2		3		4		5	
Finance & Accounting		1		2		3		4		5	
Human Resources		1		2		3		4		5	
Supply Chain Management		1		2		3		4		5	
Information Management		1		2		3		4		5	
Quality Systems		1		2		3		4		5	
Marketing & Sales		1		2		3		4		5	
Engineering Systems		1		2		3		4		5	
Manufacturing Operations		1		2		3		4		5	
Maintenance Management		1		2		3		4		5	
Materials Management		1		2		3		4		5	

Table 8-6. Diagnostic Form

Diagnostic Form				
Control point		Checkpoint		
Unit diagnosed		Date *Month/day/year*		
Diagnostic team				
Diagnostic questions		• What problems did you encounter in pursuing the company's annual policy targets for this control point? • Did you use reliable, PDCA methods? • What problems do you foresee in the near future? • When do you expect the next improvements? • What information or resources will you require to reach higher targets? • What recommendations does the team have for management?		
Notes				
scan	**plan**	**do**	**check**	**act**
1	2	3	4	5

the diagnostic questions they have prepared. The bottom of the diagnostic form is a space for notes, in a five-column format similar to that of the transformation ruler.

For the site visit, team members carry copies of the form on clipboards as a reference and a place to record and organize their observations. In addition to the general criteria of the transformation ruler, the following generic questions help frame the big issues for every category and subcategory analyzed:

- What problems did you encounter in pursuing the company's annual policy targets for this category or subcategory?
- Did you use reliable, PDCA methods and tools?
- What problems do you foresee in the near future?
- When do you expect the next improvements?
- What information or resources will you require to reach higher targets?
- What recommendations does the team have for management?

Go See—Make a Site Visit

To ground themselves in reality, team members need to take a brief tour of their own work site to make observations and review improvements made since the last diagnosis. As you will see in Stage 2 of the president's diagnosis, the visit of an external team to the work site of another team is a highly structured exercise involving extensive interactions with the external team and members of the team under review. In a local self-diagnosis, the team should walk through its own department or operation, stopping when appropriate to discuss how the diagnostic criteria apply to the team's situation. Team members should be prepared to gather whatever data are necessary to strengthen their answers or arguments in response to the diagnostic questions. Look for visual controls that the unit uses for daily work management and reporting; an example is the hoshin management board described in the previous section.

The site visit is the team's chance to observe its daily operating conditions with a fresh eye—and it's the team members' opportunity to observe, ask more specific questions, and note ideas that can be implemented more broadly. During a site visit, the team has an opportunity to see firsthand what the unit has accomplished in the categories of lean culture.

Record Observations

Make sure team members take notes on their diagnostic forms to support later discussion and scoring. To organize the notes, refer to the progress tables for the categories the team is diagnosing. Consider the symptoms or characteristics described under each of the subcategories in the progress table for each level of development, relative to what the team is seeing and hearing. Then enter these observations in the corresponding columns on the diagnostic form. The completed form provides a record that supports the post visit process in which scores are determined. The same rules for recording observations apply to the hoshin team, when it makes its site visits in Stage 2 of the diagnosis.

Diagnosis tip:
- Don't just check results. Evaluate the process through which the results were obtained.
- Discrepancies may appear among the data. In such cases, concentrate on the problem and seek its causes. Avoid looking for culprits to blame.
- Review visual information. A3s, diagrams, control charts, and similar graphic materials are helpful for communicating, clarifying, and confirming that improvement activities have been implemented.
- Allow enough time for discussion.

Analyze, Score the Development, and Create a Radar Chart

Immediately after visiting its work site, the team meets in a conference room to determine scores for the unit. Democratic voting and unanimous decision rules can lead to deadlock, so we recommend that you use a qualified consensus rule to reach final scores. Team members don't have to agree unanimously on the score, but they should be willing to support the score that's reached. Table 8-7 shows the diagnostic scorecard by which a company may be scored.

Table 8-7. Diagnostic Team Scorecard Definitions

scan	1	Score the subcategory a one (1) if the business unit being diagnosed meets the description in the transformation ruler, but does not have a documented hoshin plan to improve the situation.
plan	2	Score the subcategory a two (2) only if the business unit being diagnosed meets the description in the transformation ruler.
do	3	Score the subcategory a three (3) only if the business unit has completed all the requirements of the *do* phase for the subcategory.
check	4	Score the subcategory a four (4) only if the business unit has completed all the requirements of the *check* phase for the subcategory.
act	5	Score the subcategory a five (5) only if the business unit has completed all the requirements of the *act* phase for the subcategory. (Very few organizations meet this criteria for any of the control points, and no organizations meet this criteria for all control points.)

Review what you've observed and discuss what score to award. Although the transformation ruler incorporates the four phases of PDCA, there are actually five levels, which are defined below.

- *Level 1.* This is when you have no formal plan to improve. That is, you are in the "scan" phase for diagnosing the category or subcategory that you're diagnosing.
  Except for purposes of diagnosing your overall business operating system from a companywide perspective (i.e., the hoshin team's perspective), a formal plan does not have to be an X-matrix or a team charter. There should be evidence at the individual team level, however, of a clear focus on the overall goals of the category or subcategory and of course good project management. To achieve a Level 1 in any category or subcategory, there must be evidence of a factual understanding of the need to adopt lean or world class methods to develop competitive capabilities.

- *Level 2.* This is when you have a plan and have deployed it, but you haven't developed leaders and completed improvement projects linked to your plan. That is, you are still in the "plan" phase for the category or subcategory you are diagnosing.
  Once again, except for purposes of diagnosing the overall business operating system, deployment does not require a formal catchball process. Nevertheless, there should be evidence of a systematic approach to involving team members in the planning and executing improvements.

- *Level 3.* This is when you have developed leaders and have successfully implemented improvement projects linked to your deployed hoshin, but have not followed up with systematic visual control, or have not conducted process reviews as an integral part of your quality or business operating system, or have not completed at least one president's diagnosis. Level 3 means you are still in the Do phase.
  Except for purposes of diagnosing the human resource systems from a companywide perspective, leadership development does not need to follow strictly the methods described in Chapter 6; but there should be evidence of a systematic approach to training and coaching. Except for the hoshin team's diagnosis of the business operating system category, a "president's diagnosis" does not have to be a companywide diagnosis; but it should at least employ a well-developed set of diagnostic categories and criteria.

- *Level 4.* This occurs when the company has first met the criteria for a Level 3 in all categories of diagnosis, implemented systematic visual controls, integrated hoshin reviews into the quality or business operating system, and has completed a president's diagnosis but has not formally trained everyone in PDCA or has not integrated leadership certification (using one of the methods I describe) into succession planning. That is, you're still in the *Check* phase.

The requirements of achieving a Level 4 in any category or subcategory are to be applied strictly. Often a talented CEO or plant manager can, through force of personality, achieve world class results by aggressively implementing world class methods and tools. Without putting into place a business operating system based on hoshin kanri or systematically developing human resources with an eye to the future, however, it is doubtful that the company will able to sustain those results once the personality behind them is no longer a part of the picture. A Level 3 is the highest that any tactical, operational, or action team should be permitted to claim without evidence of a companywide Level 3 in the general management categories of the business operating system, finance and accounting, human resources, information management, and quality. By this measure, of course, extremely few companies in the world today quality for Level 4 in any of the categories of the president's diagnosis.

- **Level 5.** For a company to achieve this category is extremely rare. Level 5 is after all the level of continuous improvement, which, by definition, is never complete.

  Even once attained, a Level 5 is often transitory. Moreover, it is virtually impossible to be a "5" in all categories simultaneously, nor is it particularly desirable. To achieve a Level 5 in a particular category requires first of all a solid foundation, namely, the achievement of a Level 4 in all other categories. It also requires an enormous creative effort that requires a great deal of focus—the focus of hoshin kanri. In fact, evidence of creativity is ultimately what supports a certification at Level 5. A company, or an individual team, must demonstrate that it is routinely creating new competitive capabilities that literally break the rules, redefining the game of business.

Diagnostic team members will often disagree about scores, especially when the company first begins the diagnostic process. Be patient enough to let team members educate each other about their different points of view. If the answer isn't obvious from the criteria in the progress tables, apply the criteria in the transformation ruler. Identify the PDCA method or methods that the unit is attempting to develop and review evidence that the team can plan, do, check, and act.

Don't average scores to make the process of agreement easier. Averaging scores gives an unrealistic picture of a team's systematic development. The levels of the transformation ruler and progress tables rest upon one another, like floors of a building. In order to move from *plan* to *do*, for example, you must lay the foundation by satisfying all of the criteria for *plan*. To move from *do* to *check*, you must satisfy all the criteria for *do*. The development of the proper systems is what makes the results *sustainable*. This is why Levels 4 and 5 require much more than aggressive implementation from the company's leaders. Many Fortune 100 companies can *plan* and *do*, but they never *check* or *act*. In other words, they fail both to verify the replicability of their strategic experiments and to ensure that succeeding generations of managers and employees adhere to new standards based upon new organizational knowledge. In terms of organizational learning, plan-do companies literally forget what they have learned, consigning themselves to solving the same problems again and again. To avoid this conundrum, the general rule is for teams to score themselves (or, in the case of an external diagnosis, to score the team under review) at a *lower* level of development rather than building a false sense of accomplishment about the company's capabilities.

Once the team agrees on scores, it needs to generate a *radar chart* to display the scores in multiple categories or subcategories. Posted on visual project management boards, diagnostic radar charts provide important feedback, reminding employees and managers of the company's lean management status and inspiring continuous improvement in every part of the organization.

Returning to our Cybernautx case example, we look at how their marketing tactical team scored its criteria in a president's diagnosis.

Cybernautx Marketing End-of-Year Diagnosis

As part of its annual review, the Cybernautx marketing tactical team performed a diagnosis of its capabilities in marketing (see Figure 8-2) with a corresponding radar chart, comparing this year's diagnosis to last year's diagnosis (see Figure 8-3). The marketing department has fulfilled all the requirements of Level three, *check*, for every subcategory except supplier of choice. Although there was strong pressure to award the department a "3", the tactical team leader decided on a "2."

Stage 2: Conduct the President's Diagnosis

In preparation for the annual president's diagnosis, the hoshin team reviews and interprets the scores from the earlier self-diagnoses conducted in Stage 1 and prepares follow-up questions. The team circulates these questions to the tactical, operation, and action teams' chosen site visits in this second stage of the president's diagnosis process. After completing the site visits, the hoshin diagnostic team determines overall scores for the company and communicates these scores to the teams under review, together with written recommendations.

Hoshin, Tactical, Operational, and Action Team Exercises: Follow the headings and instructions below. From here, the hoshin team will notify each team chosen for review, as well as submit questions. The teams chosen for review will prepare a previsit report that addresses the questions submitted by the hoshin team. You will then have the president of the company prepare questions for each of the eleven criteria in the transformation ruler. The hoshin teams must then "go see" each of the chosen teams and then return to the company headquarters to calculate a companywide score using the diagnostic progress tables. To reinforce its verbal coaching and mentoring during the process, the hoshin team will provide written feedback. Step 3 of president's diagnosis is to recognize achievement. Never overlook this step.

Hoshin Team Site Visits

Your company's president should, of course, be the hoshin team leader. Toyota's president visits each of his facilities every year. So should your company's president. If your company is bigger than Toyota, or if you have an unmanageable number of sites, your president may need to delegate some of the diagnostic site visits to his or her direct reports.

As we noted above in discussing Stage 1, site visits by an external team need not be limited to the hoshin team. Tactical teams may visit operational team sites, and so forth. In addition, supply chain managers use the president's diagnosis to diagnose a supplier's engineering or manufacturing operations. With minor exceptions, all diagnostic team leaders follow the same procedures as the company president would if the diagnosis were companywide. No

Figure 8-2. Diagnisis of Cybernautx's Competitive Resource Development for Marketing as of Last Year

□ = last year's score   ○ = this year's score

	scan (mass)	plan	do	check	act (lean)
	1	2	3	4	5
Marketing & Sales					
Management		2	3		
Finance & Accounting		2	3		
People are the Key		2	3		
Supply Chain Management		2 / 2			
Information Systems		2	3		
Quality		2	3		
Voice of the Customer		2	3		
Market Segmentation		2	3		
Marketing & Sales Methods		2	3		
Perfect Service		2	3		
Knowledge of the Customer			3 / 3		
Brand Equity		2	3		

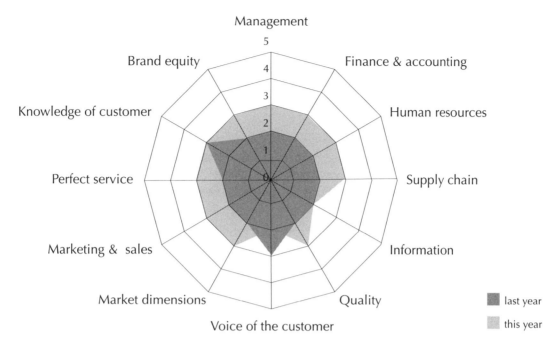

Figure 8-3. Marketing Radar Chart

matter what the focus you have or who is in charge, *all* visiting teams should be cross-functional. Your external diagnosis will have a higher degree of validity if you bring together a group of managers drawn from a variety of functions or management levels in your business unit. These points are particularly important if you're diagnosing a supplier.

Hoshin Team Notifies the Team Under Review and Submits Questions Before Site Visit

The president's diagnosis isn't a pop quiz. It's a milestone in your organizational learning process. The hoshin team notifies the team to be reviewed weeks before it visits. The hoshin team submits its questions and criteria as well as the site visit agenda at that time, so that the team chosen for review has plenty of time to prepare.

Team Under Review Prepares Previsit Report for Hoshin Team

Prior to the president's visit, the tactical, operational, or action team under review prepares a special report that addresses the questions submitted by the hoshin team. This is so the president and the hoshin team can review the team report in preparation for the site visit. The report tells what the team under review has done to carry out improvement activities in the previous improvement cycle, describes results, and explains why they do or don't meet the assigned targets. Make the report short, concrete, and to the point, with no more than two pages per hour of scheduled site visit. Brevity promotes useful interaction among the hoshin team, all teams that the hoshin team will visit, and all individual team members. Long-winded reports leave little to discuss with the hoshin team. Previsit reports may of course be supported with related A3s, attached as an appendix.

Though the remainder of the president's diagnosis follows the same steps as a team self-diagnosis, the focus of Stage 2 of the president's diagnosis is on the integration and vitality of the systems of self-diagnosis as well as progress in the development of resources and capabilities. Have teams applied the criteria properly? Is it time to update the criteria?

President Prepares Questions for the Diagnostic Forms

For the companywide diagnosis, the president should prepare questions for each of the eleven criteria in the transformation ruler. The questions may be on a broader level than the questions used in the team self-diagnosis in Stage 1. For example, the president's team should be sure to include questions addressing the firm's strategy process. This will ensure a balanced approach to monitoring important factors in the lean management transformation.

Hoshin Team Schedules a "Go See"

Schedule a full day to visit an entire plant or technical center. If the team diagnosed is an operational or action team, the visit may be shorter. When the hoshin team is on-site, remember that its purpose is to develop competitive resources through teaching, coaching, and mentoring—not to lay blame for poor performance on scapegoats. Always remember that diagnosis is primarily a fact-gathering exercise, not a bully pulpit. Listen with purpose and employ active listening skills to put team members at ease and promote open dialogue.

Active Listening Guidelines

- Open site visit meetings with these ground rules:
    - Start and stop on time.
    - Keep comments focused on the topic.
    - Share freely and ask questions.
    - Take risks—by thinking about and doing things differently.
    - Provide constructive feedback.
    - Respect each others' ideas and feelings.
    - Focus on data, not opinions.
    - Eliminate rank—all members are lieutenants.
- Encourage everyone to participate.
- Address people by name and give them an opportunity to speak.
- Make eye contact with the people who are speaking to you.
- Try to understand what people are saying from their point of view.
- Paraphrase or rephrase what has been said before you respond.
- Seek clarification by admitting that you may not understand what has been said.
- Try to remain neutral until all points of view have been presented.

Coach and Mentor

Be alert for teachable moments with employees on the team and use them well. Although a diagnosis may not be a bully pulpit, the hoshin team—or, for that matter, any team making an external diagnosis—needs to make coaching and mentoring part of what it does during its site visits. This is a technique much loved by GE's former CEO Jack Welch. Focus on the most important issues. State how a problem could have been handled better or a method could have been applied with better results. If possible, physically demonstrate what you mean to show. Otherwise, give positive examples. Time may not permit employees to show you that they grasp the diagnostic team's point, but confirm the understanding verbally. Assure employees that you will be watching, in a helpful way. Over time, as you develop trust, this simple coaching routine will grow into a mentoring relationship. Your employees will come to view you as a partner in learning.

Hoshin Team Reaches a Companywide Score

Immediately after each site visit, the hoshin team meets in a conference room to determine scores for the team. The team will follow the same instructions laid out for self-diagnosis in Stage 1. Once again, use a qualified consensus rule to reach final scores and don't average scores.

When the hoshin team returns to the company headquarters, it will calculate a companywide score. The transformation ruler makes this a simple task. The ruler's diagnostic categories and progress allow the hoshin team to combine information from the executive, sales and marketing, engineering, manufacturing, and supply chain functions. When scoring conflicts arise, use the same "no averaging" and "least developed" rules applied during the self-diagnosis. For example, if your functions have multiple sites, use the score from your least developed site. Remember: A system is no stronger that its weakest link.

While a companywide score is a good index of overall development, a radar chart provides more information about the pattern of development. Like an index, a radar chart can be seen "at a glance." Figure 8-4 shows a radar chart comparison of Cybernautx's annual diagnoses.

Figure 8-4. Comparison of Cybernautx's Annual Diagnosis

Diagnosing the Supply Chain

Companies can use the methodology of the president's diagnosis to diagnosis the status and pace of resource development of their suppliers. Be sure to provide adequate notice and training in the diagnostic criteria and scoring well in advance of your site visit. Encourage the supplier to conduct a self-diagnosis beforehand. Below is the annual diagnosis for Cybernautx's supplier, Nonesuch Casting.

> ### Nonesuch Casting's Annual Diagnosis
>
> During the year Cybernautx conducted a diagnosis of the Nonesuch manufacturing department. The results weren't bad, although Nonesuch thought that the Cybernautx diagnostic team was a little tough (see Figure 8-5). A president's diagnosis is an excellent supplement to the more usual measures of supplier quality, cost, and delivery. For many years, Toyota has used diagnostic criteria to promote the adoption of the Toyota Production System, to screen its suppliers and to identify those that have potential for serious, long-term collaboration. For a good facsimile of Toyota's criteria, see Hiroyuki Hirano's *JIT Implementation Manual* (Productivity Press).

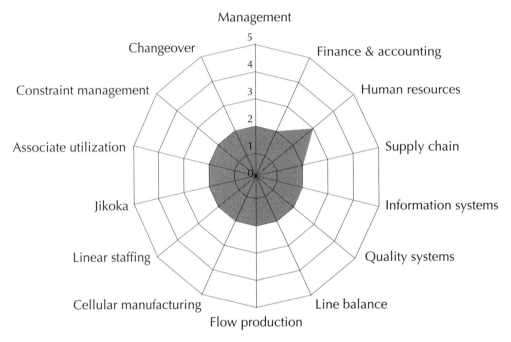

Figure 8-5. Cybernautx's Diagnosis of Nonesuch Casting

Hoshin Team Provides Written Feedback

To reinforce verbal coaching and mentoring given during the president's diagnosis, the hoshin team gives written feedback after the president's diagnosis when it transmits its scores to the tactical, operational, and action teams included in its round of site visits. You've determined a score for each team visited. Now review the picture that has emerged with the team's leaders. Identify positive results and achievements, identify improvement areas, offer implementation insights, and prescribe short-term actions and further research or training if necessary. Summarize your observations and prepare a report for the team. Be sure to develop action plans for each performance gap or weak area identified. Take immediate action where appropriate. Submit any long-term recommendations for the team to include as a part of the next year's hoshin. Whether a team has done well or poorly doesn't matter. Reinforce the positive, and suggest ways to improve whatever needs to or might be improved.

Stage 3: Recognize Achievement

To build a lean culture is to build a vital community of scientists. As we know from history, scientific investigation requires an atmosphere of collegiality and openness. So encourage development by emphasizing the positive. Once you complete the president's diagnosis, recognize the achievement of all teams and celebrate their success. Celebration is the best way to recognize the hard work of the previous year and brings together the various teams, units, and departments as one company working on a set of integrated goals.

During the team self-diagnosis in Stage 1, whenever a tactical team diagnoses an operational team, or when an operational team diagnoses an action time, the team conducting the diagnosis needs to hold a team lunch or dinner for the team that has been diagnosed to celebrate progress and to reinforce coaching and mentoring relationships. After completing the companywide diagnosis in Stage 2, the hoshin team should consider holding a conference at which exceptional teams make presentations. You may want to announce new levels of certification or offer special awards or other forms of recognition to those teams that have performed exceptionally well.

CHAPTER NINE

ACT: Institutionalizing Hoshin Kanri Through Standardized Work, Kaizen, and Leadership Development

Chapter 9 addresses the *Act* cycle and Experiment 7 of hoshin kanri so that organizations can institutionalize the hoshin system itself along with any new technologies and methodologies that you've identified in your midterm strategy and annual hoshin. The first step toward institutionalizing any process improvement is to adhere to the new standards that define it. This means the key to understanding the *Act* phase of hoshin kanri lies in the concept of standardized work, the bedrock of both lean enterprise and six sigma.

In this chapter, we will first look at how hoshin kanri effectively creates three types of standardized work at three different levels of organizational activity. We will also review the scientific meaning of adherence to standards, which creates controlled conditions for conducting each of the 7 experiments of the hoshin system. Then we look at Experiment 7 of the hoshin system: kaizen, which begins only once an organization has systematically implemented standardized work companywide. Finally, the *Act* cycle of hoshin requires that companies form a system of teachable moments and mentoring relationships. These are the key to making hoshin kanri—or any methodology, for that matter—a permanent part of your business culture.

STANDARDIZED WORK

Most often people think of standardization as pertaining to processes carried out by workers on the front line of value creation, be it in the context of the manufacturing or service industry; and this is perfectly true. Every employee engaged in creating value for customers is expected to execute repetitive processes in exactly the same way, following specific steps in an exact sequence each time the process is repeated. A standard usually represents the best way that the organization knows how to do something at any given moment in time. Assuming that the standard is a good one (we only know for sure by trying it out), this ensures a quality product. Furthermore, in a lean environment, in order to minimize waste in the process, employees execute each step within a specific window of time related to customer demand. More rigorous definitions of standardized work add another requirement, namely, that each step in a repetitive process be carried out with a strictly defined amount of work-in-process (WIP) inventory. This effectively standardizes process lead times from the perspective of how material (or information) flows from the beginning to the end of a process, because a larger amount of inventory in raw material, WIP, or finished goods will result in longer lead times.

Normally, standardized work isn't classified as part of the system of hoshin kanri. In fact, many companies that attempt to implement hoshin kanri, or parts of hoshin kanri, neither practice standardized work nor have a serious commitment to do so in the future. This is a serious error. The fact is that you can view hoshin kanri itself as *a comprehensive system of standardized work*. Hoshin kanri effectively generalizes the basic concept of standardized work to every type of job, process, and value stream. Hoshin views the work of every manager as being standardized in much the same way that the work of production workers is standardized. In a mature lean enterprise, you always define the current state in terms of standardized work, which regulates the sequence and timing as well as content of tasks and, as we will argue, business processes and even entire value streams.

As discussed below, Table 9-1 shows that there are basically three levels of standardization (A, B, C on the table), each governed by at least two of the 7 experiments. Process standards are frequently documented by means of value stream or process maps that fix process or task content, sequence, timing, and standard inventories.

- *Standardization Level A:* The first level of standardization is the normal level of standardized daily work, which regulates the content, timing, and sequence of discrete human (or machine) tasks in a business subprocess. You would normally find the process standards for this level of activity in a wide variety of standard operating procedures and current state process maps. In a lean manufacturing process, for example, process standards would be mapped using process capacity tables, line balance charts, and standard work combination sheets. (See, e.g., Hirano's *JIT Implementation Manual*, Productivity Press, 1989, section 16.)
- *Standardization Level B:* The second level of standardization occurs within the processes of individual business functions such as marketing, engineering, or manufacturing. Good examples of this type of standardization include the current state value stream maps of marketing, engineering, and manufacturing that appear in Chapter 2, Figures 2-5, 2-6, and 2-7.
- *Standardization Level C:* The third level of standardization is companywide. It defines cross-functional and interorganizational business macroprocesses that require the coordination of internal business functions and external organizations, such as customers and suppliers. A good example of this type of standardization includes the enterprise level current state process map in Figure 2-4.

If you look at Table 9-1 from the perspective of value stream mapping, it is evident that standardized work is fractal, which means that it's the same at every level, from macro to micro. Every level of mapping around the three levels of standardized work outlined in Table 9-1, is concerned with exactly the same four things:

1. The content of each "task" (which may be a "process" at the level of strategy, tactics, and operations)
2. The sequence of the tasks or processes
3. The timing of the tasks or process
4. Standard WIP inventory in between each task or process

Value Stream Mapping Tip: Current state value stream maps are effectively process standards for business macroprocesses and functional processes because they document standard task content, sequence, timing, and inventories. Interim and future state maps are created when management determines that processes must be adapted. As hoshin, tactical, and operational teams complete planned process changes, the teams update their current state maps to reflect actual practice. Ideally, in keeping with the

Table 9-1. The 7 Experiments in the Context of Standardized Work

Team		Hoshin experiment	Definition of the experiment	Type of improvement		Type of standardized work improved by the experiment	
Hoshin Team	1	Long-term strategy	A general plan of action that aims over a very long period of time—5 to 100 years—to make major changes or adjustments in the mission and/or vision of the business.	Periodic; quantum leap	A	Companywide processes and enterprise-level interactions	Standardized companywide and enterprise-wide interorganizational business processes, e.g., new product launch and supply chain management and integration
Hoshin Team	2	Midterm strategy	A partially complete plan of action including financial targets and measures of process improvement that aims over 3 to 5 years to develop capabilities and align the trajectory of business operations with the long-term strategy.	Periodic; quantum leap	A		
Hoshin Team	3	Annual hoshin	A highly concrete plan of action that aims over the next 6 to 18 months to develop competitive capabilities and align the trajectory of business operations in accordance with the midterm strategy.	Periodic; quantum leap	A		
Tactical Teams	4	Tactics	Concrete initiatives of 6 to 18 months, defined by the annual hoshin, undertaken to make develop specific new capabilities by applying new technologies and methodologies to general business processes.	Periodic; quantum leap	B	Functional processes and crossfunctional interations	Standardized processes of business functions such as the processes of marketing, engineering, etc., including their interaction with other business functions and/or organizations
Operational Teams	5	Operations	Concrete projects of 3 to 6 months, defined by the annual hoshin, undertaken to apply new technologies and methodologies to standardized processes of specific business functions.	Periodic; quantum leap	B		
Action Teams	6	Kaikaku	Concrete projects of 1 week to 3 months, usually defined after the deployment of the annual hoshin, undertaken to apply new tools and techniques in standardized daily work.	Periodic; quantum leap	C	Functional subprocesses and crossfunctional interactions	Standardized daily work, i.e., the regulation of the content, sequence, and timing of discrete tasks that define individual subprocesses and jobs
Action Teams	7	Kaizen	Problem solving in more or less real time to address defects, errors, and abnormalities that arise in the course of standardized daily work, as well as improvements resulting from employee suggestions.	Continuous; incremental	C		

principles of visual management, the teams display their current state maps in the work area for team members, other employees, suppliers, and customers to see. Many companies that practice value stream mapping fail to keep their current state maps up-to-date and thus have not documented their current standard process.

Meanwhile, interim and future state maps don't function as process standards because they do not represent current best practice. They are part of project plans to improve the current standard. Until they're actually executed, interim and future state maps represent nothing more than process improvement targets.

THE SCIENTIFIC MEANING OF STANDARDIZED WORK

The obvious point to having standards, of course, is to detect deviations from them, and to correct them as quickly as possible, ideally in real time. In a lean enterprise, these deviations include the occurrence of three evils: product defects, human errors, and abnormal process conditions.

1. *Product defects.* This entails deviations from value stream or process standards such as product standards of quality, cost, and delivery, as well as standard inventory levels and compliance with environmental and regulatory standards. For purposes of hoshin kanri, defects also include deviations from targets established by the midterm strategy and the annual hoshin, and recorded in the A3-Xs and A3-Ts.
2. *Human errors.* Deviations from standard operating procedures for any job or process, or from the critical path of any project, including hoshin, tactical, operational, and action team projects.
3. *Abnormal conditions.* These are deviations from standard conditions (including equipment conditions, safety conditions, or even general business conditions) that may lead to defects and/or errors. For purposes of hoshin kanri, abnormal conditions also include deviations from the conditions documented or assumed as a basis for the long-term and midterm strategies, the annual hoshin, and all hoshin projects.

The detection and correction of defects, errors, and abnormalities is the whole meaning of the concept of a learning organization.[1] Moreover, adherence to standards is *an absolute prerequisite for the scientific investigation of problems.* Without either the establishment or routine *adherence* to standards, *all* data—about how work was performed, the condition of equipment and processes, etc.—would be suspect. Investigating problems would be impossible. Even a room full of information technology specialists and Nobel laureates could do nothing more than speculate about causes and causal mechanisms. Without standardization, scientific experiments in continuous improvement would not be replicable. In other words, it's impossible to complete the *check* phase of the PDCA cycle. Not even spending tens or even hundreds of millions of dollars on enterprise resource planning (ERP) systems can change the fundamental scientific requirements of standardized measurement and controlled conditions.

---

1. See Chris Argyris and Donald Shön, *Organizational learning: A theory of action perspective.* (Reading, Mass: Addison Wesley, 1978). A decade after Bridgestone Tire won the Deming Prize for codifying hoshin kanri, Argyris and Shön defined organizational learning as "the detection and correction of error."

The Story of Dr. Ram

I once had a friend in India, a statistician named Dr. Ramachandrudu. We will call him "Dr. Ram" for short. Dr. Ram was a well-known quality control guru who always asked his clients—some of India's biggest companies—two questions: (1) Do you have standards? and (2) Do you adhere to those standards? It was not enough for clients to be ISO certified if they only made a show of adhering to standards once a year, when the ISO auditor visited. Dr. Ram claimed, rightly, that his clients would be wasting their money if they paid him to apply even basic statistics where there were no standards or *adherence* to standards. The reason? Within a quality system, data are generated by *deviations* from standards. Like the Tyrannosaurus Rex in the movie *Jurassic Park*, scientists can only "see" something if it *moves*—and as Einstein taught us, all motion is *relative*. Meaningful data do not exist *per se*; they are created through *measurement*. Scientifically speaking, nothing can be measured in a workplace where there are neither standards nor adherence to standards. Data observed in such a workplace are inherently flawed.

In Chapter 7, we have already addressed the manner in which hoshin kanri deals with the discovery and, to a certain extent, the correction of error. Visual management and regular meetings are primary mechanisms that promote adherence to standards. In particular, visual management ensures that there is as little ambiguity as possible about the status of any process. Ideally, it should be clear—at any level of activity and at all times—whether a process is in control or out of control. The role of visual management is absolutely critical. Knowledgeable practitioners of lean strive to create work environments (in both production and administration) in which defects, errors, and abnormal conditions are immediately clear, and thus trigger immediate corrective action. The quintessential visual management tool is poka yoke, or mistake proofing, which actually builds detection into work processes *physically*, so that the very presence of a defect, error, or abnormality triggers a physical signal, which in turn triggers the appropriate correction. Poka yoke devices can also trigger preventative action automatically, without the intervention of managers or workers. By relying extensively on poka yoke throughout their operations, lean enterprises in effect *automate* adherence to standards.

KAIZEN: EXPERIMENT 7 OF HOSHIN KANRI

Thus far, we have examined six of the seven experiments of the hoshin system. As we saw in Table 9-1, the first six experiments all focus on making discontinuous or periodic improvements in business macroprocesses, functional processes, and functional subprocesses. Such changes are normally discontinuous, because changes in the business environment that call for adjustments in company strategy are often difficult to anticipate or understand. Kaikaku, the sixth experiment of hoshin, is normally focused on business subprocesses. The most famous example of kaikaku is "five days and one night," the inappropriately named "kaizen blitz," in which several manufacturing operations (such as welding, assembly, and packaging) are combined into a single U-shaped production cell in a single week. Kaikaku events such as "five days and one night" can happen in an ad hoc manner, but within the framework of hoshin kanri they would normally be executed according to an action team plan aligned to the overall process improvement and financial targets of the annual hoshin.

Kaizen, the seventh experiment of the hoshin system, is anything but a blitz; and it is not necessarily linked formally to the annual hoshin. In fact, like standardized work, kaizen is not normally classified as part of the hoshin system. Based upon PDCA, kaizen is the continuous, incremental improvement of standardized work. While standardized work in itself can assure quality, at least for a time, it cannot ensure organizational vitality, and that vitality is the motivating force of lean enterprise. Every technique of the lean enterprise bears the stamp of PDCA and thus of kaizen, for once installed, lean methodologies are expected to *evolve*. Adherence to standards is simply not enough. The most compelling evidence for this statement lies in Toyota's famed practice of "one less." As we have seen, standardized work standardizes inventory levels, among other things. Jesus taught, "Sufficient unto the day is the evil thereof" (Matthew 6:34). Toyota disagrees. On any given day, if things are going well on the production floor, Toyota managers may decide to reduce current inventories by "one." The purpose of this exercise is to expose quality issues, equipment problems, and other bad news that stockpiles of inventory tend to hide. Inventory reduction continues "one" by "one," until problems begin to emerge, and then Toyota's problem solvers, idled by a system once under control, get to work again. This is the attitude of kaizen: Constantly push the envelope.

So important is kaizen in a lean culture that lean companies strictly separate the work of human beings from the work of machines (through the poorly understood practice of *jidoka*[2]). In a lean enterprise, machines make product; people manage the process. People are paid not to lift and carry (the wastes of motion and transportation, respectively), but to use their eyes, ears, and brains to continuously improve the process by identifying and solving problems. Kaizen defines a new and human use of human beings. Kaizen is lean thinking at idle. It's the lean enterprise breathing in and breathing out. Standardized work is merely the transmission that transfers the energy and creativity of managers and employees to value-adding processes, and ultimately to the customer.

Kaizen Implementation Tip: John Allen, former Director of Training at Toyota's Georgetown, Kentucky, facility, once explained to me that in setting up the Georgetown facility, Toyota trained literally everyone at the site in PDCA, but only *after* the installation of the Toyota Production System had been completed. The installation process had taken two years, and defined standardized work at all three levels described in Table 9-1. Only then could kaizen begin. This means, of course, that what most companies believe is "kaizen" is nothing more than catch-up. In other words, they are using "kaikaku" to install standardized work, frequently without success. To succeed in implementing standardized work, one must implement it systematically. Moreover, there must adherence to standards, just as Dr. Ram advised his clients in India. (See "The Story of Dr. Ram" above.) Once an organization learns to adhere faithfully to standards, continuous improvement may begin. To succeed, this improvement must be based upon a solid foundation of training in the scientific method. Many companies, under pressure from Wall Street, will not have the financial courage to spend enough training dollars to train everyone. They will look for "cost-effective" alternatives to Toyota's massive investments in human resources. They will also pay the price: Namely, they will be slow learners. Some will say that Ford and GM are already paying this price, with major

---

2. *Jidoka* or autonomation is one of the two pillars of the Toyota Production System. The method, which relies heavily on the use of small scale automation and *poka yoke* or mistake-proofing devices, aims at creating an environment in which production operators can safely and effectively operate multiple machines arrayed in just-in-time production cells. One important measure of autonomation is the ability of equipment to cycle through breaks, through lunch, or between shifts without attendants. Autonomation frees workers from waiting and monitoring. This not only permits operators to focus on performing standardized work correctly, it permits workers to observe and think about process and equipment conditions that affect process flow and product quality.

consequences for their stakeholders. When it comes to kaizen, organizations must be patient, think long-term, and have the courage to train workers sufficiently as PDCA scientists to make science the bedrock of their lean culture. Finally, once the training dollars have been spent, take care to treat your new, improved human assets well. These assets have legs, which is why accountants won't let you carry them on your balance sheet.

Many companies confuse the implementation of lean enterprise and six sigma with kaizen. Kaizen is not a means to becoming lean. It's the hallmark of the mature lean enterprise. The culture of kaizen—a culture in which every employee is a trained scientist engaged in the network of the seven experiments of the hoshin system—is a paramount goal of implementing lean methodologies and, of course, hoshin kanri. Implementation proceeds primarily through discontinuous leaps, that is, through kaikaku. The first leap must be to establish standardized work and thereby establish the controlled conditions upon which kaizen must be based. Companies that use hoshin primarily to develop competitive resources without concentrating on standardized work face almost certain failure, because standardized work is the essence of institutional memory. For all intents and purposes, standards that you neither document nor adhere to are forgotten.

Another way of looking at institutionalizing your improvements primarily through kaizen is to see the whole purpose of kaizen as the way for a company to maintain a vital system of learning. In this context, you can view institutionalization in terms of information processing and memory. If you use knowledge without reflection, eventually it's forgotten, even though the decline (as in ancient Egypt, for example) may be glacially slow. Knowledge that you use critically, with an eye to improvement, is less likely to be forgotten, because current knowledge (in the form of adherence to standards) creates the controlled conditions required for learning. This suggests that institutionalization has at least two steps:

1. Remembering, or adherence to standards
2. Learning, or continuous improvement

This is not to diminish the potential of hoshin kanri in managing strategic change. While hoshin can definitely mobilize management to make great changes, it is ultimately the hourly workforce—trained as PDCA scientists—that must maintain any new technologies and methodologies once they've been installed. Moreover, the results of strategic change will be far less than they can be when they're based on the real-time discovery and resolution of defects, errors, and abnormalities that only standardized work and kaizen can ensure.

Hoshin Team Exercise: The best way to test for adherence to standards and continuous improvement is, of course, to conduct a complete president's diagnosis using the transformation ruler contained on the Companion CD. In the meantime, simply "go see" by participating in a "kaizen" event in one of your facilities. Dress the part: Jeans and a sports shirt. Leave the suit and tie behind. Prepare to be a team member, not a team leader, for four to five days. The best events for this purpose deal directly with the standardized daily work of hourly associates, not high-level business processes. Avoid choosing your "best" facility for this exercise. Choose an "average" or "poor" facility. An event focusing on just-in-time production and cellular manufacturing is ideal, but any events focusing on repetitive processes (whether in manufacturing or service) would be fine.

The event facilitator—who will be a lean coordinator, a six sigma black belt, or perhaps an external sensei—will engage your team in a scientific investigation of task, sequence, and (in a lean event) timing, and work-in-process inventory. You will be provided with tools to record and analyze observations. (Remember, all lean methods and tools are based on PDCA.) Strongly resist the urge to control the situation, which will very probably be out of control, statistically (and in other ways, too). When you realize that no one does the same job the same way twice, don't look for scapegoats. Remember Deming's admonishment: It's the system, not the people. Trust the PDCA process. Work with side by side with your employees to observe, experiment, validate, and finally communicate your findings to the local management team.

The famous Japanese lean consultancy, Shingijutsu, insists that its clients' presidents and executive staff attend shop floor kaizen events, and so does my own consulting firm, taktX. In fact, my partners and I expect our clients' executives to study long and hard enough to teach these events themselves, from time to time, as a powerful demonstration of the commitment to becoming lean.

LEADERSHIP DEVELOPMENT AND SUCCESSION PLANNING

Several years ago I shared the podium with Mike DaPrile, executive vice president of Toyota, at a conference on lean manufacturing in Rochester, New York. A member of the audience asked Mr. DaPrile a question that made me sit up straight in my chair with anticipation. "What do you do?" the conference attendee asked. "I develop leaders," replied Mr. DaPrile. In other words, in his job DaPrile focuses on developing the next generation of leaders.

As one might expect, PDCA is at the heart of Toyota's leadership development process. In Steven Spear's article, "Learning to Lead at Toyota" (*Harvard Business Review*, May 24, 2004), he describes the long and surprisingly rigorous process that one American "hotshot" lived through to become a top level Toyota manager. On arriving at Toyota, the new manager was greeted by a sensei, a master of the Toyota Production System, who was to be with his new student through fourteen weeks of education and shopfloor projects. The sensei asked the student to "help a small group of 19 engine-assembly workers improve labor productivity, operational availability [the ratio of machine run time to its actual use] of machines and equipment, and ergonomic safety." Each week of the apprenticeship started and concluded with a meeting between student and sensei. On Monday, the student explained the manufacturing process he was expected to improve and the methods by which he expected to improve it. On Friday, the student explained whether or not his methods had worked, and if they had not, how they had failed. The student threw himself into the project, believing that it was his job to solve problems and make improvements himself. After all, he had two master's degrees in engineering from leading schools in the United States. At the end of the first twelve weeks of instruction, the student had made important progress, but had not reached the goals set by the sensei at the beginning of the education process. At this point, Toyota flew the student to Japan and asked him to work on the shop floor in one of Toyota's best plants. The student again tried to solve problems on his own, without engaging the hourly workers. His sensei informed him that the shopfloor workers he was trying to help had already come up with over 90 percent of the improvement ideas that the student had "discovered." After two weeks in Japan, Toyota's shopfloor leaders taught the student that instead of fixing problems himself, he should coach workers to fix problems themselves using the scientific method. Like Mike DaPrile, the new manager's job was not to be a boss and solve problems. His job was to develop leaders empowered to improve Toyota's processes on their own. Using this new knowledge upon his return to the United States, he was able to coach his American team to reach the goals set by the sensei months before.

The point to this story is that the institutionalization of hoshin kanri and lean thinking occurs in the process of leadership development and management succession. Managers who assume positions within the hierarchy must know that they too are there not to solve problems, but to develop leaders. *Succession planning*, therefore, is a critical element in institutionalizing hoshin kanri and lean thinking. Promoting the wrong sort of people can quickly lead to the "program of the month" syndrome so familiar in Western companies. In addition, succession planning must incorporate lean leadership development and certification programs, supplemented as necessary by the comprehensive development programs described in Chapter 6. The tendency in Western companies, of course, is to promote managers who get results any way they can. Often these managers have little knowledge of the processes they are managing, or of how to improve them. In a lean enterprise, it's clear that knowledge of lean processes and lean thinking are absolute prerequisites of promotion, and there are well-developed systems of education and coaching to ensure that those who rise within the organization have grasped the DNA of lean enterprise and *can effectively transmit it to others*.

Hoshin Team Exercise: Have the hoshin team review your current succession plans for top- and midlevel managers. Do promotions require any sort of certification in lean methodologies? Is hoshin kanri on the list? Are certification methods specified? Are they the same as or similar to the methods described in Chapter 6? What would Toyota's sensei in the story above have to say about your succession plan? Based on this investigation, have the team discuss changes that should be made to its succession plan to ensure that your company is capable of institutionalizing hoshin kanri and lean thinking.

THE COACHING PROCESS

In the *do* phase of hoshin, you saw how teaching is an extension of the deployment process. Coaching means helping someone to do a better job of what he or she is trying to do. The objective of coaching is not to solve the problem but to help the person you're coaching develop the ability to solve problems themselves (see Table 9-2). *Show* your students (employees) how to do a better job and don't just criticize. In the end, your employees must understand *why* their good work succeeded, so they can be successful again in the future. Coaching is the perfect complement to teaching. It provides learners with a support mechanism to encourage them to do what they know and to remind them when they forget.

Coaching follows the familiar PDCA cycle. As was the case with the techniques of training that we covered Chapter 6 in the *do* phase, much of what we know about coaching can be traced to Charles Allen and *Training Within Industry* (TWI). Hands-on learning, coaching, mentoring—all these techniques were part of America's economic response to World War I and World War II. The techniques worked then and—if Toyota's success in the automotive industry and Canon's success in consumer goods are any indication—they still work today. The two TWI books mentioned in Chapter 6, and listed in Recommended Reading, attest to the ongoing power of TWI.

Table 9-2. Coaching Cycle

plan	Identify the person, team, or organization to be coached, for what purpose, when, and where.
do	Demonstrate the standard or method to be employed.
check	Check results and the process and methods by which the results were achieved.
act	Adjust thinking and behavior by following these steps: • Explain the reasons for and advantages of the new method. • Make sure that everyone understands the principles and concepts of the new method. • Select a problem and work on it together, applying the method. • Recommend corrective action and demonstrate correct methods (conducting retraining or new training as required); propose a new challenge or, better yet, encourage the client to challenge himself. • Ask the person or team to work another problem alone. • Praise good results and reinforce correct methods

Overlapping Teams and Mentoring Relationships

When Mike DaPrile said, "I develop leaders," he might have added, "I teach, coach, and mentor people to teach, coach, and mentor others to achieve the goals of the organization." Mentoring through hoshin kanri is all about developing the next generation of managers and employees, because people are the key to developing the intangible assets of brand, technology, intellectual property, business process, and relationships. Hoshin makes this difficult job easier by creating a system of overlapping teams, minimizing the conflict between the day-to-day concerns of line management and the broader concerns of strategy.

Hoshin kanri not only creates a bundle of contracts and a system of nested experiments, it creates a set of relationships between strategic, tactical, operational, and action team leaders. The team structure of an organization that practices hoshin is often referred to as overlapping, because every manager belongs to a team within the hoshin system. Team leaders at every level in the management hierarchy teach and coach their teams to achieve their hoshin targets. Because these teaching and coaching relationships follow permanent lines of authority, in an organization governed by hoshin kanri these relationships are also permanent. This means that, over time, teaching and coaching become something greater. They become mentoring. A mentor is a trusted coach and advisor, a person who follows your career and helps you learn how to implement new technologies and methods, how to deal with the demands of hoshin projects, or how to advance through the ranks to become a leader of the next generation.

A System of Teachable Moments

The overlapping team structure of hoshin is particularly well suited to the development of leaders who are teachers. In the Introduction and again in Chapter 1, we discussed how hoshin is a system of nested PDCA cycles or experiments. As stated elsewhere in this workbook, you can also view hoshin as *system of teachable moments*. A teachable moment—a phrase coined by University of Michigan professor Noel Tichy and made famous by GE's Jack Welch—is any opportunity for leaders to teach and *mentor* their employees. Coaching is the key to institutionalizing any new method. As Jack Welch rightly insists, coaching can happen anywhere, at any time. Within a lean enterprise, coaching occurs under the following circumstances:

- As part of normal hoshin reviews, for example, as part of daily, weekly, monthly, or quarterly meetings, when tactical or action projects don't meet their targets.

- As part of the implementation of a new method, for example, during or after instruction in some knowledge or skill.
- As part of the execution of standardized daily work, for example, when defects, errors, or abnormalities occur in the normal course of business.

Hoshin kanri systematizes *all* of these moments in a way that uniquely defines lean culture. Table 9-3 describes nine different states of a lean culture, and how these states relate to each other.

Table 9-3. Window Analysis of Lean Culture

A / B	Effective standard known		Effective standard not unknown
	practiced	**not practiced**	
Effective standard known — practiced	**1** SQUARE ONE *The goal of lean enterprise culture*	**2** B reminds and coaches A back to square 1.	**5** B teaches and mentors A into square 2, and then to square 1.
Effective standard known — not practiced	**3** A reminds and coaches B back to square 1.	**4** A and B remind each other to implement the standard and move to back to square 1.	**7** B practices what he preaches and moves to square 5.
Effective standard not known	**6** A teaches and mentors B into square 3, and then to square 1.	**8** A practices what she preaches and moves to square 6.	**9** A or B or both A and B improve or invent the standard and move to square 8, 7, or 4, respectively.

We have labeled the table "window analysis of lean culture" to make an important point. The *Merriam-Webster On-Line Dictionary* defines culture as "the integrated pattern of human knowledge, belief, and behavior that depends upon man's capacity for learning and transmitting knowledge to succeeding generations."[3] This is precisely what hoshin kanri, as a system of teachable moments, achieves. Hoshin integrates this pattern of knowledge, belief,

---

3. See http://www.m-w.com/cgi-bin/dictionary?book=Dictionary&va=culture&x=11&y=11.

and behavior and at the same time promotes the transmission of that knowledge to succeeding generations of managers and employees. In Table 9-3, Square 1 is defined as a state in which *everyone knows effective standards and practices them*. In the world of lean, you measure *everything* in terms of deviations from standardized work. It doesn't matter whether you're talking about your company's vision, your suppliers' deficiencies, or what Joe the operator was supposed to do on third shift. In the diagram A and B represent any combination of individuals, teams, departments, division, or even customers and suppliers. Inside Square 1 they *all* know and practice the same effective standard.

The point to lean culture is to get to Square 1 in the diagram—and stay there. *Deviations* from Square 1, that is, deviations from standardized work, give rise to *teachable moments*. For example, let's say that A is an employee who steps outside of Square 1 because of a defect on the shop floor, or poor on-time delivery, or a kaizen event gone wrong, or a change in the competitive environment that invalidates a particular strategy or tactic in your A3-X. It now becomes B's job to teach and coach A back to Square 1. (B might be a supervisor or coworker, or the plant manager; it doesn't matter.) And as we saw in the *check* phase of the hoshin process, once a deviation is detected, this is exactly what happens. Daily, weekly, monthly, quarterly, and annual meetings, including the president's diagnosis, are all designed as formal teachable moments. The genius of hoshin kanri is that, because of the thoroughgoing process of catchball, it doesn't matter where the deviation occurs or where it's detected. In relatively short order, if not in real time, the entire organization—the entire enterprise—knows what to do and does it. In addition, because of hoshin kanri's "deselection" process, you waste no time or energy on unimportant problems. You're always focused squarely on what really matters.

Shining example of How Hoshin Kanri Drives a Learning Organization: A survey of lean manufacturing in the automotive industry found that all the world's leading automakers have at least one cutting edge, world class plant in their system. It also found that all of Toyota's plants approach this standard. Superior organizational learning appears to be the explanation for this situation. For example, when an improvement is made as the result of a kaizen in one of Toyota's plants, it will be replicated quickly in all of Toyota's plants. In the plants of Toyota's competitors, the rate of knowledge transfer is depressingly slow and ineffective. See "Big Three play catch-up to Toyota plan prowess," *Detroit News Special Report*, Sunday, February 22, 2004.

Find a Sensei

The best way to learn to coach your organization from mass to lean is to find a coach for yourself, a coach who wants to see you win the game. Here are two reasons why you should probably find yourself a sensei—a master of lean methods, including how to teach, coach, and mentor—to be your personal coach:

1. *Coaching a lean transformation requires a total grasp of its voluminous subject matter.* As the Transformation Ruler shows, practically everything about lean enterprise is different from the traditional business structures and practices pioneered by Ford and General Motors early in the 20th century. Although change is afoot in academia, this subject matter is still not taught as a central part of the curricula in schools of business or engineering. In other words, even if you graduated last year, your knowledge is already out of date. For this reason alone, you probably need a sensei,

because lean enterprise is not something you can learn on-line, or by reading a book, or by visiting lean factories (of which there are really very few), and certainly not by going back to college!

2. ***Coaching and mentoring are not skills that you normally learn when you get a master's in business or engineering, or any professional degree for that matter.*** In the "real world," the assumption is that we hire people to do the job, and if they fail, we replace them with other people who can. Developing people—that takes too much time! What we hire in people is performance. But there is a dilemma: Given the current state of our universities, we cannot buy lean human resources "off the shelf." Even if we could, we would need to change out our entire workforce. So we're faced with the prospect of growing our own human resources. What do you get from a sensei?

- *A thorough grasp—practical as well as theoretical—of lean subject matter.* A sensei is a person who has mastered the application of lean principles, concepts, systems, methods, and tools in a wide variety of circumstances. A bona fide sensei will have a grasp, in particular, of hoshin kanri as well as one or more functional lean subject areas, such as lean accounting, lean engineering (including design for six sigma), or lean manufacturing.

- *Experience in teaching how to apply lean principles, concepts, etc., clearly and persuasively at all levels of the organization.* Teaching is not a trivial skill. Teaching lean is more demanding than most teaching, because it requires people to abandon models of thinking and behavior—i.e., being the boss, being the hero, being the genius, etc.—that may have been the basis of much personal success. A sensei can persuade people to experiment with new team-based models of success—new paradigms—by speaking, discussing, demonstrating, and engaging individuals and teams in successful, concerted action.

- *Experience in coaching and mentoring others in learning to apply and teach lean methods, techniques, and tools.* It isn't enough to tell people what to do. You have to show them, more than once. In fact, you have to tell them and show them again and again, in a patient, helpful way, until they grow the new lean capabilities they need. A sensei is a person who coaches with respect and passion for the innate intelligence of human beings.

- *The knowledge of when to do, when to teach, and when to coach.* There is no such thing as "cookbook" lean. Based upon the number of lean cookbooks (including my own), we should all be lean today. But we're not. That's because becoming lean is not a recipe, it's an experience that an entire organization must live through. A sensei knows "when to hold them, when to fold them, and when to walk away." In other words, a sensei is a really good consultant who adapts to the situation at hand.

When you find your sensei, don't be in a hurry. The transformation process takes years, even if you have tried to implement lean before. Depending upon the size of your organization, the initial transfer of knowledge can take place in about 18 months, if you're systematic about it. After that, you should retain the sensei as a coach, first to coach the leaders of your business as they transform each function by teaching and coaching their own teams. It's common practice, for example, to retain a sensei or two to visit factories and engineering tech centers on a monthly or bimonthly basis after the basic training and certification of your internal leaders has been completed. Beyond this, the sensei may be engaged in developing leaders within your supply base. As you become lean, you will require your suppliers—at least your key suppliers—to become lean as well. Finally, your sensei will eventually help you master the five phases hoshin kanri: scan, plan, do, check, and act. In the *Check* phase, you should ask your sensei to attend your quarterly review meetings, and to participate in your annual president's diagnosis. In the *Act* phase, the right sensei will constantly challenge you, and help you to become better—even when you have become the best in the world.

Hoshin Team Leader Exercise: Find a sensei that fits your organization. Leaders must be teachers, coaches, and mentors. How do you measure up in this regard? Several years ago, the managers of Indiana Fasteners, a Japanese transplant serving Toyota, asked the following, pointed question of an American applicant for the position of Vice President: "Are you willing to forget everything you know about manufacturing?" Have the team review the purpose of a sensei. Think about it. Consider the reasons why you should have one, and areas in which management and the organization need mentoring. Review your options, budget, and timetable.

CONCLUSION

Lean guru John Shook has written that *hoshin kanri* is probably as revolutionary as the Toyota Production System. The history of business organization will show that it is more so. For now, however, hoshin kanri is still a kind of secret knowledge. This may not be a bad thing. Many years ago, a colleague of mine conducted a very successful week of kaizen for a client that had just begun the journey of lean transformation. The client happened to notice a blank X-matrix that my colleague was packing into his briefcase. Curiosity piqued, the client asked, "What's this?" "An X-matrix," replied my friend. "What's an X-matrix?" asked the client. "It's what lean organizations use to plan and execute strategy." "May I have a copy?" asked the client, innocently. "No," replied my friend. "You might hurt yourself. You have to be licensed first."

As I mentioned in the introduction, hoshin kanri can be a life-changing experience. In fact, I have a client—a major international company—that decided to completely reorganize as a result of its first contact with hoshin. Therefore, I wish to leave the reader with a few pieces of advice that aspiring lean thinkers should constantly bear in mind before beginning an implementation of hoshin kanri.

- In the long run, profitability is merely a reflection of how successful your organization is at pleasing its customers *better* than your competitors. This is not merely a matter of how good you are at what you do, it is also a matter of how well you organize what you know, and how your people share that knowledge amongst themselves and with your customers and suppliers.
- Lean enterprises use what they know to respond to problems in real time, not after the fact. Then they prevent problems from recurring *or ever happening at all*. In this sense, hoshin is a kind of poka yoke or mistake proofing mechanism for success in business.
- Value-adding employees working in teams, making well informed, real-time decisions on the front line, are the soul of lean enterprise; and *hoshin kanri* is the business operating system designed to guide and support them.
- Frontline employees capable of making real-time decisions do not grow on trees. You have to develop leaders at every level of the organization. Properly implemented, hoshin gives managers extra time and a framework of "teachable moments" to do this. This may one of the most important distinguishing facts about hoshin kanri.
- Hoshin creates the necessary management reporting structures, mentoring relationships, and positive attitudes that support empowered, frontline first-responders. Hoshin also ensures that project managers, supervisors, and group leaders have the necessary information to develop, guide, and support first-responders in applying the PDCA methods of lean enterprise *proactively*.
- The X-matrix (the A3-X) to which this workbook has been devoted is the essential memorandum of the hoshin process; it is a bundle of team charters (A3-Ts) that define in practical as well as strategic terms what the lean organization is all about: building and strengthening competitive capability in the concrete terms of advanced technology, top quality, low cost, and just-in-time delivery.
- Each team charter that you incorporate into your system of X-matrices should define a focused experiment to eliminate the waste and reduce the variability that stand between you and what it takes to beat the competition.

193

- Hoshin is the critical ingredient to a successful matrix organization of cross-functional teams. Through hoshin's discipline of cross-functional planning and execution, you should strive to methodically build the capability to solve complex or chronic problems that in mass production organizations are not resolved for years, or never at all.
- Once you become a lean organization, do not stop. Become a lean enterprise by applying hoshin kanri to interorganizational planning and execution, like Cybernautx did to its supplier, Nonesuch Casting.
- Don't use hoshin simply to deploy your strategy. Use it to actively manage your business *into the future*. Methodically strive to build the essential capability of lean enterprise: the capability to *adapt*.

A final warning: Like any refined tool, hoshin can cut two ways. You can use it, like Toyota, to build cutting-edge capabilities that yield products to delight customers and catch competitors off-guard. Or you can use it to ruthlessly cut costs by searching for "breakthrough" cost-down opportunities, as in some implementations of six sigma. Remember that only giving customers good value year in and year out will ensure that you meet target *profits*. This is the true purpose of hoshin kanri.

Tom Jackson
Portland, Oregon
June, 2006

RECOMMENDED READING

The President's Diagnosis

Akao, Yoji, Editor. *Hoshin Kanri: Policy Deployment for Successful TQM.* Cambridge, MA: Productivity Press, 1991.

Malcom Baldrige National Quality Award Criteria. http://www.quality.nist.gov/

Deming Prize Criteria. http://www.juse.or.jp/e/deming/index.html

EFQM Excellence Model (European Quality Award). http://www.efqm.org/Default.aspx?tabid=24

Hirano, Hiroyuku. JIT Implementation Manual. New York: Productivity Press, 1991.

Jackson, Tom L., with Constance Dyer. *Corporate Diagnosis.* Portland, OR: Productivity Press, 1996.

Juran, J.M., and Frank K. Gryna, Editors. *Juran's Quality Control Handbook, Fourth Edition.* New York: McGraw-Hill, 1988, pp. 35F.15-35F.18.

Kinni, Theodore B. *America's Best: IndustryWeek's Guide to World-Class Manufacturing Plants.* New York: Wiley, 1996.

Kobayashi, Iwao. *20 Keys to Workplace Improvement.* Portland, OR: Productivity Press, 199x.

Shingo Prize Criteria. http://www.shingoprize.org/AwardInfo/BusPrize/application_info/criteria.htm

Hoshin Kanri and Lean Management Systems

Akao, Yoji, Editor. *Hoshin Kanri: Policy Deployment for Successful TQM.* Cambridge, MA: Productivity Press, 1991.

Bechtell, Michele L. *The Management Compass: Steering the Corporation Using Hoshin Planning.* New York: American Management Association, 1995.

Dimancescu, Dan. *The Seamless Enterprise: Making Cross Functional Management Work.* New York: Harper Business, 1992.

Fukuda, Riuji. *Building Organization Fitness.* Portland, OR: Productivity Press, 1997.

Jackson, Tom L., with Constance Dyer. *Corporate Diagnosis.* Portland, OR: Productivity Press, 1996.

_____ with Karen Jones. *Implementing a Lean Management System.* Portland, OR: Productivity Press, 1996.

Kurogane, Kenji, Editor. *Cross-Functional Management: Principles and Practical Applications.* Tokyo: Asian Productivity Organization, 1991.

Mintzberg, Henry. *The Rise and Fall of Strategic Planning.* New York: Prentice Hall, 1994.

Monden, Yasuhiro. *Toyota Management System: Linking the Seven Key Functional Areas.* Portland, OR: Productivity Press, 1993.

Shiba, Shoji and David Walden. *Four Practical Revolutions in Management: Systems for Creating Unique Organizational Capability.* Portland, OR: Productivity Press/Cambridge, MA: The Center for Quality Management, 2001.

Lean Performance Measurement, Finance, and Cost Accounting

Cooper, Robin and Regina Schlagmulder. *Target Costing and Value Engineering.* Portland, OR: Productivity Press, 1997.

_____. *Supply Chain Development for the Lean Enterprise.* Portland, OR: Productivity Press, 1999.

Corbett, Thomas. *Throughput Accounting.* Great Barrington, MA: The North River Press, 1998.

Johnson, H. Thomas and A. Bröms. *Profit Beyond Measure*. New York: Free Press, 2002.

Kaplan, Robert S. and David P. Norton. *The Balanced Scorecard: Translating Strategy into Action*. Boston, MA: Harvard Business School Press, 1996.

_____. *The Strategy-Focused Organization: How Balanced Scorecard Companies Thrive in the New Business Environment*. Boston, MA: Harvard Business School Press, 2001.

Maskell, Brian and Bruce Baggaley. *Practical Lean Accounting*. New York: Productivity Press, 2004.

Sakurai, Michiharu. *Integrated Cost Management: A Companywide Prescription for Higher Profits and Lower Costs*. Portland, Oregon: Productivity Press, 1996.

Leadership, Mentoring, and Coaching

Dinero, Donald D. *Training Within Industry: The Foundation of Lean*. New York: Productivity Press, 2005.

Graupp, Patrick and Bob Wrona. *The TWI Workbook, Three Essential Skills of Supervisors*. New York: Productivity Press, 2006.

Kotter, John P. and Dan S. Cohen. *The Heart of Change: Real-Life Stories of How People Change Their Organizations*. Boston, MA: Harvard Business School Press, 2002.

Tichy, Noel M. with Eli Cohen. *The Leadership Engine: How Winning Companies Build Leaders at Every Level*. New York: HarperCollins, 1997.

Value Stream Mapping

Duggan, Kevin J. *Creating Mixed Model Value Streams*. New York: Productivity Press, 2003.

Keyte, Beau and Drew Locher. *The Complete Lean Enterprise*. New York: Productivity Press, 2004.

Shook, John and Mike Rother. *Learning to See*. Cambridge, MA: Lean Enterprise Institute.

Womack, James and Dan Jones. *Seeing the Whole*. Brookline, MA: Lean Enterprise Institute.

Problem Solving Tools

Brassard, Michael. *The Memory Jogger Plus+*. Salem, NH: Goal/QPC, 1996.

Fukuda, Riuji. *Building Organization Fitness*. Portland, OR: Productivity Press, 1997.

Michalski, Walter J. *Tool Navigator: The Master Guide for Teams*. Portland, OR: Productivity Press, 1997.

Mizuno, Shigeru, Editor. *Management for Quality Improvement: The 7 New QC Tools*. Cambridge, MA: Productivity Press, 1988.

Ozeki, Kazuo and Tetsuichi Asaka, Editors. *Handbook of Quality Tools: The Japanese Approach*. Cambridge, MA: Productivity Press, 1990.

Other Helpful Books

Cole, Robert E. *Managing Quality Fads: How American Business Learned to Play the Quality Game*. New York: Oxford University Press, 1999.

Flinchbaugh, Jamie and Andy Carlino. *The Hitchhiker's Guide to Lean: Lessons from the Road*. Dearborn, MI: Society of Manufacturing Engineers, 2006.

Neubauer, Joan. *The Complete Idiot's Guide to Journaling*. New York: Alpha Books, 2000.

INDEX

ABOUT THE AUTHOR

Tom Jackson is the former CEO of Productivity, Inc., and author of *Implementing a Lean Management System, Corporate Diagnosis* (Productivity Press), and *The President's Diagnosis* (Lean Press). Tom has been a student of lean enterprise since 1988, when he copyedited Hiroyuki Hirano's *JIT Factory Revolution* for Productivity Press. He became so fanatical about lean that he left his comfortable position at the University of Vermont to start a lean consulting company—in Malaysia! There he learned that the powerful techniques of lean enterprise—JIT, SMED, TPM, kanban, etc.—were only half of the story of Toyota's great success. The other half of the story was *hoshin kanri* and a revolution in the structure of modern business organizations. In 2003, Tom and his partner Don Makie founded taktX LLC, a lean management consultancy where Tom has applied *hoshin kanri* to the making of window and door seals, refrigerators, grain bins, and chicken feeders, the management of quality systems, and the delivery of healthcare, mental health, and social services. Tom is always thinking of new ways to get people to see both sides of lean. Learn more about hoshin kanri at Tom's web site www.hoshinkanri.biz.